THE HELLYER POCKET GUIDE

THE HELLYER POCKET GUIDE

ARTHUR HELLYER

MBE VMH

HAMLYN

First published in 1941
Fourth revised edition 1971
Ninth impression, fourth edition, 1981

This revised and updated edition published
in Great Britain 1993 by Hamlyn,
an imprint of Reed Consumer Books Limited,
Michelin House, 81 Fulham Road, London SW3 6RB
and Auckland, Melbourne, Singapore and Toronto

© 1993 Reed International Books Limited

Produced by Mandarin Offset – printed in Hong Kong

Set in Monophoto Bembo

. ISBN 0 600 57698 1

A catalogue record for this book is available at
the British Library

CONTENTS

WEIGHTS, MEASURES AND GARDEN CALCULATIONS

1. Linear Measure

METRIC

10	millimetres	= 1 centimetre
100	centimetres	= 1 metre
1,000	metres	= 1 kilometre

IMPERIAL

12	inches	= 1 foot
3	feet	= 1 yard
22	yards	= 1 chain
10	chains	= 1 furlong
8	furlongs	= 1 mile
1,760	yards or 5,280 feet	= 1 mile

2. Square Measure

METRIC

10,000 square centimetres	= 1 square metre
10,000 square metres	= 1 square metre
100 hectares	= 1 square kilometre

IMPERIAL

144 square inches	= 1 square foot
9 square feet	= 1 square yard
4,840 square yards	= 1 acre
640 acres	= 1 square mile

3. Cubic Measure

METRIC

1,000,000 cubic centimetres	= 1 cubic metre

IMPERIAL

1,728 cubic inches	= 1 cubic foot
27 cubic feet	= 1 cubic yard

4. Measure of Capacity

METRIC

1,000	millilitres	= 1 litre
	(100 cubic centimetres)	
1,000	litres	= 1 cubic metre

IMPERIAL

20	fluid ounces	= 1 pint
2	pints	= 1 quart
8	pints	= 1 gallon
4	quarts	= 1 gallon
8	gallons	= 1 bushel

5. Weight

METRIC

1,000	grams	= 1 kilogram
1,000	kilograms	= 1 metric tonne

AVOIRDUPOIS

16	drams	= 1 ounce
16	ounces	= 1 pound
14	pounds	= 1 stone
2	st, or 28 lb	= 1 quarter
4	qrs, or 112 lb	= 1 hundred-weight
20 cwt, or 2,240 lb		= 1 ton

6. Metric Equivalents

See page 8.

7. Conversion of Fahrenheit into Centigrade

To convert any Fahrenheit reading to Centigrade the formula is $\frac{5}{9}(F - 32°) = C$ when F = Fahrenheit and C = Centigrade.

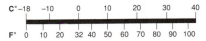

6. METRIC EQUIVALENTS

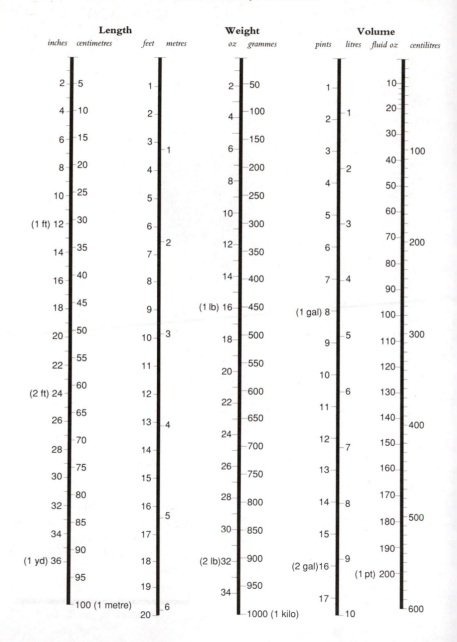

Length				Weight		Volume			
inches	centimetres	feet	metres	oz	grammes	pints	litres	fluid oz	centilitres

Length

inches	centimetres
2	5
4	10
6	15
8	20
10	25
(1 ft) 12	30
14	35
16	40
18	45
20	50
22	55
(2 ft) 24	60
26	65
28	70
30	75
32	80
34	85
(1 yd) 36	90
	95
	100 (1 metre)

feet	metres
1	
2	
3	
4	
5	
6	1
7	
8	
9	
10	3
11	
12	
13	4
14	
15	
16	
17	5
18	
19	
20	6

Weight

oz	grammes
2	50
4	100
6	150
8	200
	250
10	300
12	350
14	400
(1 lb) 16	450
18	500
20	550
22	600
24	650
26	700
28	750
30	800
(2 lb) 32	850
34	900
	950
	1000 (1 kilo)

Volume

pints	litres
1	
2	1
3	
4	2
5	3
6	
7	4
(1 gal) 8	
9	5
10	
11	6
12	7
13	
14	8
15	
(2 gal)16	9
17	10

fluid oz	centilitres
10	
20	
30	
40	100
50	
60	
70	200
80	
90	
100	300
110	
120	
130	
140	400
150	
160	
170	500
180	
190	
(1 pt) 200	600

8. Miscellaneous Weights and Measures

Litre	= ·22 gallon (1·76 pints)
Centimetre	= ·3937 inch
1 inch	= 2·54 centimetres
Metre	= 39·37 inches
1 square metre	= 1·2 square yards
1 cubic metre	= 1·31 cubic yards
1 kilogram	= 2·2 pounds

1 gallon of water weighs 10 lbs.

1 litre of water weighs 1 kilogram.

1 kilogram of any substance dissolved in 100 litres of water makes a 1 per cent solution.

1 pound of any substance dissolved in 10 gallons of water makes a 1 per cent solution, 2 pounds a 2 per cent soloution, and so on.

1 teaspoonful of water is approximately 5ml ($^1/_8$ fl oz).

1 dessertspoonful of water is approximately 10ml ($^1/_4$ fl oz).

1 tablespoonful of water is approximately 20ml ($^1/_2$ fl oz).

9. Measuring Superficial Areas

Measurements are made across the widest and the narrowest parts of the plot, the two figures are added together and then divided by two. Two similar measurements are made across the greatest and least lengths of the plot and treated in the same manner. The average width and average length obtained by this means are multiplied together to give the approximate superficial area.

If the plot or bed is rectangular, only two measurements need be made, one for width and the other for length. These are then multiplied together.

To estimate the area of a circle, measure from the centre to the edge, multiply this by itself and the result by 3·14 ($3^1/_7$).

10. Estimating Bulk

Measurements of capacity or bulk are made in cubic feet, cubic yards, cubic centimetres, cubic metres. Three, instead of two, preliminary sets of measurements must be obtained – one for average length, one for average breadth, and one for average depth – but these are made in the manner just described. All three are then multiplied together, the answer being in cubic feet if the original measurements were in feet, cubic yards if in yards, cubic centimetres or cubic metres. Cubic feet can be reduced to cubic yards by dividing by twenty-seven.

11. Estimating Gravel

Gravel is usually sold by the cubic metre or cubic yard. A thickness of 5-8cm (2-3in) of gravel is required for surfacing a path, and at this rate a cubic metre of gravel will cover 12·5 to 20 square metres while a yd³ of gravel will cover from 12 to 18 yd².

12. Estimating Paving Slabs

Crazy pavement is proportionately heavier than gravel. A metric tonne contains from 0·36-0·39 cubic metres (ton contains from 13 to 14³ (3), and the covering area depends upon the thickness. Usually 'crazy' is sold in two grades 'thin' varying from 2 to 4cm ($^1/_4$ to $1^1/_2$in) in thickness, and 'thick' from 1 to 6cm ($^1/_2$ to $2^1/_2$in) thick. The former has a covering capacity of from 11·5 to 13 square metres (14 to 16 yd²) and the latter from 6.5 to 7·5 square metres per metric tonne (8 to 9 yd² per ton) (2). Similar remarks apply to rectangular paving. York paving covers 8-9 square metres per metric tonne (10 to 11 yd² per ton). See table page 10.

13. Estimating Walling Stone

Walling stone is similar to crazy paving and its covering capacity depends upon its thickness. A usual measurement is 15cms (6in), and this has a covering capacity of about 3-3.5m² per tonne (3-4 yds² per ton) (2).

14. Estimating Soil for Filling

Soil

Table of approximate quantities of paving material required for 30-m (10-ft) length of path

Width of path	60cm (2ft)	80cm (2½ft)	90cm (3ft)	120cm (4ft)	180cm (6ft)
Bricks (flat)	71	89	107	143	214
Bricks (on edge)	107	134	160	213	320
Crazy pavement,	kg/cwt	kg/cwt	kg/cwt	kg/cwt	kg/cwt
2-4cm/¾-½in	150 (3)	190 (3¾)	225 (4½)	300 (6)	450 (9)
Crazy pavement,					
4-6cm/1½-2½in	260 (5¼)	325 (6½)	400 (8)	525 (10½)	800 (16)
York paving slabs	200 (4)	250 (5)	300 (6)	400 (8)	600 (12)
Gravel					
(5cm/2in thick)	190 (3¼)	200 (4)	250 (5)	350 (7)	500 (10)
	(1/9 yd)	(1/7 yd)	(1/5 yd)	(¼ yd)	(⅓ yd)
Gravel					
(7·5cm/3in thick)	250 (5)	310 (6¼)	375 (7½)	500 (10)	750 (15)
	(⅙ yd)	(2/9 yd)	(¼ yd)	(⅓ yd)	(½ yd)
Concrete					
(5cm/2in thick)					
Gravel	150 (3)	190 (3¾)	225 (4½)	300 (6)	450 (9)
Sand	50 (1)	65 (1¼)	75 (1½)	100 (2)	150 (3)
Cement	50 (1)	65 (1¼)	75 (1½)	100 (2)	150 (3)
Concrete					
(7·5cm/3in thick)					
Gravel	225 (4½)	275 (5½)	300 (6)	450 (9)	650 (13)
Sand	75 (1½)	80 (1⅔)	100 (2)	150 (3)	210 (4¼)
Cement	75 (1½)	80 (1⅔)	100 (2)	150 (3)	210 (4¼)

for filling up beds, etc., varies in bulk according to its texture and the amount of water that it contains. Sandy soils are the lightest and may reach 1 cubic metre to the tonne (26 to 27 ft^3 to the ton), while heavy clay barely touches 0.6 cubic metres (18ft^3) for the same weight. The average for good fibrous loam is about 0.8 cubic metres (23-24ft^3). Potting loam can be estimated at the same rate, while potting sand averages 0.9 square metres per tonne (24ft^3 per ton). Leaf-mould is much lighter, though it will vary considerably according to its age. Often these materials are sold by the load instead of by weight. The volume of a load is approximately 1 cubic metre (1 cubic yard).

15. Estimating Concrete for Pools A rough but reasonably accurate method of calculating quantities of gravel, sand, and cement required for preparing base concrete consisting of 3 parts of gravel, 1 part of sand, and 1 part of cement is to provide enough gravel to supply the whole required bulk and then add the sand and cement as extras. Their bulk will be lost in mixing and the shrinkage that takes place as the concrete dries. This method will not serve for finishing concrete made up of equal parts of small gravel, sand, and cement. In this case add together the bulk of all three ingredients, reckoning cement at 0·6 cubic metres per tonne (18ft³ per ton), and subtract one-third of the total for shrinkage.

The bulk of fully dried concrete required for a rectangular pool is obtained as follows: multiply the length by the breadth and this by the thickness of the concrete. This gives the volume of concrete for the bottom. Add twice the length to twice the width, multiply the figure so obtained by the depth and the result by the thickness of the concrete. This gives the volume of concrete for the sides. Add the sum of the two calculations together to obtain the total volume of concrete.

For a circular pool the volume of concrete for the bottom is obtained by measuring from the centre to the side and multiplying this by itself. Multiply the result by 3·14 (3¹/₇) and this, in turn, by the thickness of the concrete. The volume of concrete for the sides is obtained by doubling the measurement from the centre of the pool to the edge, multiplying this by 3·14 (3¹/₇), the result by the thickness of the concrete, and then by the depth. The sum of the two calculations is added together as before.

The simplest way of dealing with an irregular pool is to measure out a circle or rectangle which approximately covers it and calculate the volume of concrete for the bottom on this basis. The length of the sides can be measured with string.

Do not forget that all measurements must be made in the same units – yards, feet, metres or whatever is suitable.

16. Estimating Volume of Water

The approximate volume of water in a rectangular pool or tank is obtained by multiplying together the length, breadth, and depth, all in metres and then multiplying the result by 1000. This gives the volume in litres (4). For a circular pool or tank the measurement from the centre to the side (in metres) is multiplied by itself, and the result is multiplied by 3·14 (3¹/₇). The figure so obtained is multiplied by the depth (in metres), this giving the volume in cubic metres (3). To obtain the volume in gallons multiply by 1000 as before. If the volume is required in gallons make all the measurements in feet and multiply the result by 6¼.

17. Estimating Fish for Aquarium or Pool

There are two methods of calculating the maximum number of fish that can be accommodated in an aquarium. Method 1 is to allow 5cm of body length, excluding tail, to 10l of water (1in to 1gal). Method 2 is to allow 100cm of body length per square metre of surface area (4in to 1ft²). This latter system usually results in a considerably lower estimate and is the safer for general purposes.

18. Estimating Plants for Borders

When planning herbaceous borders an average of 4 plants per square metre may be adopted as a rough guide to requirements, though in actual practice the distance of planting will vary from the front to the back of the border, as the smaller marginal plants can be set much more closely than the larger kinds used in the background. As there is likely to be a greater proportion of small plants in a narrow border than in a wide one, it follows that the number of plants per square yard or metre will be greater. (See page 12.)

19. Estimating Turves for Lawns

Turves are sold at so much per hundred and are almost invariably cut in strips 30cm (1ft) wide and 1 metre (3ft) long.

Number of Herbaceous Plants required for borders of various dimensions

Width of border	Length of border							
	3m (10ft)	6m (20ft)	9m (30ft)	12m (40ft)	15m (50ft)	18m (60ft)	22·5m (75ft)	30m (100ft)
60cm (2ft)	12	24	36	48	60	72	90	120
90cm (3ft)	15	30	45	60	75	90	112	150
1·2m (4ft)	18	36	54	72	90	108	135	180
1·5m (5ft)	20	40	60	80	100	120	150	200
1·8m (6ft)	22	44	66	88	110	132	165	220
2·1m (7ft)	24	48	72	96	120	144	180	240
2·4m (8ft)	26	52	78	104	130	156	195	260
2·7m (9ft)	27	54	81	108	135	162	202	270
3m (10ft)	28	56	84	112	140	168	210	280
3·6m (12ft)	30	60	90	120	150	180	225	300
4·5m (15ft)	33	66	99	132	165	198	246	330
6m (20ft)	36	72	108	144	180	216	270	360

NOTE: The number of plants required per square metre or yard becomes progressively smaller as the border increases in width due to the greater proportion of large-growing varieties that can be accommodated. These figures must be taken as very approximate, as much depends upon the type of plant chosen.

20. Number of Fruit Trees, etc, per 100m² (100 yd²) and distances for planting

Name of Tree	Distance apart in metres (feet)	Between rows in metres (feet)	No per 100 square metres (100 yd²)
Apples, Cordon	0·6 (2)	1·8 (6)	70 (60)
Bush	3·5 (12)	3·5 (12)	8 (6–7)
Standard	7–9 (25–30)	7–9 (25–30)	1 (1)
Cherries, Bush	4·5 (15)	4·5 (15)	4 (4)
Standard	9 (30)	9 (30)	1 (1)
Cob Nuts, Bush	3·5 (12)	3·5 (12)	8 (6–7)
Currants, Bush	1·2–1·5 (4–5)	1·2–1·5 (4–5)	40–70 (36–45)
Gooseberries, Bush	1·2–1·5 (4–5)	1·2–1·5 (4–5)	40–70 (36–45)
Pears, Cordon	0·6 (2)	1·8 (6)	70 (60)
Bush	3·5 (12)	3·5 (12)	8 (6–7)
Standard	7 (25)	7 (25)	1–2 (1)
Plums, Bush	4·5 (15)	4·5 (15)	4 (4)
Standard	7–9 (25–30)	7–9 (25–30)	1 (1)
Raspberries	0·6 (2)	1·8 (6)	70 (60)
Strawberries	0·3 (1)	0·7–0·9 (2½–3)	350–450 (300–360)

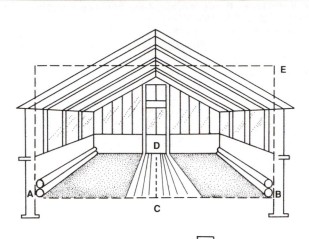

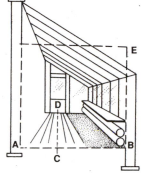

Calculating Greenhouse Volume for Fumigation
In a span-roofed house the breadth (AB), the length (CD) and the height (BE), to halfway up the roof slope are multiplied together.

Volume of a Lean-to House
Here again the breadth (AB) is multiplied by the length (CD) and the height (BE) half-way up the slope of the roof.

One hundred of these will cover 30 square metres (33⅓ yd²) of ground. The best turves for bowling greens, etc, are sometimes cut in 30cm (1ft) squares, as there is then less variation in thickness and it is consequently possible to lay them more evenly. Such turves have a covering capacity of approximately 9 square metres (11yd²) per hundred.

20. See table opposite

21. Calculating Cubic Capacity for a Greenhouse This is necessary before fumigation can be carried out, as the quantity of fumigant used is deter-

mined by the cubic capacity of the house.

The method is to multiply the length of the house by the breadth and this by the height measured midway between the eaves and the ridge. (See above.)

22. Marking out Right Angles
Stretch a line to mark one side of the angle (lawn edge, bed, or border). at the corner drive in a small peg and attach to it a piece of string 30cm (3ft) in length. From the peg measure along the base line 40cm (4ft), drive in a second peg, and attach to it a piece of string 50cm (5ft) in length. Draw the two loose ends of string

together and at the point at which they meet drive in a third peg. A line stretched between the first and third peg will make a right angle with the base. (See illustration right.)

23. Marking out Circles and Ovals

A circle is very simple to make. Drive in a peg at the centre, attach to it a piece of string half the diameter of the required circle and draw the end of this around the centre, scratching out a line meanwhile with a pointed stick or indicating it with a trickle of finely powdered lime or silver sand.

An oval bed is a little more difficult. First peg down two lines bisecting each other at right angles to mark the extreme length and breadth of the bed. Then the two focal points are ascertained by attaching a string half the length of the oval to one of the pegs marking the extreme width and drawing the free end round so that it touches the longer line first on one side and then on the other of the shorter line. Strong pegs are driven in at each of

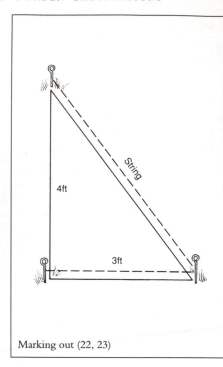

4ft

String

3ft

Marking out (22, 23)

24. Table for Calculating Dilutions

	Quantity of water required				
	100 galls	**50 galls**	**25 galls**	**10 galls**	**5 galls**
Quantity of concentrate required	10 galls	5 galls	2½ galls	8 pts	4 pts
	9 galls	4½ galls	2¼ galls	7¼ pts	3¾ pts
	8 galls	4 galls	2 galls	6½ pts	3¼ pts
	7 galls	3½ galls	1¾ galls	5½ pts	2¾ pts
	6 galls	3 galls	1½ galls	5 pts	2½ pts
	5 galls	2½ galls	1¼ galls	4 pts	2 pts
	4 galls	2 galls	1 galls	3⅓ pts	1½ pts
	3 galls	1½ galls	6 pts	2½ pts	1¼ pts
	2 galls	1 galls	4 pts	1½ pts	16 fl oz
	1 galls	½ galls	2 pts	16 fl oz	8 fl oz

NOTE The above calculations are not mathematically exact but are worked to the nearest unit that would be employed horticulturally.

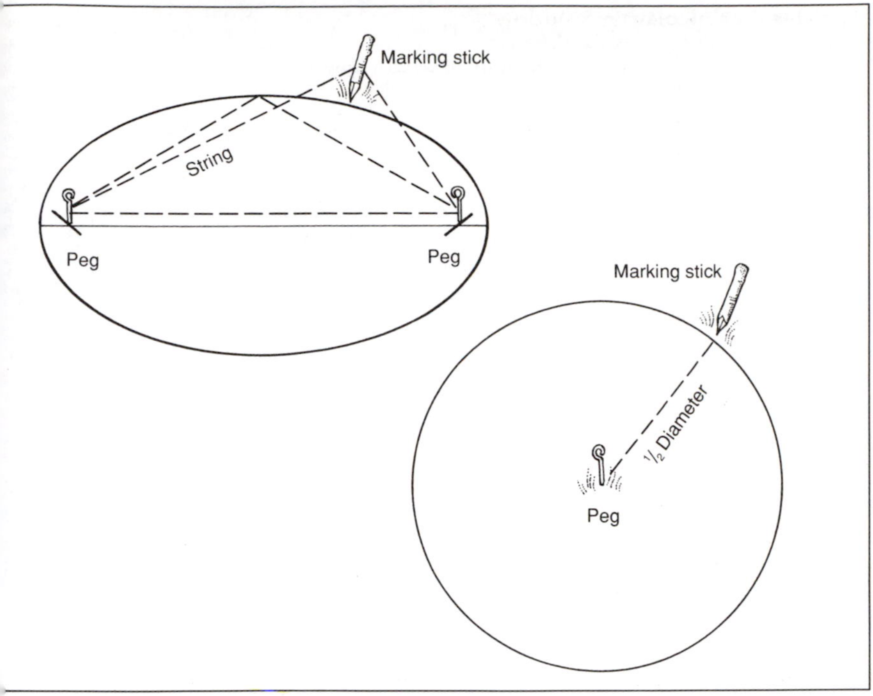

Quantity of water required				
2 galls	**1 gall**	**1 qt**	**1 pt**	**%**
1⅗ pts	16 fl oz	4 fl oz	2 fl oz	10
1⅖ pts	14 fl oz	3½ fl oz	1¾ fl oz	9
1³⁄₁₀ pts	13 fl oz	3 fl oz	1½ fl oz	8
1⅒ pts	11 fl oz	2¾ fl oz	1⅜ fl oz	7
1 pts	10 fl oz	2½ fl oz	1¼ fl oz	6
16 fl oz	8 fl oz	2 fl oz	1 fl oz	5
12 fl oz	6 fl oz	1½ fl oz	6 dr	4
10 fl oz	5 fl oz	1¼ fl oz	5 dr	3
6 fl oz	3 fl oz	6 dr	5 dr	2
3 fl oz	12 dr	3 dr	1½ dr	1

N.B. Using metric measures it is very easy to calculate dilutions since 10 cc of a concentrate made up to 1 litre with water gives a 1 per cent dilution, 20 cc a 2 per cent dilution and so on.

25. Table for Calculating Solutions

	Quantity of water required						
	1 gall	2 galls		3 galls		4 galls	
	oz	lb	oz	lb	oz	lb	oz
	¼	0	½	0	¾	0	1
	½	0	1	0	1½	0	2
	¾	0	1½	0	2¼	0	3
	1	0	2	0	3	0	4
	1½	0	3	0	4½	0	6
	2	0	4	0	6	0	8
	3	0	6	0	9	0	12
	4	0	8	0	12	1	0
	5	0	10	0	15	1	4
	6	0	12	1	2	1	8
	7	0	14	1	5	1	12
	8	1	0	1	8	2	0

The left-hand vertical label reads: **Weight of chemical or other substance required**

NOTE The above calculations are not mathematically exact but are worked to the nearest unit that would be employed horticulturally.

26. Table for Calculating Fertilizer Quantities (See footnote, right)

Amounts required at same rate for various areas			
Per sq yard	Per acre	Per acre	Per sq yard
½ oz	150 lb	1 cwt	⅓ oz
1 oz	300 lb	2 cwt	⅔ oz
1½ oz	450 lb	3 cwt	1 oz
2 oz	600 lb	4 cwt	1½ oz
3 oz	8 cwt	5 cwt	2 oz
4 oz	10¾ cwt	6 cwt	2½ oz
5 oz	13½ cwt	7 cwt	2¾ oz
6 oz	16¼ cwt	8 cwt	3 oz
7 oz	19 cwt	9 cwt	3¼ oz
8 oz	21½ cwt	10 cwt	3¾ oz
9 oz	24½ cwt	15 cwt	5½ oz
10 oz	27 cwt	20 cwt	7½ oz
11 oz	30 cwt	25 cwt	9¼ oz
12 oz	32½ cwt	30 cwt	11 oz
13 oz	35 cwt	35 cwt	13 oz
14 oz	38 cwt	40 cwt	15 oz
15 oz	40½ cwt	45 cwt	16¾ oz
16 oz	43 cwt	50 cwt	18½ oz

Quantity of water required									
5 galls		10 galls		20 galls		50 galls		100 galls	
lb	oz	lb	oz	lb	oz	lb	oz	lb	oz
0	1¼	0	2½	0	5	0	12½	1	9
0	2½	0	5	0	10	1	9	3	2
0	3¾	0	7½	0	15	2	5½	4	11
0	5	0	10	1	4	3	2	6	4
0	7½	0	15	1	14	4	11	9	6
0	10	1	4	2	8	6	4	12	8
0	15	1	14	3	12	9	6	18	12
1	4	2	8	5	0	12	8	25	0
1	9	3	2	6	4	15	10	31	4
1	14	3	12	7	8	18	12	37	8
2	3	4	6	8	12	21	14	43	12
2	8	5	0	10	0	25	0	50	0

N.B. Using metric measures it is very easy to calculate solutions. If a fertilizer is to be dissolved in water at a rate of 75g to 10l, then for 50l of solution, simply multiply 75 by 5, giving 375g.

these points. A piece of twine, twice the length of the distance from one of these pegs to the farthest extremity of the bed, is then knotted into a loop, thrown over the two focal pegs and drawn around them with a sharp-pointed stick which is used to scratch the outline of the oval on the soil. (See illustration on previous page.)

27. Marking Irregular Outlines
Present-day tendency is to get away from formality by introducing irregular outlines into the garden. These cannot be drawn geometrically. Instead, mark them out roughly with small sticks and then outline them more definitely with finely powdered lime or silver sand poured from a bottle or through a narrow-necked funnel. If the curve does not please, it is only a small matter to brush the lime or sand away and mark out a different line.

(See table 26, left)
NOTE. These calculations are not mathematically correct but are worked to the nearest unit that would be used horticulturally.
N.B. Using metric measures it is very easy to calculate spreading rates. If a fertilizer is to be applied at 30g to 1 square metre, then for 15 square metres, simply multiply 30 by 15, giving 450g.

SOIL CULTIVATION, MANURES, AND FERTILIZERS

SOIL CULTIVATION

28. Digging Technically this means turning soil over to the full depth of an ordinary spade, approximately 25cm (10in). First a trench should be opened across one end of the plot, 25cm (10in) deep and about the same in width. The soil removed is wheeled to the other end. Then a further narrow strip is turned over into the trench, the process being repeated backwards across the plot until the far end is reached, when the barrowed soil is used to fill in the last trench. Care must be taken to turn each sod right over so that weeds or grass are completely covered up.

To save barrowing soil over the length of long plots, these are divided longitudinally into any number of convenient sections of even number. The gardener works down one, back up another, and so on, finishing at the same end as that at which he or she started.

If grassland is to be dug, the turves should be well chopped as they are turned over, otherwise decay will be slow. A dusting of sulphate of ammonia or Nitrochalk, 60g per square metre (2oz per yd²), will hasten decay, as will a dressing of well-rotted dung. If bulky manure is to be incorporated by digging, spread it first on the surface at the required rate and then turn it in in the process of digging.

29. Trenching This term is used to describe two distinct operations. Full trenching involves digging the soil 90cm (3ft) deep and bringing the lowest spit to the top. This is seldom practised, as sub-soil is relatively infertile and it is best to keep the richer surface soil on top. This may be done by a special method of trenching as follows: the plot, if large, is divided into strips as for plain digging, but the preliminary trench is at least 60cm (2ft) wide. Some gardeners prefer to work with a 1m (3ft) trench, as this gives more room for movement.

The soil from this trench is wheeled to the far end of the plot (Fig 1 in diagram facing). The bottom of the trench is divided in half and a further depth of 25cm (10in) is dug out of the front portion and carted back (Fig 2, facing). The subsoil so exposed is broken up with a fork. The step of soil left at the back of the trench is turned over with a spade on top of this subsoil (Fig 3), thus exposing a further strip of subsoil to be forked. Now another trench, half the width of the first, is marked out and the topsoil is turned right over on top of the step formed by the second-spit soil in trench No 1 (Fig 4). The second-spit soil in trench No 2 is turned on top of the subsoil exposed in trench No 1 (Fig 5) and the subsoil in trench No 2 is broken with a fork. Another half-measure trench is marked off and turned over in the same way (Fig 6). This sequence is continued until the ground is all dug, the last trench being filled with two heaps of soil from the first.

BASTARD OR HALF TRENCHING, also known as double digging, is midway between trenching and digging and involves turning over the soil one spade deep and forking the spit immediately below, without altering its position.

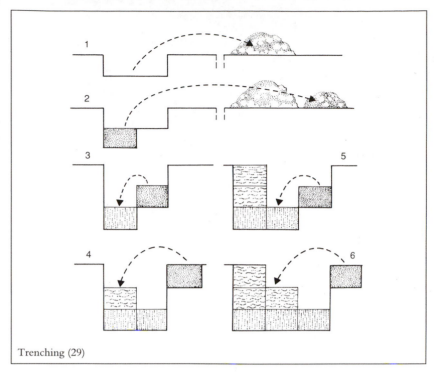

Trenching (29)

If manure is to be incorporated with the soil, either by trenching or by bastard trenching, fork it into the second spit as thoroughly as possible and turn a little in with the top spit as described under 'Digging' (28), but do not get any quite close to the surface, where it would impede planting or sowing.

30. Ridging This is most serviceable in autumn or early winter. The soil is thrown or drawn into steep ridges, the object being to expose a large surface to the beneficial action of wind, rain, frost, and thaw. Two methods are employed. One is to pull the soil into ridges with a draw hoe as described under 'Earthing Up' (37). The other is to mark the plot into 1m (3ft) wide strips, each of which is dug separately lengthwise, ie starting at one end and working backwards down

the length of the strip with narrow trenches. In digging, the centre spadeful is always turned inwards to lie on top of the centre one and so form a ridge as shown in the illustration on the next page.

31. Stripping Turf If turf on new land is reasonably free from deep-rooting perennial weeds such as convolvulus (bindweed), coltsfoot, dock, perennial thistle, horsetail (equisetum), and ground elder, it may be turned in by digging or trenching and will in time rot and enrich the soil. Dressing with a nitrogenous fertilizer or manure as described under 'Digging' (28) will hasten the progress. Very weedy turf or turf containing pests such as leather-jackets, wireworms, and cockchafer larvae is best stripped and stacked for twelve months to rot. The stack may be of any size but will rot

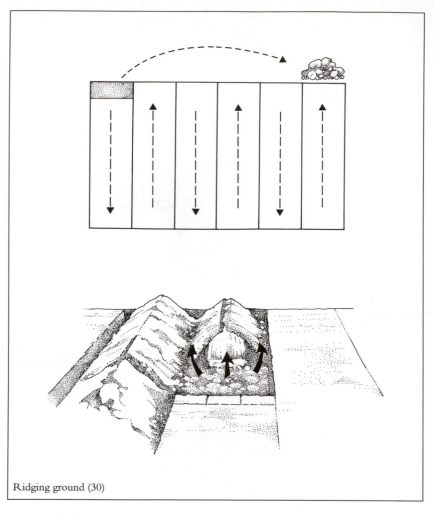

Ridging ground (30)

most rapidly if in a sheltered, shady place. Dust alternate layers with sulphate of ammonia or fresh soot and fresh hydrated lime. The sulphate of ammonia or soot should not be mixed with lime in the same layer.

32. Drainage This may be necessary on heavy or low-lying land if surface water lies for a long time. Land drains are of two types, stone drains and pipe drains.

STONE DRAINS may be prepared with any hard rubble, broken clinker, etc. Trenches are cut about 30cm (10in) wide and 50cm (18in) or more in depth, with a fall of at least 30cm (1ft) in 6m (20ft) in one direction. The bottom 20cm (9in) of the trench is filled with the stones, clinkers, or rubble. About 3cm (an inch) or so of finer rubble or gravel is placed on top. This is covered with inverted turves and the trench is finally filled with soil. All drains should communicate at their lowest points with a main drain, ditch, or large soakaway.

PIPE DRAINS are laid in trenches cut in the same manner. A little gravel, broken clinker, or small rubble is placed in the bottom of each trench. Special earthenware land-drain pipes are laid end to end but not quite touching on this layer. They are surrounded and just covered with small rubble. Inverted turves are placed on top and the trench is filled with soil. Plastic land-drain pipes are another alternative. Again, all drains must communicate at their lowest points with a main drain, ditch, or soakaway.

A SOAKAWAY is made by digging a large hole, preferably deep enough to penetrate impervious subsoil such as clay and reach more open or stony soil below. This hole should be filled to within about 30cm (1ft) of the surface with clinkers, brick ends, or other hard rubble, the remainder being covered with small rubble, turves, and soil as for land drains.

Drainage can often be improved without making land drains by digging or trenching-in plenty of strawy manure, sifted cinders, sharp boiler ashes, or coarse sand. In bad cases faggots of bushy wood may be laid in the bottom of each trench as work proceeds. Household ashes are of no use for improving the drainage of soil, as they are too soft and fine in texture. See also 'Lime' (61).

33. Forking Mainly used for breaking down the surface of ground already dug or trenched and for mixing fertilizers and manure with the soil. Sometimes a digging fork with broad, flat tines is substituted for a spade for ordinary digging or trenching, especially if ground is heavy or wet. When a fork is used to break surface clods the back is employed with swinging, sideways blows.

34. Hoeing There are several types of hoe, serviceable according to soil and requirements.

THE DRAW HOE has a blade at right angles to the handle. It is employed with chopping, drawing motions, the operator moving forwards and thus treading on the hoed ground. It is useful for breaking down rough surfaces, having off thick growth of weeds, drawing deep drills for large seeds and potatoes, or drawing soil towards plants.

THE CANTERBURY HOE has three broad prongs at right angles to the handle and is used like the draw hoe for breaking down clods.

THE DUTCH HOE has a flat blade approximately in the same plane as the handle and is the best tool for keeping the surface soil loose and cutting off light weed growth and mixing top dressings with the soil. It is employed with sweeping backward and forward movements. The blade passes just beneath the surface and the operator moves backwards so that the hoed soil is not trodden on.

CULTIVATORS AND PATENT HOES of many kinds have been devised and some are serviceable. Particularly useful are the clawed cultivators with three or five tines, used principally instead of a fork for breaking clods and loosening the surface round plants in growth.

SURFACE CULTIVATION has three main objects – to break the surface into fine particles and thus make it suitable for seeds and small plants; to maintain a loose surface layer or dust mulch of soil, which has a tidy appearance and acts as a kind of blanket over the lower soil; and to destroy weeds.

35. Raking This is required in final preparation of seed beds and beds intended for small plants, and also for removing moss and creeping weeds from lawns. Raking of soil should be done only when the surface is reasonably dry. Excessiveness fineness is not an advantage and may cause surface caking. The ideal will depend on the size of the seeds or plants. The smaller these are the more the soil should be raked. For lawns a spring-toothed rake is better for regular use than the ordinary rigid rake, as it is less likely to tear out grass or otherwise damage the surface of the lawn.

36. Seed Sowing Apart from forking, hoeing, and raking the surface to a fine crumbly condition known as *'a good tilth'*, seed beds must be trodden to give even firmness throughout. Tread slowly backwards and forwards across the surface, choosing a time when the soil is drying white on top. Boards about 30 by 15cm (1ft by 6in) may be fixed to the boots to hasten treading. Rake the surface level after treading is finished.

DRILLS FOR SEEDS may be drawn with the edge of a dutch hoe, the corner of a draw hoe, or a pointed stick. Small drills may be made by pressing a broom handle into the surface. Wide drills for peas and beans may be made with a spade used flat to scoop out the soil 5-8cm (2-3in) deep. Cover seeds by drawing the displaced soil back with the rake. Finally use the rake vertically with gentle ramming motions to firm the soil over the seeds.

37. Earthing Up This means drawing the soil towards plants. It is practised for two reasons, first to exclude light and secondly to provide plenty of loose soil in which such plants as potatoes and artichokes may form their tubers. Exclusion of light is principally required with leeks and celery to blanch the stems and make them palatable, but it is also an important object in earthing potatoes, as if the tubers are exposed to light they become green, bitter, and poisonous. A draw hoe is commonly used for this task and the soil is drawn up a little at a time rather than in one operation.

38. Planting This may be done with dibber, trowel, spade, or special tool according to the type of plant.

THE DIBBER is serviceable for planting seedlings rapidly. Its drawback is a tendency to consolidate the soil unevenly and cramp roots in a narrow hole. Special steel-shod dibbers may be purchased or good dibbers can be made from old spades or fork handles cut to a length of about 50cm (18in) and sharpened to a point. Avoid making holes too deep. When the roots have been dropped into position, push the dibber into the soil again alongside the plant and, with a levering movement towards it, press the soil firmly around the roots.

A TROWEL is the best tool for planting most small and medium-sized plants. Long-handled trowels save stooping but place greater strain on the wrist muscles. Holes made with the trowel should be of ample size to accommodate all roots disposed naturally. Work the soil by hand round these and firm on all sides with the foot or knuckles. Loose planting is a common cause of failure, as loose soil dries rapidly and plants cannot make sturdy growth in it.

A SPADE may be used for planting all large things such as shrubs, fruit trees, and bushes, etc. Holes should be wide and comparatively shallow so that roots may be spread out laterally to their full extent. The uppermost should, as a rule, be covered with from 10-15cm (3-6in) of soil. Break the soil finely, scatter round the roots, a little at a time, and jerk the tree or shrub gently meanwhile so that soil settles between the roots. When all are covered tread firmly, scatter more loose soil on top, and water in if dry.

WATER all newly planted seedlings and plants freely during dry weather until established. Quick-acting fertilizers should not be given to anything freshly planted.

SPECIAL TOOLS are employed for certain purposes. A bulb planter which removes a neat core of turf is serviceable for naturalizing daffodils, etc, in grassland. It has a wide handle, a shaft similar to that of a spade, a crossbar near the bottom and a circular blade.

39. Mulching This consists of spreading a layer of manure, leaf-mould, peat, grass clippings, or some similar substance over the surface of the soil. Its object is twofold, first to feed plants and second to act as a blanket to the lower soil in which roots are growing. Mulches are most serviceable in the spring and early summer, particularly round newly planted subjects. Mulching material should be loose. If it becomes beaten down by rain or other causes, it should be shaken up again with a fork. A thick mulch of grass clippings maintained on rose beds from late spring to late summer has proved a useful preventive of rose black spot (667).

40. Top Dressing is allied to mulching, but is employed solely to feed plants. Usually some fairly concentrated and readily soluble fertilizer or manure is employed such as sulphate of ammonia, superphosphate of lime, sulphate of potash, dried blood, etc. Care must be taken not to give an excessive quantity. Top dressings are most useful for plants in full growth or bearing. They should be spread evenly over the full presumed root spread and must not be heaped around the stems.

41. Plant Foods Plants require many different chemicals, but three only are likely to be deficient under normal conditions in most places. These are nitrogren, phosphorus (supplied as phosphoric acid), and potash. Occasionally iron, magnesium, manganese, boron, and a few other chemicals must be added to these, but as wrong use of these may cause damage the advice of an expert should usually be obtained if their application is contemplated. In general, nitrogen tends to promote stem and leaf growth, phosphorus root growth, and potash fruitfulness and ripening, but one tends to interact with another so that, for example, lack of potash may prevent the plant making proper use of the nitrogen available in the soil and so on.

A 'balanced' manure or fertilizer is one that supplies the essential ingredients in approximately the right proportions for the crop in question. Most animal manures are not balanced in this sense though they may contain all necessary foods. Chemicals usually supply one plant food each, though a few, such as nitrate of potash (64) and phosphate of potash (68), supply two. In order to obtain a well-balanced chemical fertilizer several chemicals must be mixed in correct proportions (81) to (99).

By law it is necessary that the nitrogen, phosphoric acid and potash content of mixed commercial fertilizers should be quoted. This is done on the basis of percentage of each of these foods in the complete mixture. The analysis is always given in the order as above and is occasionally abbreviated to figures only. Thus a fertilizer described as 7 : 5 : 4 would contain 7% nitrogen, 5% phosphoric acid and 4% potash.

MANURES

42. Manure from Stables and Byre Bulky manures of this type contain nitrogen, phosphates, and potash, but not in the right proportions for all plants. Consequently it is necessary to 'balance' these animal manures with appropriate chemicals. Animal manures, by virtue of the humus they produce, improve the texture of the soil, making light soils more retentive and improving the drainage of heavy soils. Cow and horse manure are excellent for general use: the former is most suitable for light and the latter for heavy soil. Pig manure is rich in nitrogen and best for poor, sandy soils. Horse, cow, and pig manures should be stacked in the dry and allowed to rot for some months. When fresh the food they contain is not available for plants. Bacterial action causes decay and breaks down some parts of the manure into simple, inorganic chemicals. Average dressings are 50kg (1cwt) (a good barrowload) to from 5-10 cubic metres (6-15 yds²).

Rotted dung may be spread thinly as a mulch or top dressing round plants in full growth or bearing. It may also be used in liquid form (49). Rotted dung may be dug in at any time of the year. If fresh dung must be used, it is best applied to vacant ground in the autumn. Fresh horse manure can be used for mushrooms (148) and hotbeds (506). Analyses vary greatly according to the food on which the animals have been fed, bedding used, its age, storage conditions, etc. If stored well, dung tends to become richer, bulk for bulk, with age. Averages for good rotted samples of mixed farm manure are: nitrogen 0.5-1%, phosphoric acid 0.25-0.05%, potash 0.5-1%. Urine is, in general, richer in nitrogen and potash.

43. The Compost Heap This may be built with any vegetable refuse. Old plants, pea and bean haulms, grass clippings, leaves, straw, hay, green manure crops, and even paper and soft hedge clippings may go into it. If the greater part is soft green refuse, no further steps need be taken to ensure decay. Make the heap about 1m (3ft) high, 1m (3ft) through, and of any convenient length, turn it after a month, so far as possible bringing the inner portions out and turning the outside in. When the heap has decayed to a brown, manure-like mass it can be dug in at the same rate as animal manure. If there is much dry or hard rubbish, such as hay, straw, cabbage stumps, hedge clippings, or paper, a rotting agent such as Nitrochalk, sulphate of ammonia, or one of the special proprietory products should be used. Dust each 15cm (6in) thick layer lightly with the chemical (with sulphate of ammonia it is advisable to treat alternate layers with hydrated lime instead) and wet thoroughly any part of the material that seems dry. When turning, add more water to dry parts.

44. Indore Process This is a controlled method of compost making. As far as possible animal and vegetable refuses are mixed in definite proportions with dung and urine. Excessive acidity is counteracted with calcium carbonate (chalk) or potassium carbonate. Occasionally slaked lime is employed. No other chemicals are used, but wood ashes are mixed in if available. Rotting is usually in pits 1m (3ft) deep, not more than 4.5m (5yds) wide, and any convenient length. Air vents are made with a crowbar every metre or so (every few feet). The heap or pit is turned twice, the first time after a month and again after a further month. Water is used freely if necessary to prevent the compost becoming dry.

45. Green Manures A quick-growing crop such as mustard, rape, vetches, or annual lupins may be sown and dug in just as it is about to come into flower. This adds organic matter to the soil, improves its texture, and holds up soluble foods which might otherwise be washed out. Where lupins, vetches, and other legumes are grown the nitrogen content of the soil is increased, as these plants harbour bacteria which fix nitrogen from the air. Mustard may be sown up to late summer for autumn digging, rape or annual lupins until midsummer, while vetches are best sown in spring. Dust the ground with Nitro-chalk or sulphate of ammonia at 65g per square metre (2 oz per yd²) as the green crop is dug in, to hasten decay and prevent temporary nitrogen shortage.

46. Hair The scrapings from hides treated in tanneries are sometimes available and are a useful source of humus and slowly available nitrogen. May be dug in freely at any time.

47. Hops Spent hops contain about 0·5% nitrogen, 1–2% phosphoric acid and a very small quantity of potash. They decay slowly and improve soil texture. They can be dug in freely at any time of the year in the same way as such bulky manures as stable manure and cow dung.

48. Leaf Mould Easily made in the garden, by collecting deciduous leaves, preferably oak and beech, in autumn. These are built into heaps and left for at least a year. The resulting leafmould can be dug in or used as a surface mulch to improve soil texture and moisture holding. It is usually acidic.

49. Liquid Manures These may be prepared with animal manures from stable, byre, pigsty, etc, or with soot or chemicals. The advantage of applying manures or fertilizers in liquid form is that they are more rapidly available, but plants cannot make use of the fresh organic substances they contain even in solution (42). It is only after such compounds have been broken down by bacterial action that they are available as plant food. In consequence, it is useless to prepare liquid manure from undecayed animal droppings. Liquid manure of animal origin may be prepared by diluting urine, or by steeping a bag of rotted manure in a tub of water. In either method the liquor must be diluted to the colour of straw. Applications may be given frequently to orna-mental plants, fruits, and vegetables in full growth.

50. Mushroom Compost Mostly composted straw and a useful addition to light, sandy soils. It often contains chalk, however, and is not recommended for alkaline soils. It may also contain pesticides used for growing mushrooms, so organic gardeners may prefer not to use it. Allowing it to weather for some months may allow the pesticides to break down gradually before use.

51. Poultry Droppings Droppings of all types of poultry may be used as manure. They contain a higher percentage of nitrogen and phosphates than stable and farmyard manure, but less potash, and must be balanced by appropriate chemicals (41). Weight for weight they are about four times as rich as animal manure. Fifty kilos (1 cwt) of moist droppings will dress from 20–35 square metres (24–40 yds²). If dried and powdered or pelletted the quantity would have to be even more reduced, and such manure is best employed like a chemical fertilizer at 250–380g per square metre (8–12oz per yd²). Poultry manure should be stored under cover. An average analysis of a moist sample is nitrogen 1·5%, phosphoric acid 1·5%, potash 0·5–0·75%. If thoroughly dried, this would rise to nitrogen 4%, phosphoric acid 3%, potash 1·5%. Can also be used to make liquid manure in the same way as other animal manures but should be well diluted (49).

52. Sewage Sludge When processed, is a useful substitute for farmyard manure and can be dug in at rates up to 100kg per 25 square metres (2cwt per rod or 30yds²), An analysis should be given, however, as some samples are too poor to be of much value. The analysis should show 2% or more of nitrogen and about 1·5% of phosphoric acid.

53. Seaweed A valuable substitute for

dung. Compared with this, seaweed is rich in potash and almost lacking in phosphates, so is even more in need of balancing with chemicals (43). Seaweed may either be dug in as gathered at rates of about 50kg to 7 square metres (1cwt to 8yds²) or may be dried and dug in at about 50kg to 20 square metres (1cwt to 24yds²). The bladder seaweeds and driftweeds with long, broad fronds are the best kinds. Analysis varies according to variety. An average for fresh seaweed is nitrogen 0·3%, phosphoric acid 0·1%, potash 1%.

54. Shoddy Waste from wool factories which decays slowly in the soil and may be used as a substitute for farmyard manure. Pure wool shoddy is more valuable than samples containing cotton. Shoddy is a bulky nitrogenous manure and improves the texture of the soil. Average rate of application approximately 250-500g per square metre (½-1 lb per yd²). Analyses show from 5 to 15% nitrogen.

Fertilizers

55. Basic Slag A slow-acting phosphatic fertilizer which also supplies lime. It is a steel-industry by-product and must be ground by machinery; the coarser the grinding the slower its action. Slag may remain in the soil for several years. Quality varies, and analysis may show anything from 8 to 22% phosphoric acid. Also the solubility, and consequently the availability, of the phosphoric acid varies. This is quoted on basis of solubility in citric acid. Over 80% soluble is good; below 40% poor and exceptionally slow acting. Most useful for autumn or winter application at rates from 130-250g per square metre (4-8oz per yd²).

56. Blood Contains nitrogen. Commercial dried blood is a fine dry power

containing about 7-14% nitrogen. This can be applied at rates up to 65g per square metre (2oz per yd²). Most serviceable for spring and early summer use and for plants in full growth or bearing.

57. Bonemeal An invaluable source of phosphates. Bonemeal is slow acting but this will depend on the grinding. The finer this is the more rapidly will the fertilizer be available. Analysis shows from 1 to 5% nitrogen (the high figure for raw bones containing gelatine not present in prepared bonemeal or bone flour), phosphoric acid 20 to 25%. Rates of application up to 130g per square metre (4oz per yd²) or 130g per 35 litres (4oz per bushel) of potting soil. Most useful for autumn and winter application and in potting composts.

58. Coal Ashes Of no value as a fertilizer. Sharp boiler ashes may be used to lighten clay soils.

59. Fish Meal The dried refuse from factories engaged in the smoking or canning of fish. It contains nitrogen, phosphorus and other plant foods and may be used at 60-90g per square metre (2-3oz per yd²). Average analysis: nitrogen 6-10%, phosphoric acid 4·5-9%, potash 0·5-0·75%. Prepared fish manure usually contains other chemicals to make it a balanced food and should be used according to manufacturers' instructions.

60. Hoof and Horn Meal A steady-acting manure which is of great value in the garden and especially with potting composts (96). With these it may be mixed at the rate of 50g per 35 litres (1½ oz per bushel). Outdoors it may be employed at rates of up to 66g per square metre (2oz per yd²). Average analysis: 12-14% nitrogren, 1-3% phosphoric acid.

61. Lime Strictly speaking, lime is calcium oxide, but the term is loosely applied in gardens to several other compounds of calcium. Though required by plants as food, calcium itself is almost invariably present in the soil in sufficient quantity for this purpose. Calcium oxide, calcium hydroxide, calcium carbonate and (less commonly) calcium sulphate are added as soil sweeteners, to liberate other chemicals and to improve the texture of heavy ground. For these purposes all forms of lime, including chalk, are identical except that some act more rapidly and others have better moisture-holding qualities.

HYDRATED LIME (air-slaked lime) is the quickest-acting form which can be used with safety around plants. A powder for use at rates up to 500g per square metre (1lb per yd^2).

CHALK (calcium carbonate) is slower in action, though this depends very much upon the fineness of grinding. Is especially suitable for light soil, as it holds moisture. Can be used at rates up to 1kg per square metre (2lb per yd^2).

GROUND LIMESTONE is another form of calcium carbonate. It is even slower acting, but again much depends on fineness. Can be used in the same way as chalk.

QUICKLIME (calcium oxide) is quick acting but caustic, unpleasant to handle and rarely used. It kills insects, etc, in the soil.

GYPSUM (calcium sulphate) is commonly used for improving soil structure and particularly for heavy clay soils. On heavy soils a dressing of 250g per square metre (8oz per yd^2) can be given.

MAGNESIAN LIMESTONE is a special form of limestone which contains magnesium as well as calcium carbonate. It may be used with advantage on all soils lacking in magnesium.

FERTILIZERS which contain *free lime* and therefore add it to the soil are nitrate of lime, Nitro-chalk, and basic slag.

Superphosphate of lime contains no free lime and cannot be employed in place of lime.

METHOD OF TESTING SOIL FOR LIME
Take a typical sample of soil, break up finely and half fill a tumbler with it. Pour in dilute hydrochloric acid. If there is much effervescence, free lime is present; if there is little or no effervescence, there is little or no free lime. This is a very rough and ready method of testing, however, as 'free lime' is not essential to the health of either plants or soil. What is important is 'available lime' i.e. lime in a particular physical association with the finest soil particles (colloids). This 'available lime,' is not shown by the acid test. A truer estimate can be obtained by means of a chemical 'soil indicator' giving a pH reading. If this shows pH 7·0 the soil is neutral. If the figure is higher than 7·0 the soil is alkaline, if below this figure it is acid. As a rule lime will be required only when the figure drops below 6·5 and even then not by any means for all plants. Rhododendrons and heathers thrive in soils as acid as pH 5·0.

62. Rock Phosphates. A source of slowly available phosphoric acid comparable with basic slag as a phosphatic fertilizer. Most useful for permanent crops and pastures. Rate of application 100-130g per square metre (3-4oz per yd^2). Best used in autumn or winter. Average analysis from 25 to 35% phosphoric acid. The finer the mineral is ground the better.

63. Muriate of Potash A relatively pure form of potash which must be used with caution, as it is injurious to some tender roots if brought directly into contact with them. Muriate of potash is frequently used in compound fertilizers and is readily soluble. Rate of application 15-30g per square metre ($1/2$-1oz per yd^2). Tends to make potatoes more waxy in texture. Best applied in autumn or winter. analysis: potash 40-60%, common salt 13-18%. (Correctly known as potassium chloride.)

64. Nitrate of Potash This is also known as saltpetre. It contains both nitrogen and potassium in readily assimilable form and is of great value as a liquid manure for pot plants if dissolved in water at the rate of 30g per 10 litres ($\frac{1}{2}$ oz per gall). Is too expensive for outdoor use. Analysis: nitrogen 12-14%, potash 44-46%. Do not confuse with potash nitrate (69).

65. Nitrate of Soda A very soluble salt rich in nitrogen. Sometimes used as a top dressing in summer, either alone or in combination with other quick-acting fertilizers. Has a caustic effect upon foliage and may do damage if applied carelessly. Nitrate of soda must not be mixed with superphosphate of lime. It tends to make clay soils more sticky. Rate of application 15-30g per square metre ($\frac{1}{2}$-1oz per yd^2), 2·5-5g per litre ($\frac{1}{4}$ - $\frac{1}{2}$ oz per gallon). Analysis: 16% nitrogen.

66. Nitrate of Lime Like Nitrochalk, a quick acting, granular nitrogenous fertilizer for general use in spring and early summer. Rate of application 30g per square metre (1oz per yd^2). May be used as a rotting agent on compost heaps (43). Analysis: nitrogen 15·5-16%.

67. Nitro–chalk A quick-acting proprietary fertilizer in granular form which supplies the soil with nitrogen and lime. Particularly valuable for acid and lime-free soils. Rate of application 30g per square metre (1oz per yd^2). Most suitable for spring or early summer application. May be used as a rotting agent on compost heaps (43). Analysis: nitrogen 15·5%, carbonate of lime 48%.

68. Phosphate of Potash Contains both phosphorus and potassium. Is very soluble and most serviceable as a liquid stimulant for pot plants in full growth. Use at 5g per litre ($\frac{1}{2}$ oz per gall). Too expensive for use outdoors. Analysis of commercial phosphate of potash is phosphoric acid 51%, potash 35%.

69. Potash Nitrate Often sold as Chilean potash nitrate and not to be confused with nitrate of potash, a quite different chemical. This is a quick-acting fertilizer supplying nitrogen and potash. Rate of application 15-30g per square metre ($\frac{1}{2}$-1oz per yd^2). Most suitable for spring or early summer application. Average analysis: nitrogen 15%, potash 10%, but some samples contain a higher proportion of potash and are correspondingly more valuable.

70. Potash Salts A general name given to various natural deposits containing muriate of potash in combination with other salts, such as common salt and magnesium sulphate. Others, not usually specifically named, contain higher percentages of potash. Should be bought on potash analysis, eg 30% potash salts are worth half again as much as 20% potash salts. Rate of application 15-30g per square metre (1-2oz per yd^2). They are best applied in autumn or winter.

Saltpetre, see **Nitrate of Potash (64).**

71. Salt (sodium chloride) Now illegal for use as a weed–killer and rarely used as a fertilizer, but is a source of sodium and helps to liberate potash already in the soil. Rate of application 30g per square metre (1oz per yd^2). Best used in winter or early spring. Is sometimes given to asparagus and seakale beds.

72. Sequestrols Some necessary elements rapidly become insoluble (and therefore unavailable as plant food) through chemical interaction in the soil. This is likely to occur with iron and manganese on alkaline soils, with copper on acid sandy or peaty soils and with zinc on sandy neutral or alkaline soils. Ordinary salts of these chemicals such as sulphate of iron and sulphate of manganese may then prove ineffective and instead special organic compounds known as sequestrols or chelates must be used. In these the necessary element is held for a considerable time immune from chemical reaction, yet available to plants. Sequestrols or chelates are sold as manufactured products sometimes individually, sometimes combined with other plant foods. Since they vary in formulation label instructions must be followed.

73. Soot A good sample may contain as much as 6% nitrogen in the form of sulphate of ammonia. Fresh soot is rather caustic and may be used as a soil fumigant to destroy insects and slugs. For use as a fertilizer it is best stored in the dry for three or four months. If exposed to rain or mixed with lime it quickly loses its value, though lime makes it yet more effective as a soil fumigant. Soot also enables soil to absorb sun heat more readily. Rate of application up to 200g per square metre (6oz per yd²). May be used at any time.

74. Steamed Bone Flour Virtually identical from the garden standpoint with fine bonemeal (57) except that all gelatine has been extracted so the flour is very dry, and mixed with other fertilizers it prevents them caking.

75. Sulphate of Ammonia A nitrogenous fertilizer used in a similar manner to nitrate of soda. On the whole a safer chemical to use, as it is not quite so quick acting or caustic. Tends to increase the acidity of acid soils. Must not be mixed with lime but may be mixed with superphosphate of lime, sulphate of potash, and muriate of potash. Rate of application 15-30g per square metre (½ -1oz per yd²). Best used in spring or early summer. Analysis: 20·6% nitrogen.

76. Sulphate of Iron If iron is lacking in the soil it may be applied in this form. Dressings at the rate of up to 30g per square metre (1oz per yd²) may be made in spring. Is also used as a fungicide to kill toadstools, etc, or moss on lawns and root-rot fungi at rates up to 250g per 10 litres (4oz per gall) of water. See also Sequestrols (72).

77. Sulphate of Magnesium If magnesium is lacking, this is the form in which it is usually supplied. The common salt as purchased is Epsom salt and contains water of crystallization which reduces its concentration to 10% magnesium. The rate of application for this commercial product is 30g per square metre (1oz per yd²) or 30-60g per 10 litres (½-1oz per gall) of water.

78. Sulphate of Potash The best form of potash for general use. It is noncaustic and reasonably quick acting. May be used at any time of the year. Rate of application 15-30g per square metre (½ -1oz per yd²). Analysis: 48% potash. Frequently increases disease resistance.

79. Superphosphate of Lime The best form in which to apply phosphates where a quick result is desired. Contains no free lime and will not affect acidity. Rate of application 30-100g per square metre (1-3oz per yd²). Most suitable for application in spring or early summer, but is apt to burn delicate foliage or flowers. Analysis: 18% phosphoric acid.

80. Wood Ashes A useful but variable source of potash. The amount present will depend upon the type and age of the wood burnt and the method of storage. Much potash may be washed away if wood ashes are left in the open. A good sample will contain 15% potash, a poor one as little as 4%. Apply up to 250g per square metre (8oz per yd²), at any time of the year.

COMPOUND FERTILIZERS

81. General Description The following formulae supply nitrogen, phosphoric acid, and potash and so fulfil the requirements stated under (41) for complete plant foods. There are also many proprietary compound fertilizers specially blended for certain plants.

A useful formula that can be used when preparing mixed fertilizers to give a definite percentage of certain plant foods is as follows:

$$N \left(\frac{100}{N^1}\right) + P \left(\frac{100}{P^1}\right) + K \left(\frac{100}{K^1}\right) + x = 100$$

Where N, P, and K represent respectively the percentages of nitrogen, phosphoric acid, and potash required in the mixture, while N^1, P^1, and K^1 represent the corresponding percentages in the individual ingredients, x will be the amount of non-active 'filler' (eg sand or fine peat) required to give bulk to the mixture. Note that this formula is serviceable only when each ingredient supplies one only of the plant foods required.

82. Potato Fertilizer (for early varieties).

Sulphate of ammonia	5 parts by weight
Superphosphate of lime	8 parts by weight
Sulphate or muriate of potash	3 parts by weight

Mix well and apply before or at planting time at the rate of 130g per square metre (4oz per yd²).

83. Potato Fertilizer (for late varieties).

Sulphate of ammonia	3 parts by weight
Superphosphate of lime	4 parts by weight
Sulphate of potash	2 parts by weight

Mix well and apply before or at planting time at the rate of 160g per square metre (5oz per yd²).

84. Root Crop Fertilizer (carrots, parsnips, beetroot, etc).

Sulphate of ammonia	1 part by weight
Superphosphate of lime	4 parts by weight
Sulphate of potash	2 parts by weight

Mix well and use prior to sowing at the rate of 130g per square metre (4oz per yd²).

85. Cabbage Crop Fertilizer (cabbages, savoys, brussels sprouts, kale, broccoli, etc).

Sulphate of ammonia	2 parts by weight
Superphosphate of lime	3 parts by weight
Sulphate of potash	1 part by weight

Mix and use prior to planting at the rate of 90g per square metre (3oz per yd²).

86. Pea and Bean Fertilizer

Sulphate of ammonia	1 part by weight
Superphosphate of lime	3 parts by weight
Sulphate of potash	2 parts by weight

Mix and use prior to sowing at the rate of 60g per metre (2oz per yd) of row.

87. Tomato Fertilizer

Sulphate of ammonia	2 parts by weight
Superphosphate of lime	3 parts by weight
Sulphate of potash	2 parts by weight

Mix well and use as a top dressing at the rate of one teaspoonful per plant every week or ten days from the time the first fruits begin to swell.

88. Fruit Tree Fertilizer

Sulphate of ammonia	2 parts by weight
Sulphate of potash	1 part by weight

Apply at the rate of 90g per square metre (3oz per yd²) in early spring. Every alternate year give, in addition, basic slag, at the rate of 130g per square metre (4oz per yd²) in mid-autumn.

89. Vine Fertilizer (for winter use)

Hoof and horn meal	2 parts by weight
Bonemeal	4 parts by weight
Sulphate of potash	1 part by weight

Mix well and use at the rate of 200g per square metre (6oz per yd²).

90. Vine Fertilizer (for summer use)

Dried blood	2 parts by weight
Superphosphate of lime	2 parts by weight
Sulphate of potash	1 part by weight

Mix well and use at the rate of 130g per square metre (4oz per yd²).

91. Chrysanthemum Fertilizer (1)

Hoof and horn meal	2 parts by weight

Bonemeal	4 parts by weight
Sulphate of Potash	1 part by weight
Ground chalk	1 part by weight

Mix in potting soil at the rate of 200g per 35 litres (6oz per bushel).

92. Chrysanthemum Fertilizer (2) (for summer feeding)

Sulphate of ammonia	2 parts by weight
Superphosphate of lime	4 parts by weight
Sulphate of potash	1 part by weight

Mix well and use in water at the rate of 30g to 12 litres (1oz to 3gall) once a week from about mid-summer till buds start to show colour.

93. Carnation Fertilizer

Sulphate of ammonia	2 parts by weight
Superphosphate of lime	3 parts by weight
Sulphate of potash	1 part by weight

Mix well and use $\frac{1}{2}$ teaspoonful per plant every week or ten days while in full growth and forming flower buds.

94. Rose Fertilizer (Tonk's formula)

Nitrate of potash	10 parts by weight
Superphosphate of lime	12 parts by weight
Sulphate of magnesium	2 parts by weight
Sulphate of iron	1 part by weight
Sulphate of lime (gypsum)	8 parts by weight

Crush and mix thoroughly and apply in mid-spring at the rate of 130g per square metre (4oz per yd²).

95. General Garden Fertilizer

Sulphate of ammonia	5 parts by weight
Superphosphate of lime	7 parts by weight
Sulphate of potash	2 parts by weight
Steamed bone flour	1 part by weight

Mix well and use as a top dressing, or prior to sowing or planting in spring or summer at rates from 90-160g per square metre (3-5oz per yd²) or in water at 60-100g per 10 litres (1 to 2oz per gall). This is an exceptionally well-balanced fertilizer.

96. Fertilizer for Mixing with General Potting Composts (John Innes formula). See (497).

97. Fertilizer for Mixing with

General Seed Composts (John Innes formula). See (493).

98. Fertilizer for Revitalizing Weak Lawns

Sulphate of ammonia	1 part by weight
Dried blood	2 parts by weight
Sulphate of potash	2 parts by weight
Sharp sand	20 parts by weight

Mix well and give two applications during the spring, each at the rate of 200g per square metre (6oz per yd²).

99. Lawn Sand

Sulphate of ammonia	3 parts by weight
Sulphate of iron	1 part by weight
Fine silver sand	20 parts by weight

Mix well and apply as necessary at the rate of 130g per square metre (4oz per yd²) during dry weather in spring and summer. This mixture burns out broad-leaved weeds and moss but stimulates the finer grasses.

MISCELLANEOUS NOTES

100. Mixing by Parts This system has been adopted in the foregoing recipes of mixed fertilizers because it is the most elastic and easily adjustable to individual needs. Note that all parts are by weight, not by bulk. The individual part can be of any convenient weight so long as the same unit of weight is used throughout the preparation of one mixture. For example, supposing 100g is chosen as the unit and the general fertilizer (95) is to be mixed, then 7 times 100g namely, 700g - of superphosphate will be required, 500g sulphate of ammonia, 200g sulphate of potash, and 100g steamed bone flour, making 1500g of fertilizer altogether, or enough to treat 10 square metres at 150g per m².

101. Fertilizers and Manures which must not be Mixed Some substances interact chemically with one another and lose their value. Such should never be mixed. The most important are sulphate of ammonia, Nitro-chalk, or soot with chalk or lime or any substance containing free lime, such as basic slag; and lime with dung or poultry droppings. Nitrates must not be mixed with acid substances. Superphosphate of lime can sometimes be acid, and must not be mixed with chalk, lime, or substances containing free lime.

102. Plant Hormones Strictly, this term applies to certain substances produced by plants which regulate growth but it is also used for some synthetic chemicals producing similar effects. A better term for these is 'growth regulators' For the amateur gardener, their main use

is in rooting powers and liquids, to improve success rates when propagating by cuttings, and in hormone weed-killers.

Growth regulators in excess are toxic to plants and this makes them useful as weed-killers. Some are used to kill annual and perennial broad-leaved weeds, theoretically without harming grasses and similar plants, and are sprayed on to the plants so that the solution is absorbed through the leaves and stems. These weed-killers are also absorbed through the roots. Plants sprayed with them curl and become distorted, gradually turn brown and eventually die. Hormone weed-killers must be used with care, according to the manufacturer's instructions.

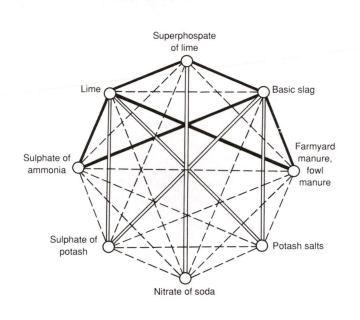

A Fertilizer mixing chart. Fertilizers connected by a thick black line should never be mixed, while those joined by double lines must only be mixed when for immediate use. Those connected by dotted lines can be mixed quite safely.

THE VEGETABLE GARDEN

MISCELLANEOUS NOTES

103. Rotational Cropping This idea has been taken over from farmers, who employ a definite rotation of crops from one year to the next with the object of making the very best use of the ground. Root crops may be used to clean newly broken ground prior to the cultivation of cereals, after which the land is allowed to lie fallow for a year or is put down once more to grass. No such clearly defined annual system of rotation is practicable on the allotment or in small gardens, partly because it is necessary to keep much of the ground in constant use, and partly because of the difficulty of devising any rotation which will give an ideal sequence of crops together with a sensible division of the ground according to the requirements of the consumer.

One advantage of rotation is that it conserves the food reserves of the soil and so reduces the need for manuring. Green crops and potatoes make a comparatively high demand on the nitrogen in the soil, and both benefit greatly from applications of well-rotted animal manure. Such manure is harmful to carrots, parsnips, and beetroots, which require abundant potash rather than nitrogen. A fundamental point in any system of garden rotation should be that, so far possible, green crops and potatoes should be followed by roots.

A type of rotation that can be followed roughly in most gardens is to divide the ground into three approximately equal sections and devote one mainly to green crops, one to potatoes, and one to roots, peas, and beans and other vegetables.

Then in the second year everything can be shifted on one place, the greens coming to the potato plot, the potatoes going on to the ground cleared of roots, and the roots occupying the plot cleared of greens. The third year there is a similar shift on, and the fourth year the crops come back to their original plots (104). Onions may well stand outside such a system of rotation and have a more or less permanent bed to themselves.

104. Suggested Three-year Rotation (see table overleaf). The scheme is applicable to plots of any size or shape, so no particular dimensions are necessary. The only essential is that sections A, B, and C should be of approximately the same area. They need not be of the same shape. The second year the order of the crops from top to bottom is C, A, B, D; the third year B, C, A, D; the fourth year the same as the first year. Onions are not included in the rotation because they appear to derive greater benefit from being grown on the same plot for a number of years. If, however, it is preferred to include them they should go to plot C.

105. Intercropping Some crops take up a good deal of space above ground without anything like occupying all the ground with their roots. Examples are the taller varieties of peas and runner beans. Space is necessary with these to prevent one row from shading the next so heavily that the plants would fall into ill health. But some crops appreciate shade, and it is an obvious deduction to plant these between tall subjects that require a lot of room. That is the simplest form of intercropping. Cleverly practised, it can be a great space saver in the garden.

104. Suggested Three-year Rotation

	THREE YEAR ROTATION PLAN
A	Cabbages, cauliflowers, brussels sprouts, kale, savoys, and other brassicas. Preceded by, or intercropped with lettuces, radishes, and other small salads. Plot dressed with animal manure or compost and limed (not together). Crops fed while in growth with nitrate of soda or sulphate of ammonia.

B	Potatoes. Followed by broccoli, spring cabbage, coleworts, leeks, and late-sown turnip (for tops).
	    Plot dressed with animal manure or compost, but *not* lime.
	    Complete fertilizer applied just prior to planting potatoes (83).

C	Carrots, parsnips, turnips, and beetroots.
	    Peas and beans with summer spinach and lettuces between.
	    No animal manure or compost except for pea and bean trenches. Wood ashes forked in. Complete fertilizer (low nitrogen ratio) applied just prior to sowing (93).

D	Onions. Plot dressed with animal manure or compost and wood ashes. Nitrate of soda after thinning.

Winter greens or other plants raised in a reserve bed may be ready for planting out before any ground is vacant for them, though another crop is nearing maturity and will shortly be harvested. Under such circumstances it is in order to plant the new crop between the old. Do not inter-crop in this way too long in advance of the time of harvesting the preceding crop or the result may be starved and drawn plants.

106. Catch Cropping Sometimes ground has to be prepared some consider-able time before it will be needed, and it may be possible to get a quick-growing crop in before that for which the ground was actually intended is ready to go in. This is known as catch cropping, and is a method of economizing both space and time in the vegetable garden. Lettuces, radishes, spring onions (for use in salads), summer spinach, mustard and cress are a few of the best catch crops, and they may be sown in celery trenches or on the ridges on each side of such trenches, on the ground prepared for the later kinds of winter greens or for very late sowings of quick-maturing peas and in other similar places.

107. Successional Sowing If all the seeds of such things as lettuces, radishes, spinach, early carrots, early turnips, or peas are put in at one time the result will be a glut for a few weeks followed by a complete lack of supplies. The right course is to make a number of small sow-ings at intervals of a fortnight or three weeks so that a continuous supply of the

108. Approximate yield of vegetables

Vegetable	Per square metre	Per square yard	Per metre of row	Per ft of row
Beans, broad	1·2kg	2·3lb	750g	8oz
Beans, French	700g	1·5lb	375g	4oz
Beans, runner	12kg	24lb	6kg	4lb
Beans, haricot★	200g	5–6oz	100g	1oz
Beetroot	2·5kg	5·5lb	1·3kg	14oz
Broccoli	3kg	6lb	1·7kg	19oz
Brussels sprouts	1kg	2lb	850g	9oz
Cabbage (spring)	2kg	4lb	1kg	11oz
Cabbage (autumn and winter)	3·5kg	7lb	2·2kg	1·5lb
Cauliflower	2·5kg	5lb	1·6kg	1lb
Carrots (main)	3kg	6·5lb	1·1kg	12oz
Carrots (early)	1·5kg	3·75lb	450g	5oz
Endive	10–12 heads	10 heads	2–3 heads	1 head
Kale	2·3kg	5lb	1·5kg	1·3lb
Leek	2·3kg	5lb	1·2kg	13oz
Lettuce	12–14 heads	10–13 heads	5–6·5 heads	1·5–2 heads
Mushrooms	4·8kg	10lb	–	–
Onions	2·5kg	5·5lb	900g	10oz
Parsnips	2·3kg	5lb	1·2kg	13oz
Peas	700g	1·5lb	500g	6oz
Potatoes (main)	2·5kg	5lb	2·2kg	1·5lb
Savoys	2·8kg	7lb	2·2kg	1·5lb
Shallots	3·6kg	8lb	900g	10oz
Spinach (summer)	1·5kg	3·75lb	450g	5oz
Swedes	2·7kg	6lb	1·3kg	14oz
Turnips (main)	2·7kg	6lb	1·3kg	14oz
Tomatoes (under glass)	6·8kg	15lb	3·5kg	6lb per plant
Tomatoes (outdoor)	4·8kg	10lb	2·5kg	4lb per plant

★ Seeds only

vegetable is ensured.

There are early, mid-season, and late varieties of many vegetables. One important difference in these is in the time they take to reach maturity. For example, an early pea may be ready for picking twelve weeks after sowing, whereas a mid-season variety sown at the same time will not be ready for a further fortnight, and a late kind may take a full sixteen weeks. By a wise selection of these different kinds it will also be possible to lengthen the season and maintain continuity of supply.

For very late sowings an early variety is often selected. This is explained by the fact that there is such a limited period of good weather left for growth that only a naturally quick-growing variety can mature in time. This is particularly noticeable with peas, carrots, and turnips.

109. Continuity Chart for Principal Vegetables

Vegetable	mid winter	late winter	early spring	mid spring	late spring
Artichokes	███	███	██		
Beet	░░░	░░░	░░░	░░░	░░░
Beans, broad	░░░	░░░	░░░	░░░	░░░
– French	░░░	░░░	░░░	░░░	░░░
– runner	░░░	░░░	░░░	░░░	░░░
Broccoli, heading	███	███	███	███	███
– sprouting		███	███	███	███
Brussels sprouts	███	███			
Cabbages	███	███	███	███	███
Carrots	░░░	░░░	░░░	░░░	░░░
Cauliflowers	░░░	░░░	░░░	░░░	░░░
Celeriac	░░░	░░░	░░░		
Celery	███	███	███	███	
Endive	███	███	███		
Kale	███	███	███	███	███
Kohl Rabi					
Leeks	███	███	███	███	
Lettuces					
Onions	░░░	░░░	░░░	░░░	░░░
Parsnips	███	███			
Peas	░░░	░░░	░░░	░░░	░░░
Potatoes	░░░	░░░	░░░	░░░	░░░
Savoys	███	███	███	███	
Shallots	░░░	░░░	░░░	░░░	░░░
Spinach	███	███	███	███	
Spinach beet		███	███	███	███
Turnips	░░░	░░░	░░░	░░░	░░░
Turnip tops			███	███	███
Vegetable marrows	░░░	░░░	░░░	░░░	
	mid winter	late winter	early spring	mid spring	late spring

Key ███ Times at which vegetables are available from the open ground.

early summer	mid summer	late summer	early autumn	mid autumn	late autumn	early winter

early summer	mid summer	late summer	early autumn	mid autumn	late autumn	early winter

Key   Additional period during which vegetables may be stored or preserved. With careful management it may be possible to extend the season of some crops even further.

110. Vegetable Sowing and Planting Chart

SEEDS TO BE SOWN OR THINNED IN THE ROW

Vegetable	Seeds for 10m/50ft row	When to sow	Distance between rows	Distance to sow or thin
Beans				
– broad	284ml/½pt	early win	60cm/2ft	15cm/6in
– French	142ml/¼pt	early – mid spr	45cm/18in	20cm/8in
– haricot	142ml/¼pt	mid – late win	45cm/18in	20cm/8in
– runner	284ml/½pt	late spr – early sum	2.5m/8ft	20cm/8in
Beet	7g/¼oz	mid spr – early sum	30cm/12in 35cm/15in	15-20cm/6-8in
– seakale	7g/¼oz	early spr – late sum	45cm/18in	22cm/9in
Carrot	7g/¼oz	early spr – early sum	20cm/8in 35cm/15in	5-10cm/2-4in
Endive	3·5g/⅛oz	mid spr – late sum	30cm/1ft	22cm/9in
Kohl Rabi	3·5g/⅛oz	mid spr – late sum	45cm/18in	30cm/1ft
Lettuce	3·5g/⅛oz	mid spr – late sum	22cm/9in 30cm/1ft	15-22cm/6-9in
Onion	5·5g/⅙oz	early spr	30cm/1ft	15cm/6in
Parsley	7g/¼oz	early spr – late sum	22cm/9in	13cm/5in
Parsnip	7g/¼oz	late win – early spr	45cm/18in	20cm/8in
Peas	142ml/¼pt	early spr – early sum	60-150cm/2-5ft	7·5cm/3in
Radish	14g/½oz	early spr – late sum	15cm/6in	
Spinach				
– summer	7g/¼oz	early spr – mid sum	30cm/1ft	20cm/8in
– winter	7g/¼oz	late sum	30cm/1ft	15cm/6in
– beet	7g/¼oz	early spr – late sum	45cm/18in	22cm/9in
Swede	7g/¼oz	late spr – early sum	35cm/15in	20cm/8in
Turnip	7g/¼oz	early spr – mid sum	30cm/12in 35cm/15in	10-20cm/4-8in

Depth to sow	When ready for use	Remarks
2·5cm/1in	sum	Autumn sowing should only be attempted in fairly sheltered places.
2·5cm/1in	mid sum – mid aut	Gather the beans while still young.
2·5cm/1in	mid aut onwards	Leave beans to ripen in pod, and then shell out and store dry for winter use.
2·5cm/1in	mid sum – mid aut	Plants may be grown as bushes by frequent pinching of runners.
2·5cm/1in	mid sum onwards	Globe varieties are best for early use; cylindrical rooted kinds for storing.
2·5cm/1in	All year round	The leaves are cut as required, and boiled in the same way as spinach.
0·5cm/¼in	early sum onwards	Sow stump-rooted varieties for early use and intermediate kinds for storing.
1cm/½in	late sum – early spr	Specially welcome in winter.
1cm/½in	mid sum – early aut	Withstands drought remarkably well.
1cm/½in	early sum – early aut	Winter supplies obtained by placing seedlings in frames in mid autumn.
1cm/½in	late sum onwards	Lift in early autumn for storing.
1cm/½in	early sum – early aut	Winter supplies obtained by placing seedlings in frame in mid autumn.
2·5m/1in	early aut onwards	Roots may be left in the ground all winter, or lifted and stored.
2·5cm/1in	early sum – mid aut	Make frequent small sowings so that a successional supply is maintained.
0·5cm/¼in	mid spr – early aut	Early supplies may be obtained by sowing in late winter on a hotbed.
2·5m/1in	early sum – early aut	Make small successional sowings.
2·5m/1in	mid aut – mid spr	A sheltered position should be chosen.
2·5m/1in	mid sum onwards	Continues to crop for a long time.
1cm/½in	mid aut onwards	A wholesale and profitable vegetable.
1cm/½in	early sum onwards	For summer supplies it is best to sow in a partially shaded position.

▶

110. Vegetable Sowing and Planting Chart contd.

SEEDS TO BE SOWN IN A SEEDBED AND TRANSPLANTED TO WHERE THEY ARE TO BE GROWN

Vegetable	Seeds to supply 100 plts	When to sow	When to transplant
Borecole (kale)	3·5g/⅛oz	mid – late spr	mid – late sum
Broccoli	5·5g/¼oz	early – late spr	late spr – mid sum
Brussels sprouts	3·5g/⅛oz	early – mid spr	late spr – early sum
Cabbage, summer autumn, winter	3·5g/⅛oz	early – mid spr	late spr – mid sum
Cabbage, spring	3·5g/⅛oz	mid – late sum	early – mid aut
Cauliflower	3·5g/⅛oz	late win – mid spr	late spr – early sum
Celery	1g/¹⁄₃₂oz	late win – mid spr	early – mid sum
Cucumber (ridge)	100 seeds	mid – late spr	early sum
Leek	2g/¹⁄₁₆oz	early spr	early sum
Onion (for transplanting)	2g/¹⁄₁₆oz	late sum – mid win	mid spr
Savoy	14g/½oz	mid – late spr	early – late sum
Tomato	7g/¼oz	early spr (under glass)	early sum
Vegetable marrow	100 seeds	mid – late spr	early sum

Remarks Key

1 There are numerous varieties, including the well-known curled kales.

2 Varieties can be obtained to give a succession from autumn until late spring.

3 Plant very firmly in soil that has not been over manured.

4 Varieties should be chosen to give the required succession.

5 Not all kinds are suitable for summer sowing. Consult catalogue on this point.

6 More delicate in flavour than the broccoli, and also more tender.

7 Raise the seedlings in a geenhouse or frame.

8 Pinch out tips of main runners, to encourage formation of side growths.

108. Approximate Yield of Vegetables The figures (page 35) can only give a rough guide to average production. Yield varies greatly according to soil, weather, and degree of cultural skill. Figures 50% in excess of those given may be obtained under favourable conditions.

Almost all the weights quoted are for maincrop varieties allowed to mature. Earlies may be harvested at practically any stage of growth, so no reliable weights can be given. Exception is made with early carrots, as figures are taken from the average market yield of shorthorn varieties allowed to develop.

109. Continuity for Principal Vegetables (see table pages 36–37)

110. Vegetable Sowing and Planting (see table pages 38–41)

111. Germinating Period of Veg-

Distance between rows	Distance between plants	Depth to sow	When ready for use	Remarks
75cm/2½ft	45cm/18in	1cm/½in	late aut – late spring	1
75cm/2½ft	60cm/2ft	1cm/½in	mid aut – late sum	2
75cm/2½ft	60cm/2ft	1cm/½in	early aut – late win	3
60cm/2ft	45cm/18in	1cm/½in	mid sum – late win	4
45cm/18in	30cm/1ft	1cm/½in	early spr – early sum	5
75cm/2½ft	60cm/2ft	1cm/½in	late sum – early win	6
90cm/3ft	30cm/1ft	0·5cm/¼in	early aut – early spr	7
120cm/4ft	90cm/3ft	2·5cm/½in	mid sum – early aut	8
45cm/18in	22cm/9in	0·5cm/¼in	early aut – late spr	9
30cm/1ft	15cm/6in	0·5cm/¼in	early sum	10
60cm/2ft	45cm/18in	1cm/½in	mid sum – early spr	11
90cm/3ft	45cm/18in	0·5cm/¼in	late sum – mid aut	12
120cm/4ft	90cm/3ft	2·5cm/1in	mid sum – mid aut	13

▶

9   Earlier supplies can be obtained by sowing in a warm greenhouse in mid-winter and transplanting outdoors in mid-spring.

10   White Lisbon onions can be sown more thickly in late summer for use as salading in the spring.

11   A hardy and profitable vegetable.

12   Earlier plants for cultivation throughout in the greenhouse can be raised from seed sown in mid–late winter.

13   Pinch main runners of trailing varieties to induce formation of side growths.

etable Seeds The table of germination times (page 42) is necessarily only approximate. Actual times will vary greatly according to soil, warmth and weather. Given a sufficiently low temperature or dry soil, seeds will remain dormant indefinitely. The times given overleaf are for normal conditions at the usual sowing times.

CULTIVATION OF VEGETABLES ALPHABETICALLY ARRANGED

The following notes are based on kitchen and not exhibition requirements. Vegetables required for show must, in general, be given considerably more space and a higher rate of feeding.

112. Artichokes, Jerusalem Much like a perennial sunflower, and belongs to

110. Vegetable Sowing and Planting Chart contd.

◄

ROOTS AND TUBERS FOR PLANTING

Vegetable	Roots for 10m/50ft row	When to plant	Distance between rows	Distance between plants
Artichoke – globe	10/16	mid spr	90cm/3ft	90cm/3ft
Artichoke, – Jerusalem	2·1kg/7lb	late win	75cm/2½ft	35cm/15in
Asparagus	26/40	mid spr	35cm/15in	35cm/15in
Onion sets	150g/⅓lb	early spr	30cm/1ft	15cm/6in
Potatoes – early	2·4kg/8lb	early spr	75cm/2½ft	30cm/1ft
– mid-season	2·1kg/7lb	mid spr	90cm/3ft	35cm/15in
– late	2·1kg/7lb	mid spr	90cm/3ft	35cm/15in
Rhubarb	10/16	early spr	90cm/3ft	90cm/3ft
Shallots	600–900g/ 2–3lb	late win – early spr	30cm/1ft	15cm/6in

GERMINATING PERIOD OF VEGETABLE SEEDS

Name	Time (days)	Name	Time (days)	Name	Time (days)
Beans		Cress	5–8	Parsnip	21–28
– broad	8–12	Cucumber	5–15	Pea	7–12
– French	10–14	Endive	14–21	Radish	6–10
– runner	10–14	Kale	7–12	Savoy	7–12
Beet	18–24	Kohl Rabi	7–12	Spinach	
– seakale	18–24	Leek	21–24	– summer	10–15
Borecole	7–12	Lettuce	10–15	– winter	10–15
Broccoli	7–12	Mustard	4–8	– beet	18–24
Brussels Sprouts	7–12	Onion		Swede	7–12
Cabbage	7–12	– spring-sown	21–25	Tomato	7–14
Carrot	17–24	– late summer-		Turnip	7–12
Cauliflower	7–12	sown	12–18	Vegetable Marrow	6–10
Celery	18–28	Parsley	28–42		

Depth to plant	When ready for use	Remarks
5cm/2in	mid sum – mid aut	The flower heads are cut before they begin to expand.
15cm/6in	late aut – early spr	May be used as a windbreak.
5-7.5cm/2-3in	late spr – early sum	Do not cut asparagus for at least two years and never after early summer.
half-covered	mid sum onwards	A good method for those who cannot practise autumn sowing.
10-12.5cm/4-5in	early-mid sum	It is an advantage to sprout the tubers in a light frost-proof place before planting.
10-12.5cm/4-5in	late sum onwards	Dig when the skins are firm.
10-12.5cm/4-5in	late sum onwards	Dig when the skins are firm.
buds just showing above ground	early spr – mid sum	Earlier supplies can be obtained by covering the roots with barrels in mid winter.
half-covered	mid sum onwards	First class for pickling.

the same family. One important difference is that it has tuberous edible roots not unlike those of the potato. Soil is not a matter of first importance. Heaviest crops are obtained through autumn or winter digging and application of manure or vegetable compost at 50kg to 10 square metres (1cwt to 12yd²). Position in sun or partial shade. Plant in late winter with spade or trowel, 35cm (15in) apart in rows 75cm (2½ft) apart. Holes should be 15cm (6in) deep. No subsequent cultivation required except periodic hoeing. Tubers are ready between late autumn and early spring and may be dug as required or lifted at once and stored in sacks or clamp like potatoes.

A proportion of the tubers may be set aside for replanting, but no sprouting is required.

113. Artichokes, Globe Highly ornamental plants grown for their flower-heads, which are eaten before they open, when the fleshy scales are regarded as a delicacy. Plants can be raised from seed sown in a frame in early spring or outdoors in mid-spring, but this is not recommended. The best method is to detach offsets early in mid-spring, selecting from the best plants. These are replanted in well dug, fairly rich soil and open position. Space 90cm (3ft) apart each way. Mulch with manure in late spring. Cut off all flower stems the first season. Cropping is most profitable in the second and third years, after which beds should be remade. Remove dead leaves in mid autumn and cover crowns with bracken or straw until early spring. Cut heads regularly as soon as they are plump and the scales fleshy.

114. Asparagus Plants can be raised from seed sown in a greenhouse or frame in early spring or outdoors in late spring, but it is better to purchase two-year-old roots early in mid-spring. These will start to crop two years after planting. Plant 35cm (15in) apart in rows 35cm (15in) apart. Common practice is to make bed 120cm (4ft) wide containing three rows each raised above ground level to improve winter drainage, or plants may be grown on the flat 35cm (15in) apart in rows 1m (3½ft) apart and after two years soil is drawn over the plants as when earthing up potatoes. Either way, soil must be deeply dug and liberally manured. Top dress each early spring with short, well-rotted manure or hop manure. Do not cut after early to mid-summer but allow plants to make foliage, which should be cut off above soil level in mid- to late autumn.

115. Aubergine (Egg Plant) These are grown for their fleshy fruits. Seeds are sown in pans or boxes in a warm greenhouse during mid- to late winter. Seedlings are pricked off and later potted singly into small pots from which they are worked on into 15 or 17·5cm (6 or 7in) pots for fruiting. Soils and treatment throughout this period are the same as for tomatoes (168) except that side shoots are not removed; the points of growth are pinched out when seedlings are 15cm (6in) high and each plant is restricted to about six fruits. Water freely.

116. Beans, Broad Two types are grown – the Longpod, and the Windsor. The first is sufficiently hardy for autumn

sowing in many districts; while the second is best for bottling or freezing.

For spring sowing, manure or compost may be applied at 50kg to 12 square metres (1cwt to 15yd²). It is an excellent plan to follow the crop after brassicas or potatoes, for which the ground has already been manured. Prior to autumn sowing, dust the ground with basic slag 100g (3oz), and sulphate of potash 30g per square metre (1oz per yd²). These fertilizers may also be used prior to spring sowing, plus sulphate of ammonia, at the rate of 30g per square metre (1oz per yd²), if no manure is available.

Sow 15cm (6in) apart in drills 2.5cm (1in) deep and 60cm (2ft) apart. Autumn sowings should be made in mid- to late autumn, spring sowings during early and mid-spring. An early crop can be obtained by sowing seeds 5cm (2in) apart each way in boxes in mid- to late winter and germinating in a warm greenhouse, or a month later in a frame set on a hotbed. Seedlings are planted outdoors in about mid-spring, spaced as seeds outdoors.

Pinch out the growing points as soon as the plants have set two or three clusters of pods each. Gather beans frequently as they attain suitable size. Good varieties are Aquadulce for autumn sowing and Witkiem Major and Green Longpod for spring sowing. The Sutton is a fine dwarf variety. Hylon has very long pod, and is good for showing.

Black fly and chocolate spot are common foes (667).

117. Beans, Haricot These are really French beans (118), but are grown for their ripened seeds, which are stored and used during winter. Preparation of ground and cultivation are the same as for French beans, and it is only in the harvesting that there is any difference of treatment. Pods should be allowed to hang until they turn rown, when the whole plants are pulled up, tied in small bundles, and hung head downwards in a shed or room to dry off. Then the seeds can be shelled out and stored in dry bins for the winter. Reliable varieties are Chevrier Vert and Comtesse de Chambord (white seeded).

Mosaic and anthracnose are the commonest diseases (667).

118. Beans, French There are two main types, the dwarf and the climbing. The former are of more use to the amateur, as they require no staking. Soil should be prepared as for broad beans (116), and the same fertilizers used. Sow in mid- to late spring outdoors. Earlier crops can be obtained by sowing seeds 5cm (2in) apart each way in boxes in mid-spring, and germinating in a greenhouse or frame. The seedlings should be planted outdoors in early summer. Seeds shown outdoors should be spaced 20cm (8in) apart in drills 2·5cm (1in) deep and 45cm (18in) apart. These are also correct spacings for seedlings. Gather beans frequently while still quite tender. Water freely during dry weather. Surplus beans may be frozen, stored in salt, or allowed to dry, the seeds being used as haricots.

Reliable varieties are Tendergreen, Masterpiece, and The Prince. Mont d'Or is an excellent yellow waxpod.

Foes as for haricot beans (117).

119. Beans, Runner Soil should be prepared as for broad beans (116). Manure or compost, though not essential, is useful. An economical method is to prepare a trench 45cm (18in) wide and deep for each row and mix manure thoroughly with the soil in this. Fertilizers as for broad beans.

Sow outdoors in late spring. The plants are even more tender than French beans. Alternatively, plants may be raised in boxes as described for French beans (118) and be planted out in early summer.

Seeds or plants should be spaced outdoors 20cm (8in) apart in a double line 25cm (10in) apart. If more than one such double line is required, a space of at least 2·5m (8ft) must be left between each. Stakes at least 2·5m (8ft) in length must be placed in position, one to each plant, before the beans commence to climb.

An alternative method of cultivation is to sow or plant 60cm (2ft) apart in rows 90cm (3ft) apart and pinch out the tips of young shoots repeatedly from early to late summer. This makes the plants become bushy, and no stakes are required.

Good varieties are Sunset, Streamline, Kelvedon Marvel. Hammond's Dwarf Scarlet is bushy, short and needs no staking.

Flower dropping is the commonest trouble. It is usually caused by cold nights, but may be aggravated by dry soil.

120. Beetroot There are three distinct types of beetroot, grown for their roots — the globe, or round-rooted, the intermediate, or cylindrical-rooted, and the long. The first is valuable for early crops, but the others are capable of giving heavier crops and should, in consequence, be planted for the maincrop. Spinach and seakale beetroots are grown for their stems and leaves and not for their roots, and are separately dealt with (162), (165). Dig the soil thoroughly, working in manure or compost at the rate of 50kg to 17 square metres (1cwt to 20yd²), if none has been applied for a previous crop, and, just prior to sowing, rake in a dressing of the following mixture at 100-130g per square metre (3-4oz per yd²): 1 part of sulphate of ammonia, 1 part of sulphate of potash, 5 parts of superphosphate of lime.

Seed for an early crop may be sown in mid-spring and for the main crop in late spring. Draw drills 2·5cm (1in) deep and 30-35cm (12-15in) apart, and sow seeds in small groups 15cm (6in) apart for round and 20cm (8in) for intermediate and long-rooted varieties. Reduce seedlings to one at each cluster. After thinning, dust sulphate of ammonia or nitrate of soda between the rows at the rate of 30g (1oz) to every 3·5m (12ft). Germination of beetroot seed is usually rather poor. Soaking in water for 30 minutes prior to sowing may help.

Lift early kinds from early to midsummer onwards, as required. Maincrop beetroot should be lifted in early autumn and stored in sand or peat in a dry, frost-proof place. Twist off the tops.

Good kinds are Avon Early, Detroit-Little Ball, Cylindra, and Cheltenham Greentop.

Foes seldom give much trouble, but cutworms may damage the roots while leaves are occasionally attacked by leaf miners (667).

121. Broccoli, Heading Closely allied to cauliflower, and sometimes called winter cauliflower, from the culinary point of view it is identical except that flavour is less delicate. It is also hardier and has a much longer season. Where possible, follow broccoli after early potatoes or some other crop that has already had manure, and give chemicals only. It will then only be necessary to clear off weeds and other rubbish, dust the surface with the fertilizers, fork in, and tread firmly. Recommended chemicals are hydrated lime at 250g per square metre (8oz per yd²); basic slag at 100g per square metre (3oz per yd²); and either sulphate of potash or muriate of potash at 30g per square metre (1oz per yd²). If ground manured for a previous crop is not available, work in a moderate dressing of dung or compost, about 50kg to 15 square metres (1cwt to 18yd²); then give the chemicals described above as a top dressing.

Seed should be sown outdoors in mid- to late spring. For early supplies it is an advantage to sow a few seeds in a frame in early spring. In all methods sow thinly in drills 1cm (½ in) deep and 15cm (6in) apart.

Plant from late spring to midsummer with a trowel and press soil firmly around the roots. Water freely if the weather is dry, but when possible plant during showery weather. Space 60cm (2ft) apart in rows 75cm (2½ft) apart.

As the plants approach maturity, bend inner leaves inwards over the curds for protection.

Varieties may be grouped as early, mid-season, and late. The first are ready from mid-autumn to mid-winter, the second from mid-winter to mid-spring, and the third carry on the supply until early summer. Standard kinds are: *early*, Superb Early White; *mid-season*, Leamington, Snow's Winter White, Saint David, Purple Cape; *late*, Late Queen, St George, Birchington, May Blossom.

Club root, cabbage caterpillars, flea beetle, and cabbage root fly are the commonest foes (667).

122. Broccoli, Sprouting Grown for the flowering shoots, which are cut off when 15-23cm (6-9in) in length. Sprouting broccoli are hardier than heading kinds, and the sprouts are produced successively for a long time. Soil should be well dug and moderately enriched with manure at about 50kg to 10 square metres (1cwt to 12yd²), unless plants follow a crop for which manure has been applied, when give soot at 250g per square metre (8oz per yd²) or the fertilizer mixture as recommended for heading broccoli (121).

Seed should be sown in mid-spring in the same manner as for heading broccoli. Plant seedlings from early summer to early autumn 45cm (18in) apart in rows

75cm (2½ft) apart. Sprouts should be cut as they become available.

Good varieties are Calabrese Romanesco, Christmas Purple Sprouting, and early and late purple and white sprouting.

Club root, cabbage caterpillars, flea beetle, and cabbage root fly are the commonest foes (667).

123. Brussels Sprouts Soil preparation should be thorough. Work in well-rotted animal manure or compost at the rate of 50kg to 10-17 square metres (1cwt to 12-20yd²), or, better still, choose a plot that has been manured for some previous crop, such as potatoes. Then chemicals only will be required. Sulphate of ammonia may be applied in spring at 15g per square metre (½oz per yd²); supplement with sulphate of potash, 15g per square metre (½oz per yd²), and superphosphate of lime, 65g per square metre (2oz per yd²). Six or eight weeks after planting, give another dressing of sulphate of ammonia, Nitro-chalk, or nitrate of soda at 15g per metre (½oz per yd) run. Do not apply fertilizers after late summer.

Seed should be sown in a frame or greenhouse in early spring or outdoors in mid-spring as described for heading broccoli (121) and young plants treated in a similar manner. Plant out very firmly in mid- to late spring, or, if the sprouts are to follow some other crop, as soon as this can be cleared. Set plants 60cm (2ft) apart in rows 75cm (2½ft) apart.

Picking may begin as soon as the most forward buttons attain usable size. Do not strip the plants, but leave smaller sprouts to gain size. The tops can be cut and used as 'greens' in early to mid-autumn and this will help sprouts to swell.

Pear Gynt, Citadel, Rampart, Bedford-Fillbasket, Rubine, Noisette are good varieties.

Club root, caterpillars, root fly, flea beetle, aphid and white fly are the pests most to be feared. Gall weevils, often present, do little harm (667).

124. Cabbage By judicious selection of varieties and by successional sowing it is possible to maintain a supply of cabbage throughout the year. Soil should be well prepared. Manure or compost at the rate of 50kg to 8-10 square metres (1cwt to 10-12 yd²) will be well repaid, but may be omitted for late-summer-planted cabbages following a crop such as potatoes or peas, for which manure has already been given. If the manure is omitted, a top dressing of soot at 130g per square metre) (4oz per yd²) or sulphate of ammonia at 30g per square metre (1oz per yd²) will be sufficient.

Usually two sowings are enough, one made outdoors in mid-spring and the other between mid- and late summer. If a midsummer supply is required, a third sowing should be made in a frame or greenhouse in late winter or early spring. Sometimes a fourth sowing is made outdoors in late spring or early summer to give cabbages in mid-winter. Details of sowing are the same as for heading broccoli (121), and planting is carried out in the same manner except that it will be sufficient to allow 30cm (1ft) between the plants and 45cm (18in) between the rows for spring cabbage – that is to say, those that are planted out in autumn and harvested the following spring – and 45cm (18in) between plants and 60cm (2ft) between rows for autumn and winter cabbage.

Reliable kinds are as follows: *For spring sowing*, Golden Acre-Progress, Primo, Greyhound, Winnigstadt, January King, and Christmas Drumhead; *for summer sowing*, April, Offenham - Flower of Spring, Harbinger, Spring Hero, and Durham Early; *for late winter sowing*, Golden Acre - Progress.

Club root, caterpillars, cabbage root fly, cabbage aphid, flea beetle and white fly are the worst foes (667).

125. Cardoons Ornamental plants grown for their blanched stems, which are used, both cooked and raw, in salads. Plants may be raised from seed sown in a warm greenhouse or in a frame in mid-spring, two or three seeds in each 7.5cm (3in) pot. Reduce seedlings to one per pot and harden off for planting out in late spring. The plants should be 45cm (18in) apart in rows 90cm (3ft) apart. Situation should be open and the soil well dug and manured. Blanching starts in early autumn, when plants are well grown, and is done as for celery (129), or by tying corrugated brown paper or clean straw around the stems. Usually about eight weeks are required to obtain well-blanched stems.

126. Carrots These may be divided according to the length of their roots, viz long, intermediate or short, and also according to shape, viz tapering or stump rooted (cylindrical). The short, stump-rooted varieties are used for early crops; longer stump-rooted varieties are the most popular for general use, long tapered carrots being grown primarily for exhibition.

Soil for intermediate and long types must be dug deeply, but stump-rooted varieties will thrive with shallower cultivation. Dung and compost should not be applied, though it is an advantage if ground can be chosen that has been manured for some previous crop. Prior to sowing give sulphate or muriate of potash at 30g per square metre (1oz per yd²), superphosphate at 65g per square metre (2oz per yd²), and sulphate of ammonia 15g per square metre (½oz per yd²).

Sow the seed of a stump-rooted variety for the earliest crop in a sheltered position outdoors in very early spring. Even

earlier sowings can be made in a frame or under cloches. Sow thinly in drills 0·5cm (¼ in) deep and 20cm (8in) apart. No thinning will be required until the most forward are ready for use; the remainder will be left to grow on. Make further small sowings of a stump-rooted variety every three weeks or so until the early summer to give a successional supply of young roots for summer and early autumn use. Sow maincrop carrots for storing in mid-spring. Drills should be 1cm (½ in) deep and 30-45cm (12-15in) apart, and the seedlings must be thinned to about 10cm (4in) apart. Maincrop carrots should be dug in early autumn before the roots get too tough and start to crack. Store in sand or ashes.

Reliable varieties are Champion Scarlet Horn, Chantenay Red Cored, Early Nantes, James's Scarlet Intermediate, St Valery, and Autumn King.

Carrot fly is the commonest pest (667).

127. Cauliflower Not so generally useful as broccoli, as the season is shorter and the plants less hardy. The flavour is very delicate. It is almost impossible to give too much manure or compost. The situation should be sunny, but reasonably sheltered. Seed may be sown in boxes in a warm greenhouse in late winter or direct in a frame in early spring. Outdoor sowing cannot be attempted till mid-spring, and then plants are usually too late to be of much use. Another plan is to sow outdoors in early autumn and transfer seedlings to a frame or cloche in mid- to late autumn, spacing them 7·5cm (3in) apart each way. They are transplanted to the open ground the following mid-spring to crop in late summer.

Plants from late winter and early spring sowings should be hardened off in readiness for planting out in late spring or early summer. Set them 60cm (2ft) apart in rows 75cm (2½ ft) apart. A week or so later give a sprinkling of nitrate of soda or Nitro-chalk at 30g per square metre (1oz per yd²).

Reliable varieties are Dok-Elgon, All the Year Round, Novo, White Chief, Snowball, Veitch's Autumn Giant, and Walcheren.

Club root, cabbage caterpillars, cabbage root fly and flea beetle are the commonest foes (667).

128. Celeriac A useful substitute for celery for cooking and one that will grow in poorer and drier soil. Seeds should be sown in a cool greenhouse or frame during early to mid-spring and seedlings hardened off for planting out in late spring. Choose an open site and dig the soil well, enriching with manure if possible. Plant 30cm (1ft) apart in rows 45cm (18in) apart. No earthing up is required. Roots can be lifted in mid-autumn and stored in sand or ashes in a shed. Marble Ball is a good variety.

129. Celery Soil must be deeply dug and well manured. The usual practice is to prepare trenches either 35 or 45cm (15 or 18in) wide, the former for single, the latter for double rows. If there is more than one such trench they must be at least 90cm (3ft) apart. All soil is removed to a depth of 45cm (18in). The bottom is broken up with a fork and manure or compost worked in. A layer 23cm (9in) thick of good top-spit soil and manure in about equal parts is placed on top and then a further 15cm (6in) of soil only.

Seed is sown in shallow boxes in late winter for an early crop or in early to mid-spring for a later supply. First sowing should be made in a warm greenhouse, later ones in a frame. The seedlings are picked off as soon as they can be handled, and are spaced 5cm (2in) apart each way. Plant out in early to mid summer 30cm (1ft) apart, down the middle of the trench in the narrow trenches or one row on each side in the wide ones. Water in very freely. Subsequently water liberally in dry weather, and give one or two light dressings of nitrate of soda at 30g to 4 metres (1oz to 12ft) of trench. Earthing up will be necessary with most varieties, but self-blanching celeries can be obtained. Work must not be started till plants are fully grown. This will be between early and mid- to late autumn. Remove offshoots round the base, tie stems together, and draw soil round them in a steep ridge. Celery is fit for use about six weeks after earthing up. It can be left in the open all the winter, and be dug as required, but it is advisable to protect the plants by placing two boards on edge along each ridge,

Varieties are Solid White and Standard Bearer.

The best of the self-blanching varieties is Golden Self-Blanching. This is particularly valuable for early use. Raise as ordinary celery but plant out on the flat, not in trenches. Ground should be rich and well dug. Space 23cm (9in) apart each way and make a number of short rows rather than a few long ones. When well grown, place boards on edge round the bed to help blanch the outside plants.

Celery leaf miner and celery leaf spot are the worst foes. There is also a heart rot disease (667).

130. Chicory The blanched leaves and stems make a useful addition to autumn and winter salad. Seeds should be sown outdoors from mid-spring to early summer in drills 30cm (1ft) apart. Soil should be well dug and prepared as for lettuce (146). Thin seedlings to 23cm (9in) apart. The roots are lifted in late autumn and heeled in in a sheltered place in sand or ashes. They are forced as required in complete darkness, the whole process being identical to that applied to seakale (161).

131. Chives These are used as a substitute for onions for flavouring and also for salads, and are appreciated on account of their mild flavour. Chives will grow in almost any soil and situation. Plants should be obtained in very early spring and, after being divided into small tufts, planted 15cm (6in) apart in rows 20-23cm (8-9in) apart. When chives are required for the table, cut off some of the shoots close to soil level. When the beds become overgrown, the plants can be lifted and divided.

132. Coleworts Also known as collards, these are really small, quick growing cabbages, taken as a catch crop from the spring-cabbage bed. They take up little room, and are often cut and used as greens before they have formed hearts. They can be sown in midsummer and used immediately from early to mid-winter, when autumn cabbages are over and before the spring crop has attained sufficient size. Culture is exactly as for cabbage (124), and the plants are put out in their final quarters in mid-autumn. A convenient method is to have a row of coleworts between each two rows of spring cabbage, spacing the plants 22cm (9in) apart in the rows.

Foes are the same as for cabbage.

133. Corn Salad A useful and easily grown addition to summer salads. Seed may be sown thinly either broadcast or in drills 10-12·5cm (4-5in) apart at frequent intervals from early spring until midsummer. Plants will thrive in any open or partially shaded position and reasonably rich soil. Leaves should be cut when the plants are a few inches high and before they run to flower.

134. Couve Tronchuda A relative of the cabbage, less widely grown now than in the past, but worth seeking out. Cultivation is exactly the same as for autumn cabbage (124). Seed should be sown in early or mid-spring and plants put out on well-manured soil in early summer. Allow them at least 60cm (2ft) each way and water well in dry weather. Gather the mid-ribs of the outer leaves first and the hearts last.

Cress See **Mustard and Cress (149)**.

135. Cucumbers, Ridge Beds should be prepared in the open in the same manner as for vegetable marrows (170), except that it is an advantage to build the soil and manure into a low mound or ridge so that the plants are as fully exposed to the sun as possible. Seed is sown singly in small pots in a frame or greenhouse as advised for marrows. The plants, after hardening off, are planted on their mounds in early summer. Plant 90-120cm (3-4ft) apart, and pinch out the tips of each runner when it has made about six leaves. Later, train the side shoots evenly to cover the surface of the bed, fixing them in position with wooden or galvanized-wire pegs. Water freely and feed once a week with weak liquid manure as soon as the first fruits start to swell. Fertilize female flowers (distinguishable by the embryo cucumbers immediately behind them) with pollen from the male blooms. All-female varieties do not need to be fertilized. Cutting should begin as soon as the most forward cucumbers are of usable size and should continue regularly throughout the season.

Varieties are King of the Ridge, Sweet Success (female), Kyoto.

136. Cucumbers, Frame These may be grown in either greenhouses or frames. Amateurs will be well advised not to sow before late winter in a heated greenhouse, or mid spring in an unheated one. In a frame on a hotbed (506) sowing may start in early to mid-spring. The seeds are best sown singly in small pots in the same manner as vegetable marrows (170), and the early treatment is similar.

Planting should be done when the seedlings have two rough leaves each. To avoid disease do not use greenhouse borders, but instead plant the seedlings either singly in 25cm (8in) pots or two to a grow-bag. The pots should contain sterilized compost such as John Innes No.3. Place a stake to each plant and make it secure.

Train the main stem towards the apex of the house, pinching out its tip when it reaches this, and tie in side growths to horizontal wires 35cm (15in) apart and 22cm (9in) below the glass. Pinch out the tip of each side growth two leaves beyond the first fruit. In frames pinch out the tip of each plant when it is about 15cm (6in) high. Spread out the side shoots that result evenly around each plant and peg to the soil. They are, in turn, stopped when they have formed about six leaves. It is the tertiary side shoots from these that will produce fruits. Male flowers should be removed, as, unlike ridge cucumbers, it is undesirable that the female flowers should be fertilized. If an all-female variety is grown, this procedure is not necessary.

Water freely and syringe twice daily with tepid water to keep the atmosphere moist. Little air will be needed at first, but open the top ventilators when the temperature reaches 24°C (75°F). As soon as surface roots appear, a top dressing of the same compost as that used in the pots should be given. This may be repeated whenever more surface roots appear. Liquid manure is not required until plants are fruiting freely, when weekly or bi-weekly doses will be appreciated. Shade is necessary from late spring.

Telegraph, Butchers' Disease Resister, and Conqueror are reliable free-cropping varieties. The last-named is particularly good for unheated greenhouses or frames. Pepinex has nearly all female flowers.

Red spider and white fly are the commonest pests. Gummosis, foot rot, wilt, and mildew are the worst diseases (667).

137. Endive One of the virtues of this is its hardiness, which makes it possible to secure supplies in winter at a time when lettuces are difficult to produce. Soil should be rich in order to ensure quick growth and tender leaves. Dung at the rate of 50kg to 7 square metres (1cwt to 8yd²) may be supplemented by a top dressing of superphosphate at 30g per square metre (1oz per yd²) just prior to sowing. During the summer one or two top dressings of nitrate of soda, Nitro-chalk, or sulphate of ammonia may be given between the rows at the rate of 30g to 4m (1oz to 12ft), but should be discontinued after late summer.

Seed may be sown in small quantities at intervals between mid-spring and late autumn, but it is the later sowings that are most useful. Sow thinly in drills 1cm (½in) deep and 30cm (1ft) apart, and thin seedlings to 22cm (9in) apart. The thinnings can be transplanted elsewhere, and in mid-autumn it is a good plan to place some in a frame or cloche to maintain supply if the weather is severe. Blanching must be done when the plants have attained sufficient size for use. The simplest method is to cover the centre of each plant with an inverted plate or saucer and leave this undisturbed until the leaves have become white, about six weeks.

Varieties are Moss Curled, Green Curled, and Batavian Green.

138. Garlic Useful as a flavouring. The cultivation of garlic is similar to that of shallots (163). Old cloves or clusters or bulbs are split up in late summer or spring and replanted 15cm (6in) apart in rows 30cm (1ft) apart. Just cover the bulbs with soil. Lift in mid-summer when the foliage turns yellow and lay in a sunny place for a few days to dry off. Then store in a dry, cool, but frost-proof place.

139. Good King Henry Used as a substitute for spinach and a valuable plant as it is perennial, very hardy, and will grow almost anywhere. Seed can be sown outdoors in early to mid-spring, or plants can be purchased and established at the same time. Seedlings or plants should be spaced 30cm (1ft) apart in rows 45cm (18in) apart. Choose a sunny position and reasonably rich soil. A plantation will continue to crop for many years, and young leaves can be gathered throughout the spring and early summer as required.

140. Gourds and Pumpkins These are used for jam making and also for pies. Cultivation is identical with that of marrows (170), with the exception that the fruits are allowed to grow fully and become ripe before they are cut. They may be stored in a cool, dry place for many months.

141. Horseradish Obtain good roots in early spring, and plant in holes made with a long dibber. These holes should be 30cm (1ft) apart each way and deep enough to allow the roots to be dropped in and covered with 10cm (4in) of soil. No further cultivation, beyond occasional weeding and hoeing, will be necessary. Instead of leaving the bed from year to year to become over-crowded, all roots should be lifted in early winter and the thickest and straightest laid in sand, ashes, or dry soil in any shed or outhouse for use, the remainder being trimmed up, tied in small bundles, and placed in sand or ashes outdoors, ready for re-planting the following early spring. The only preparation needed for the soil is thorough digging and the application of a little manure or compost.

142. Indian or Sweet Corn (Maize) A favourite vegetable in America and now more widely grown in this country. It is the seed heads or cobs which are eaten, and these are cut while the seeds themselves are still milky if opened up. Seed is sown singly in small pots in mid-spring and germinated in a frame or, alternatively, seeds are sown in late spring outdoors where the plants are to grow. If the latter procedure is adopted, the seeds should be sown in twos or threes 45cm (18in) apart in rows 90cm (3ft) apart. This is also the correct spacing for planting seedlings raised in pots. Seedlings are planted outdoors in late spring to early summer after proper hardening off. Fairly rich soil is required and a sunny, preferably sheltered position. Water freely or mulch with grass clippings as the cobs commence to form. At this period go over plants occasionally and shake the plumes of male flowers to scatter pollen over the female 'tassels' which protrude from the ends of the cobs. Examine cobs for gathering when tassels wither, and remove as soon as the seeds become milky. Only sweetcorn varieties are used for cooking, others for ornament and stock feeding.

Reliable varieties are Earliking, First of All, Aztec, Kelvedon Glory and John Innes Hybrid.

143. Kale (Borecole) This name covers a group of vegetables rather than one kind. They are of great importance on account of their hardiness, ease of culture, and heavy-cropping qualities. Culture is in all details the same as for sprouting broccoli (122). Plants are put out in mid- to late summer often on the ground cleared of early and mid-season peas and potatoes, and are in use from late autumn to late spring.

Varieties grown for their leaves cooked as greens are Curled Scotch, Dwarf Green Curled and Frosty. Varieties grown for their young shoots are Pentland Brig, Cottager's Kale, Thousand-headed Kale, Fribor and Hungry Gap.

Foes as for cabbages (124).

144. Kohl Rabi This is grown for its swollen stems, which are cooked and eaten like turnips. Good crops can be obtained during summers which are too hot and dry for turnips. Soil preparation is exactly as for turnips (169), and the same fertilizers should be employed. Seed is sown thinly in drills 1cm ($\frac{1}{2}$in) deep and 45cm (18in) apart, and the seedlings are thinned to 30cm (1ft) apart. If this is done a little at a time, some of the later thinnings will have grown sufficiently to be of use for the pot.

Successional sowings, from mid-spring until mid- to late summer are necessary to even out the supply.

145. Leeks These make heavy demands on the land. Farmyard or stable manure or good vegetable compost should be dug in during autumn or winter at the rate of 50kg to 8 square metres (1cwt to 10yd^2). Just prior to planting out, a dressing should be given of a mixture of 3 parts of superphosphate, 1 part of sulphate of ammonia, and 1 part of sulphate of potash, used at the rate of 65g per square metre (2oz per yd^2). Seed is sown thinly in drills 0·5cm ($\frac{1}{4}$ in) deep and 22cm (9in) apart between early and mid-spring. For an early crop and exhibition, seed is sown in a warm greenhouse in mid- to late winter.

Planting is done with a stout, steel-shod dibber. With this, holes are prepared 22cm (9in) deep and 22cm (9in) apart in rows 45cm (18in) apart, and one plant dropped well down into each. Do not make any attempt to refill the holes with soil, but simply water the plants in thoroughly. This deep planting will blanch the stems without need for much further earthing up. For exhibition, leeks are planted with a trowel in shallow trenches prepared as advised for celery (129), and the soil is gradually drawn around the stems as they lengthen. This method results in very large, well-blanched stems. Nitrate of soda, Nitro-chalk, or sulphate of ammonia may be used at 30g to 3m (1oz to 10ft) of row, or soot at 30g to 120cm (1oz to 4ft) when plants are well established. Lifting and storing are unnecessary. Leeks are quite hardy and may be left in the ground all the winter, being lifted as the occasion arises when required for use.

Varieties of merit are Winter Crop, Musselburgh and The Lyon – Prizetaker.

Principal foes are as for onions (150).

146. Lettuce There are three types, the cabbage, cos and loose leaf. Choice may be determined by personal taste, some people liking the crispness of the cos, while others prefer the softness of the cabbage and loose-leaf types. Soil must be rich and well prepared to encourage quick growth. Manure or compost should be worked in prior to planting at the rate of 50kg to 8 square metres (1cwt to 10yd^2). Just prior to seed sowing, the soil should be dressed with a mixture of 5 parts of superphosphate, 2 parts of sulphate of ammonia, and 2 parts of sulphate of potash at the rate of 100g per square metre (3oz per yd^2).

Seed should be sown thinly in drills 1cm ($\frac{1}{2}$in) deep and 30cm (1ft), apart for the bigger varieties or 22cm (9in) for small kinds such as Tom Thumb. Small successional sowings should be made about once every three weeks from the early or mid-spring to the late autumn. Earlier supplies can be obtained by sowing in late winter in a greenhouse or in a frame or cloche on a hot-bed (506). Sow broadcast in shallow boxes; prick seedlings out 5cm (2in) apart each way into similar boxes as soon as they can be handled. Then the plants can be gradually accustomed to outdoor conditions in readiness for planting out in mid-spring.

Winter supplies can be obtained by sowing in a frame during the early to mid-autumn and transplanting the seedlings to another frame or greenhouse when they can be handled. It is very important with all lettuces grown under glass to plant shallowly. The lowest leaves must be above soil level or damping off may occur.

Thinning out of seedlings raised in the open should be done as soon as they have two or three true leaves each. Leave the plants standing 15-22cm (6-9in) apart in the rows. The thinnings can be replanted in another bed.

An occasional dusting of soot at 30g to 1m (1oz to 4ft) or of nitrate of soda, Nitro-chalk, or sulphate of ammonia 30g to 3·5m (1oz to 12ft) may be given between the rows. Discontinue application of fertilizers as hearts form.

Reliable kinds are - *Cabbage type:* Continuity, All the Year Round, Avon-defiance, Webb's Wonderful, and Tom Thumb; *Cos type:* Little Gem and Paris White. For autumn and winter use, Arctic King and Imperial (cabbage) and Winter Density (cos) are reliable. For frame or greenhouse culture the cabbage varieties May Queen, Premier and Marmer are recommended. Salad Bowl is a good loose-leaf (heartless) variety. Butter-crunch is intermediate and semi-hearted.

Aphids on leaf and root, cutworms, and slugs are the pests most to be feared. Grey mould, mildew and damping off, the worst fungal diseases (667).

147. Mint Choose an open position and one where the plants can spread some distance without becoming a nuisance. Roots should be obtained in early spring and be strewn thinly all over the selected site, then covered with 4cm (1½ in) of finely broken soil. Almost any ground will grow mint, but it is an advantage if a little manure or compost can be dug in

first. If a winter supply is required, some roots should be lifted in mid- to late autumn, placed in shallow boxes and lightly covered with soil. Then place them in a warm greenhouse, where they will soon produce fresh green shoots.

Mint rust is the only important disease (667).

148. Mushrooms These can be grown in sheds, outhouses, cellars, frames and greenhouses if darkened, and outdoors. Outdoor beds are unreliable, as an even temperature and cool, damp atmosphere are essential for success. Fresh horse manure or straw or chaff treated with special proprietary preparations are necessary for making the compost. If manure is used it should be strawy and free from shavings and must be obtained from horses that are in good health. Remove twigs or other refuse and make into a stack 90cm (3ft) high. Cover with 2·5cm (1in) of soil. After a week shake and mix thoroughly; water any parts that appear dry and stack again but without soil. Continue in this manner every four or five days for about three weeks. By this time the manure and straw should have rotted to an even texture and dark brown colour and should smell sweet, without trace of ammonia. Place in boxes 22-30cm (9-12in) deep or build into beds 20-25cm (8-10in) deep, 60-90cm (2-3ft) wide, and any convenient length. For outdoor cultivation, ridge beds 90cm (3ft) wide and 75cm (2½ ft) in height are to be preferred. In either method the manure should be trodden down firmly little by little as the bed is filled. Place a thermometer in the bed and wait till the temperature falls to between 21° and 24°C (70° and 75°F). Then break up purchased spawn into pieces the size of a walnut and place one every 22cm (9in), at 2·5cm (1in) beneath the surface. Cover with a layer of straw 15cm (6in) thick under cover, or 30cm (1ft) outdoors. Ten days to a fortnight later examine the bed to discover whether the spawn is running, ie producing white filaments of mycelium. If so, remove the straw and case the bed with peat or good soil to a thickness of 4cm ($1\frac{1}{2}$in) for ridge beds, 2·5cm (1in) for flat beds. Re-cover outdoor beds with straw or matting. Under cover, if temperature can be controlled, maintain at about 18°C (65°F) until mushrooms appear, when it may fall to 13°-16°C (55°-60°F). Maintain a damp atmosphere throughout. Water if beds become dry, but avoid watering overmuch. Indoor beds can be made at any time; outdoor beds are best made in midsummer.

A simpler method is to buy a bucket or bag of ready-spawned compost, but use it promptly.

Maggots are the principal foes (667)

149. Mustard and Cress Two of the most easily and rapidly grown salad vegetables. Sowing may commence under glass in mid-winter in a temperature of 16°-18°C (60°-65°F). Outdoors it is not wise to start sowing until mid-spring or to continue after late summer. Shallow boxes are used for greenhouse cultivation, and these may be filled with any fine soil. Sow evenly and fairly thickly, press into the surface with a smooth flat piece of wood and do not cover with any soil. Place a slate or board over each box, but tilt this as soon as seedlings appear and remove a day later. Water when necessary with lukewarm water. Outdoor seeds can be broadcast on the surface of finely broken soil and pressed in as described, and then covered with a sack or mat until germination takes place. Cut with a pair of scissors just above soil level when seedlings are 5-7cm (2-3in) in height. Cress takes twelve to eighteen days to reach cutting stage; mustard eight to twelve days.

Damping off is the only serious disease (667).

150. Onions Dung or compost should be dug in as long as possible in advance of seed sowing at 50kg to 10 square metres (1cwt to 12yd²). Bonfire ashes can also be worked in at 250g per square metre ($\frac{1}{2}$lb per yd²). Alternatively, give sulphate or muriate of potash just before sowing at 30g per square metre (1oz per yd²). In any case apply either basic slag or bonemeal at 130g per square metre (4oz per yd²), with the dung, or superphosphate of lime, 65g per square metre (2oz per yd²), before sowing. Seed for the main crop should be sown as early in spring as the state of the ground will permit. Sow thinly in drills 1cm ($\frac{1}{2}$in) deep and 22cm (9in) apart. Later, thin seedlings to 15cm (6in) apart. This can be done gradually, the thinnings being used for salads.

For an early supply, seed may be sown in the same way at the end of summer. The seedlings will then stand the winter without thinning, and in the spring some can be used for salad and some be planted 15cm (6in) apart in rows 30cm (1ft) apart in a well-prepared bed. Bulbs can be used direct from the ground from early summer to early autumn, while from the spring sowing bulbs will be lifted in early autumn and stored for autumn and winter. An alternative method is to sow thinly in boxes in a warm greenhouse in midwinter and harden off (507) for planting out in mid-spring.

Give one or two top dressings of nitrate of soda, 30g to 3m (1oz to 12ft) of row, during late spring and early summer, to encourage growth. In late summer the leaves should be bent over at the neck to check further growth and encourage ripening of the bulbs. Lifting should be done with a fork in early autumn. Leave the bulbs on the ground or place them in a greenhouse, frame, or shed to dry out for a few days and then store in a cool, dry place. Bulbs with thick soft necks do not keep well. Another method of growing onions is by sets or small bulbs. These are planted in mid-spring 15cm (6in) apart in rows 30cm (12in) apart. The sets should be pressed firmly into the soil to a third of their depth.

Varieties for spring sowing are Ailsa Craig, Hygro, Bedfordshire Champion, and Buffalo. For autumn sowing, Reliance and Autumn Queen are recommended. White Lisbon is useful for salads. Stuttgarter Giant and Sturen are good varieties for sets.

Mildew, neck rot, white rot, eelworms, and onion fly are the worst foes (667).

151. Parsley In order to ensure an all-year supply, three sowings should be made, the first in early to mid-spring, the second in early summer, and the third in mid- to late summer. The first two can be made in any open position, but the last should be made in as sheltered a position as possible. Even so, it is advisable to transplant some of the seedlings to a frame, or alternatively cover them with cloches, in mid-autumn. Ground should be moderately rich, and the seed should be sown as thinly as possible, in drills 0·5cm (¼ in) deep and 15 or 20cm (6 or 8in) apart. Thin out seedlings to 12cm (5in) apart.

152. Parsnips Soil should be dug deeply to encourage the production of long, unforked roots. Manure is not desirable before sowing, but choose, if possible, a plot that has had manure or compost for some previous crop. In any case apply prior to sowing a mixture of 4 parts of superphosphate, 1 part of sulphate of ammonia, and 1 part of sulphate or muriate of potash at the rate of 100g per square metre (3oz per yd²). Lime is neces-sary on acid soils and should be applied as hydrated lime, 250g per square metre (8oz per yd²), during the autumn or winter. Sow seed as early in spring as the weather will permit. Drills should be 2·5cm (1in) deep and 45cm (18in) apart, and later, seedlings must be thinned out to 20cm (8in) apart. Give one top dressing of nitrate of soda, Nitro-chalk, or sulphate of ammonia at the rate of 30g to 3m (1oz to 12ft) of row after thinning. Roots may be left in the ground all the winter if desired, and be dug as required. It is usually convenient, however, to lift a proportion in late autumn and store in sand or ashes in a shed or other place.

For exhibition roots, deep holes are made 30cm (1ft) apart in rows 60cm (2ft) apart with a crowbar and filled with fine soil. Two seeds are sown in the top of each hole in early spring and seedlings are thinned later to one per hole. The roots follow the line of least resistance and so are perfectly straight.

Reliable varieties are Avonresister (resistant to carrot fly), Tender and True, The Student, and Hollow Crown Improved.

Carrot fly, which causes a rusty condition of the roots often erroneously called 'canker' is the commonest pest.

153. Peas Digging should be done thoroughly as early in the autumn as possible. Dung or compost should be applied at the same time at the rate of 50kg to 12 square metres (1cwt to 15yd²) unless the peas are to be grown on ground that has been well manured for a preceding crop. Fertilizers should be used just before seed sowing, whether manure is given or not. Use a mixture prepared with 3 parts of superphosphate, 2 parts of sulphate of potash, and 1 part of sulphate of ammonia, and scatter at 65g per metre (2oz per yd) of row for a width of 30cm (1ft) on each side of the drill.

A first sowing of a hardy early pea may be made in a sheltered place outdoors in very late winter. If mice are a problem, it may be advisable to set traps at intervals along the row, partly covered with tiles or slates to keep the bait dry. Scoop out a trench the width of a spade and just over 2·5cm (1in) in depth and sow a double line of peas in this, one at each side, the peas themselves being about 7cm (3in) apart in the lines. Then cover with soil. A second sowing of an early variety should be made in early spring and a third in mid-spring. The first maincrop peas should also be sown in mid-spring. Another sowing of maincrops may follow at the end of the month, a final sowing being made in late spring or very early summer with, if desired, a few rows of a first early variety sown in early to mid summer to give the chance of young peas in mid-autumn if the season is favourable. Successive rows should be at least as far apart as the eventual height of the peas. It is an advantage if the taller peas can be sown in rows running north and south.

Sticking will be necessary for all peas over 45cm (18in) in height and is an advantage even with dwarf peas. Water freely during dry weather. If water is scarce, spread a mulch of strawy manure or grass clippings 5-7cm (2-3in) thick for a width of 30-60cm (1ft) on each side of the row.

Reliable kinds are as follows: *Earlies* – Little Marvel, Feltham First, Kelvedon Wonder, Early Onward, Pilot. *Maincrop* – Alderman, Senator, Miracle, Onward, Lord Chancellor.

The principal foes are mildew and thrips (667).

154. Potatoes These are first rate for cleaning newly broken grassland, as their heavy growth smothers weeds and their big root systems break up the clods of soil, leaving the land in good condition for succeeding crops. Soil should be dug at least 25cm (10in) deep as early in the autumn as possible and left rough for the winter. Manure or compost may be applied at 50kg to 12·5 square metres (1cwt to 15yd^2). Lime should not be used unless the ground is known to be sour, when application should be restricted to about 190g per square metre (6oz per yd^2) of hydrated lime. This may be given as a top dressing six or eight weeks after digging in the manure. Fertilizers should be employed, whether or not dung is available. See (82), (83).

The best planting sets come from districts in which virus diseases are almost unknown. New stock should be imported from virus-free districts every year. Sets should be obtained as early as possible. Immediately on arrival, stand them with their eyed ends uppermost in shallow boxes and place these in a light but frost-proof place.

Early potatoes may be planted outdoors in a sheltered position in early spring. Maincrop varieties are planted during mid-spring. Spacing for earlies should be 30cm (1ft) apart in rows 75cm (2½ ft) apart; for maincrop kinds 35cm (15in) apart in rows 90cm (3ft) apart. Methods of planting vary greatly. One of the simplest is to take out with a spade a V-shaped trench about 12cm (5in) in depth. The tubers are spaced in this, care being taken to keep the shoots uppermost and not to break any, and the soil removed is drawn back with a rake or draw hoe. Large tubers may be cut so that each section has at least two sprouts.

Earthing up must begin as soon as the shoots appear through the soil. This is particularly important in the case of the earliest-planted potatoes, as the sprouts may be killed by late spring frosts. Pull soil over them with a draw hoe and continue to earth up week by week until the ground is all drawn up in flat-topped ridges about 22cm (9in) in height. Digging of earlies can start as soon as the tubers are of usable size. For late varieties digging should be delayed until the skins of the tubers are mature and will not rub off readily. Exception to this rule may be necessary if disease is severe, when it may be desirable to lift the crop without delay to save what there is. Potatoes for eating must not be allowed to green. This can be prevented by storing them in sacks in a dark, dry shed, outhouse, etc, temperature 5°-7°C (40°-45°F), or in clamps in the open. These are ridge-shaped mounds of tubers 1·2-1·8m (4-6ft) through at the base, covered with 15cm (6in) of clean straw and 22cm (9in) of soil. Clamps must be made in a well-drained place. It is an advantage to place straw beneath the potatoes. A handful of straw should be drawn through the soil every 90cm (3ft) along the ridge for ventilation.

Varieties are numerous. A few of the best are as follows – *Earlies:* Ulster Chieftain, Home Guard, Arran Pilot, Sharpe's Express, Duke of York, Ulster Chieftain, Pentland Javelin (scab resistant and partially eelworm resistant) and Epicure. *Second Early and Maincrop:* Arran Banner, King Edward, Catriona, Pentland Dell, Majestic. For partial eelworm resistance Cara and Klondyke.

The principal diseases are potato blight, virus, scab and blackleg. Slugs, eelworms, cutworms and wireworms are pests which do much damage (667).

155. Radishes Soil can scarcely be too rich, and liberal dressings of dung or compost may be given. There is no better place for the earlier sowings than the beds prepared for winter greens. Radishes sown there in early or mid-spring will be used before most of the greens are ready for planting out. Seed should be sown in small batches every fortnight from early

spring until late summer. Even earlier supplies can be obtained by sowing in a frame or cloche in late winter. Sow seed thinly all over the bed and cover lightly by sifting a little dry soil over it. Growth will be rapid, and no further attention should be necessary until the roots are large enough for pulling. Use the most forward first. Winter radishes can be obtained by sowing suitable varieties in mid- or late summer in rows 22cm (9in) apart and thinning to 10cm (4in).

French Breakfast, Scarlet Globe and Inca are good varieties for spring and summer use; Black Spanish and China Rose for winter use.

156. Rhubarb Soil should be rather rich, and plenty of dung or compost can be dug in if available. Dust the surface with basic slag at the rate of 190g per square metre (6oz per yd²). Strong roots should be obtained in early spring and planted with a spade 1m (3ft) apart each way. The crowns should just appear on the surface of the ground when all the soil has been returned. Plant firmly, treading the soil around the roots. The young stems are pulled away from the crowns as they attain sufficient size. It is a mistake to take too many from one plant as this weakens it, and for the same reason it is not wise to continue pulling after midsummer. Outdoors, without any forcing, supplies will be available from about midspring onwards, but earlier sticks can be obtained by covering roots with barrels, drainpipes, boxes, or special forcing pots in mid-winter and heaping manure or leaves over these. All light must be excluded.

If rhubarb is required earlier in the year, it will be necessary to force in a heated greenhouse or shed. Roots should be dug as required from late autumn onwards, and be exposed for a day or so to frost. Then they are packed into boxes with light soil around them and are placed under the staging in the greenhouse or in any other convenient place from which light can be excluded, and in which a temperature of from 16° to 24°C (60° to 75°F) can be maintained. Water moderately at first, but freely as growth begins.

Rhubarb can also be raised from seed sown thinly in a frame in early spring. Thin seedlings to at least 15cm (6in) and transplant to permanent quarters the following spring.

Champagne, The Sutton, and Victoria are reliable varieties and give sticks of fine red colour. Timperley Early is a particularly good variety for forcing.

157. Sage Plants should be obtained in the spring and planted at least 45cm (18in) apart in any sunny and ordinary, though preferably well-drained, soil. If at any time it is desired to work up a further stock, cuttings can be rooted during late summer or early autumn. Prepare these from firm young growths 7-10cm (3-4in) in length. Sever each immediately below a joint, remove the lower leaves and insert in sandy soil in a frame or under a cloche, keeping shaded and well watered until rooted.

158. Salsify Grown for its roots, which look much like those of parsnip (152) and are cooked in the same way. Cultivation is also similar to that of parsnip, and the soil is prepared in the same way. Sow seed in mid-spring in drills 1cm (1/2 in) deep and 30cm (1ft) apart; thin seedlings to 15-20cm (6-8in) apart. Lift roots in late autumn and store in sand or ashes until required.

159. Savoy This is a type of cabbage with crinkled leaves. Savoys are very hardy and of great value during the winter months. Cultivation is identical with that of winter cabbage (124) and seed should be sown during late spring and early summer. Plants should be put out in

succession during summer, the later ones following early potatoes and peas. Varieties are numerous and should be chosen for succession. Good kinds are Best of All, Christmas Drumhead, Ormskirk Early, Medium and Late, Rearguard, Ice Queen and Wirosa.

Foes as for cabbage (124).

160. Scorzonera A root vegetable very little grown in this country. Cultivation is similar to that of parsnip (152), and soil is prepared in the same way. Seed should be sown in mid- to late spring and roots lifted in early to mid autumn for storing in sand or ashes in a frost-proof frame. The roots are boiled in the same way as those of parsnip (152) or salsify (158).

161. Seakale Grown for blanching both outdoors and under glass. Plants may be raised from seed sown outdoors in mid-spring, but two years must elapse before seedlings are strong enough for forcing. A better method is to purchase crowns and maintain a stock by root cuttings. These are prepared from thongy roots about 15cm (6in) in length. Plant either crowns or root cuttings in early spring 30cm (1ft) apart in rows 45cm (18in) apart, dropping them into dibber holes and just covering with soil. Take care that root cuttings are planted the right way up. By late autumn they will have developed into strong crowns, some of which may be lifted for forcing. Trim off side roots from which further cuttings can be prepared, tie in bundles, and lay in sand or ashes until early spring. Stack the crowns right way up beneath a cool and shady wall and surround with sand or ashes. Pot up a few crowns at a time, three or four in an 18cm (7in) pot, and bring into a heated greenhouse, placing beneath the staging and keeping quite dark. Cut growth at soil level when 15-22cm (6-9in) in length. The shoots should be perfectly white and are served as a substitute for asparagus. In mid-winter, crowns left outdoors can be covered with boxes or inverted flower pots, or soil or ashes may be piled over them to effect blanching.

162. Seakale Beet This closely resembles spinach beet and cultivation is identical. The only point of difference is that the mid-rib of each leaf is very large and fleshy and can be used as a substitute for seakale, the green portion of the leaves being stripped off and boiled as spinach. For other details see spinach beet (165).

163. Shallots Soil should be well cultivated, but need not be so rich as for onions. It is an advantage if a plot can be chosen that has been manured for the preceding crop. In any case, apply a mixture of 3 parts of superphosphate, 2 parts of sulphate or muriate of potash and 1 part of sulphate of ammonia, at 100g per square metre (3oz per yd²) prior to planting. This is done as early in late winter as the weather will allow. Good bulbs saved from the previous crop are pushed firmly two-thirds their depth into the soil. They should be spaced 15cm (6in) apart in rows 22cm (9in) apart. The bulbs should be ripe and ready for harvesting in early to midsummer. A week or so before this, draw the soil away from the clusters of bulbs so that they are exposed to the light and can swell readily. After lifting with a fork, lay the clusters on the surface or in a frame for a few days to dry off. Then separate the bulbs and store them in a dry, cool place. Hâtive de Niort is the most shapely variety but Giant Red and Giant Yellow crop more heavily.

Foes are as for onions, but virus disease

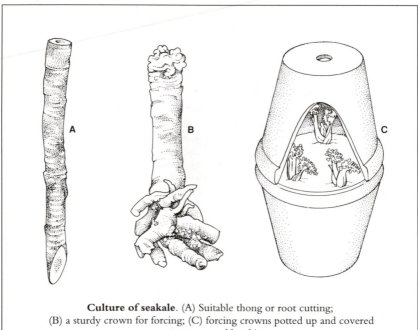

Culture of seakale. (A) Suitable thong or root cutting; (B) a sturdy crown for forcing; (C) forcing crowns potted up and covered to ensure proper blanching.

is also sometimes very troublesome (667).

164. Spinach Soil for summer spinach should be rich and rather moist. Dung or compost may be used at 50kg to 8 square metres (1cwt to 10yd²). It is often possible to take a catch crop (106) of spinach off ground already prepared for some other vegetable, but which will not actually be required for a month or so. For summer supplies it is an advantage to sow in partial shade, and in dry places spinach may be grown in furrows about 7cm (3in) deep and 25cm (10in) wide as these can be easily flooded with water.

For winter spinach a sheltered but sunny position should be chosen, and the soil must not be quite so rich. Sulphate of potash, at 15g per square metre ($\frac{1}{2}$oz per yd²), should be applied prior to sowing.

Sowing of summer spinach should start in early spring and continue at intervals of three or four weeks until midsummer. Then in late summer a sowing of winter spinach may be made. The seed should always be sown very thinly in drills 2·5cm (1in) deep and about 30cm (1ft) apart. Thin out seedlings to 10cm (4in) apart as soon as they can be handled and a little later to 20cm (8in). Give a light top dressing of nitrate of soda, Nitro-chalk, or sulphate of ammonia at 30g to 3m (1oz to 12ft) between the rows, after thinning summer spinach, and in early spring for the winter kind. The outer leaves should be cut as soon as they attain sufficient size.

165. Spinach Beet A form of beetroot, also known as perpetual spinach, grown solely for its leaves. These are cut as they become large enough, and are used as a substitute for spinach. The plants continue to crop for months and are very hardy. Soil is prepared as for summer spinach (164), but there is no need to choose a partially shady position for either summer or winter supplies. Seed should be sown twice to ensure an all-year supply, the first time in early to mid-spring, and the second in late summer. Sow the seeds in pairs about 22cm (9in) apart in rows 45cm (18in) apart and, if all germinate, single them out later.

166. Swedes These are grown in exactly the same way as turnips (169) and are especially serviceable for storing for winter use. For this purpose seed should be sown during late spring or early summer in drills 1cm ($\frac{1}{2}$in) deep and 38cm (15in) apart. Thin to 20cm (8in) apart and lift for use as required or store a few like parsnips (152). Purple Top, Bronze Top, and Marian are the varieties principally grown.

Foes as turnips (169).

Sweet Corn, *see* **Indian Corn (142).**

167. Thyme Plants will succeed in any sunny position and ordinary soil, but prefer one that is rather light and of a well-drained nature. It is best to start with young plants purchased in the spring and planted 20-22cm (8-9in) apart each way. Alternatively, seeds may be sown thinly in mid-spring, either in a frame or in a sheltered border outdoors and covered with 0·5cm ($\frac{1}{4}$in) of soil. Seedlings should be transferred to a sunny bed of finely broken soil in late spring to early summer, and planted 5-7cm (2-3in) apart each way to develop into sturdy young plants for removal to their final quarters the following spring.

168. Tomatoes For an early crop under glass, seed should be sown in a warm greenhouse during mid- to late winter. In unheated houses it is not wise to start until mid-spring. For outdoor planting, seed is best sown in a warm greenhouse in early spring. In all methods the seeds should be sown very thinly in well-drained pots or boxes filled with a good seed compost (493). Cover with a light sprinkling of fine soil and place a pane of glass and a sheet of paper over each receptacle until germination takes place. Then give as much light as possible. Prick off into similar trays and compost when the seedlings have formed two rough leaves each, spacing them 5cm (2in) apart each way. When they are about 10cm (4in) in height, pot singly in 7·5cm (3in) pots, and when these are full of roots remove to 10 or 13cm (4 or 5in) pots. For these later pottings use a rougher compost (497). This same compost, with the loam in lumps about the size of a small hen's egg, will also do for the final potting or planting. The plants can be fruited singly in 25cm (9in) pots; in growbags; in 10in diameter bottomless rings standing on a 6in thick layer of washed boiler ashes or small gravel; or they may be planted 45cm (18in) apart in rows 75cm ($2\frac{1}{2}$ ft) apart direct in a bed of soil prepared on the floor or staging of the house.

Remove all side growths, and keep each plant to a single stem. Water freely and, when flowers appear, syringe the plants each morning to assist pollination. Top dress the soil with well-rotted compost of finely broken cow or horse manure when roots appear on the surface, and from the time the first fruits start to swell feed once a week with tomato fertilizer (87).

Temperature throughout should range from 16°–21°C (60°–70°F). It will not matter if it runs up to 27°C (80°F) at times so long as ample water and ventilation are given. When in full crop each plant may easily require 4l (1gall) or more of water daily. Top ventilation should be given whenever outdoor conditions allow, and side ventilators and doors left open in hot weather.

Outdoors, tomatoes may be planted in early summer. Set them 45cm (18in) apart, and if there is more than one row, let these be at least 90cm (3ft) apart and run north to south. Remove all side shoots and pinch out the top of each plant when it has formed four trusses of flowers. Stake each plant securely, and in addition tie up each truss of fruit so that it gets as much sun as possible. In early autumn it may be advisable to remove some of the lower leaves. Tomatoes can also be grown by the ring culture method or in grow bags.

Bush tomatoes are grown in the same manner except that they are not restricted to a single stem but are allowed to bush out and each stem is tied to a stake or horizontal wire.

Some reliable varieties are Eurocross, Ailsa Craig, Alicante, Grenadier, Herald, Best of All, Moneymaker, Grower's Pride, Red Ensign, Supercross, Amberly Cross. Golden Sunrise has yellow fruits. For outdoor planting, Harbinger, Sweet 100 and Outdoor Girl are recommended. A good bush variety is The Amateur. Tiny Tim can be grown in a windowbox.

Foes most to be feared are leaf mould, potato blight, virus, streak, wilt (sleepy disease), collar rot, and white fly (667).

169. Turnips Dung or compost must not be used, but it is an advantage if a plot can be chosen that has been manured for a previous crop. Then it will be sufficient to dig thoroughly in autumn or winter and dust the surface with superphosphate at 100g per square metre (3oz per yd²) and sulphate of potash at 15g per square metre ($\frac{1}{2}$ oz per yd²) prior to sowing. If such ground is not available, it will be advisable in addition to give a dressing of soot at 250g per square metre (8oz per yd²) or sulphate of ammonia at 15g per square metre ($\frac{1}{2}$ oz per yd²) at the same time. Small successional sowings should be made every three or four weeks from early spring until midsummer to supply young roots to be pulled as required. For winter storing, a sowing may be made soon after midsummer. Turnip tops for use as greens in the spring are produced by sowing seed in drills 45cm (18in) apart in early sutumn and leaving the plants unthinned to stand the winter. Seed for the successional sowings may be sown in drills 1cm (½ in) deep and 30cm (12in) apart, but for the winter crop the distance between the rows should be increased to 40cm (15in). Similarly, it will be sufficient to thin the summer crops to 10cm (4in) apart, but the winter turnips must have twice this room. Winter turnips should be lifted for storing in mid-autumn. They are pulled out, the tops are cut off, and the roots are stored in a shed or cellar. Varieties are Golden Ball, Purple Top, Milan, and Early Snowball for summer supplies. Greentop White for winter and supplying turnip tops.

Club root, cabbage gall weevil, and flea beetle are the principal foes (667).

170. Vegetable Marrow The old practice of growing marrows on heaps is not good, as it is difficult to keep them supplied with sufficient moisture. A better plan is to dig out a trench 60cm (2ft) wide and as much in depth and to fill this with a mixture of soil, dung, compost, old leaves, etc. Then, if a little extra soil is built in a low ridge around the bed, it will be a simple matter to flood the whole with water in dry weather. Seed should be sown in mid-spring singly in small pots filled with any good compost, and germination effected in a frame or greenhouse. Outdoors it is not safe to sow until late spring. Planting should not be done until early summer. Plant bush varieties 90cm (3ft) apart, trailing 120cm (4ft) apart.

The runners of trailing varieties should be pinched out when they have extended 90cm (3ft). This will force the plants to make side growths, which usually bear female flowers, and consequently fruits, more freely than the main growths. Fertilize the female flowers, which can be recognized by the embryo fruits just beneath them, by inverting male blooms over them. Cutting should start as soon as the first marrows are of usable size. Only

Fertilizing a female marrow flower.
The female flower has an embryo marrow behind it. The male flower bearing the pollen should be brought into close contact with the sticky stigma of the female flower.

towards the end of the season should a few be allowed to remain to ripen. These, if cut without injury, may be stored for winter use in a cool, dry place.

Good trailing varieties are Long Green Trailing, Long White Trailing. Good bush varieties are White Custard, Green Bush and White Bush. Courgette is a very prolific trailing variety grown to be cut when the fruits are about 15cm (6in) long.

171. Watercress One of the most valuable salad vegetables from the point of view of vitamins. May be grown without running water by digging a trench 60cm (2ft) wide and 30cm (1ft) deep, in a sunny position, placing 15cm (6in) of rotten manure in the bottom, covering with 8cm (3in) of soil and sowing seed thinly in mid-spring and again in late summer, or planting cuttings. The trench should be flooded with water fairly frequently while the plants are in growth. Permanent beds are usually made of concrete and are about 120cm (4ft) wide and 15-25cm (6-10in) in depth. The flow of water should be controlled by suitable sluices or valves. Some 8cm (3in) of good soil should be placed in the bottom of the bed and a little clean gravel or sand on top. Cuttings from selected plants are dibbled into this bed 15cm (6in) apart each way. Usually two plantings are made, one in late spring or early summer and the other in mid-autumn. Restrict water to a depth of 4cm (1½in) at first, but increase slowly according to the growth of the plants. About 7·5-10cm (3-4in) is sufficient under ordinary conditions.

The principal disease is mildew (667).

THE FRUIT GARDEN

MISCELLANEOUS NOTES

172. Arrangement of Trees There are several ways of arranging trees in an orchard. The principal are as follows: square. all trees at equal distances in rows at right angles to one another; quincunx, as the last with one tree in the middle of each square; triangular, trees at the points of an equal-sided triangle, this being repeated right through the plantation. Cordons and trained trees are almost always planted in straight, parallel rows or against walls and fences.

In large orchards it is a frequent practice to plant permanent, slow-maturing trees or small fruits (eg currants, gooseberries, etc) in between. These latter are known as fillers and are removed after from 10 to 15 years, by which time the permanent trees are beginning to require all the space. A drawback to mixed plantations is the difficulty of carrying out spraying and feeding programmes suitable to all the trees.

173. Cultivation of Orchards Growth is always slower when the ground beneath trees is grassed than when it is cultivated, but trees tend to be more fruitful and bear fruit of better colour and quality when grassed under. In consequence young trees are usually grown on cultivated ground, but this may be grassed down after eight to ten years, or after four years, for trees grown on dwarfing stocks. Another scheme with much the same object is to keep ground cultivated until fruit is well formed and then allow the growth of summer weeds for a few weeks, digging or ploughing these in later. The weeds must not be allowed to seed.

On no account must deep cultivation be carried out near established fruit trees, or surface roots will be destroyed. Near large fruits, eg apples, pears, plums, cherries, etc, it is not safe to dig more than 10cm (4in) deep. For bush fruits, eg currants and gooseberries, 5-7·5cm (2-3in) should be regarded as the maximum; strawberries, raspberries, etc, 2·5-5cm (1-2in).

174. Unfruitfulness This may be due to one or other of several causes. Most fruits are only formed if the flowers are fertilized with pollen. In some varieties, eg apple Bramley's Seedling, and pear Pitmaston Duchess, the flowers carry little or no pollen and fertilization can take place only if another variety of the same kind of fruit which bears pollen liberally is grown near by. In other instances, eg most sweet cherries and, to a lesser extent, apples, pears, and plums, pollen is borne freely but is partially or wholly ineffective on flowers of its own variety and sometimes also with flowers of certain other varieties. Varieties which will not produce fruit with their own pollen are said to be 'self-sterile'; those which will bear some fruit with their own pollen but more when cross-pollinated, are described as 'partially self-fertile', while those with pollen which is wholly effective on their own flowers are 'self-fertile'. Where the pollen of one variety will not fertilize the flowers of another, 'incompatibility' is said to exist between the two.

In planting an orchard it is important that varieties should be assorted in such a manner that the pollen of one fertilizes the flowers of another. Note that flowers can be fertilized only with pollen of the same kind, apples with apples, pears with pears, etc.

Even when the right kind of pollen is available in sufficient quantity it must be carried from flower to flower. This is largely the work of bees and other insects. Lack of these may cause unfruitfulness. This can be overcome by introducing bees or by hand fertilizing the flowers by carrying pollen to them on a camel-hair brush.

Cold, damp weather at blossom time may keep insects away, while frost may kill the blossom outright. This is a particular danger with early-flowering fruits such as peaches, nectarines, cherries, and plums. Under-nourishment of trees may also prevent effective fertilization. This can be remedied by proper feeding.

Young trees that are growing very freely often fail to produce any blossom at all. Their excessive vigour can be checked by opening a trench round them in mid-autumn and severing the coarser roots (root pruning), or by removing a ring of bark 0·5cm ($1/4$in) wide from around the main trunk or the base of each main bough at blossom time (bark ringing). This latter method should not be practised with stone fruits (eg plums, cherries, etc), as it is liabled to cause gumming (667) or possibly silver leaf infection.

175. Lorette Pruning In addition to the methods described under particular fruits a system of pruning has been devised by a Frenchman, M. Lorette, and bears his name. It is particularly applicable to trained apples and pears and, though primarily designed for the French climate, has proved very successful in some places in this country. The object is to force the stipulary buds, at the base of each side growth, to form fruit buds and so, in time, very compact spurs. Normally, these buds remain dormant and are all so small that they can scarcely be seen.

Briefly the system is as follows: between mid- and late spring shorten leaders by about one-third their length. In early summer prune side growths produced from the remaining portion of each leader if they have attained the thickness of a lead pencil at the base. Only 0·5cm ($1/4$in) of each is retained. The terminal growth may be retained as a leader. In midsummer any further side growths that were not thick enough to be pruned in early summer are dealt with in a similar manner. In late summer the process is repeated on still later side growths, and also any which may have grown from old fruit spurs or other parts of the tree. Any which are still weak should be bent down and tied in that position. No winter pruning is practised.

176. Starting Dormant Buds Sometimes numerous buds remain dormant, with the result that whole lengths of branch are bare and profitless. This can be overcome by *knife-edge ringing*, ie drawing the edge of a knife right round the stem above the bare portion so that the bark is severed to the wood beneath, or *notching*, ie removing a triangular section of bark immediately above each dormant bud. Either operation should be done in late spring.

177. Suckers All fruit trees and bushes are liable to produce suckers. These are not necessarily harmful. That depends partly upon whether the trees are grafted or on their own roots. Most apples, pears, plums, damsons, cherries, peaches, nectarines, and apricots are grafted, or budded, which is simply a form of grafting. The roots are provided by a stock which is of different character from the tree growing upon it. Any suckers, ie growths from the root, will therefore be part of the stock. They will, in consequence, produce crab apples, quinces, etc, according to their nature, not good garden apples, pears, etc. Such suckers must be removed right to the root from which they grow. If any stumps are left, these will soon throw out further shoots. Such suckers if retained will tend to crowd the tree with useless growth and sap its strength. If desired, these suckers may be detached in autumn, with a portion of root, and be replanted elsewhere to be grafted or budded in due season.

Most of the smaller bush fruits, ie gooseberries, currants, raspberries, etc, are grown from cuttings, layers or suckers and are, consequently, on their own roots. Suckers from these partake of the characteristics of the parent and are not harmful unless they are overcrowding the plant with growth or preventing easy access to it. See (216), (244), (246), (254), (274), (362).

178. Fruit Tree Bands Bands of grease–proof paper covered with a tacky substance are placed around the trunks or main boughs of apples and also, to a lesser extent, pears, plums, and cherries in early autumn to trap various insects which crawl up or down the trunks during the winter and spring. These bands should be 90cm (3ft) above ground level and at least 10cm (4in) wide. Special banding compound should be purchased to smear on these and must be renewed occasionally during the winter if it loses its tackiness. The bands must be kept in position until mid–spring. Alternatively special vegetable greases can be purchased to be smeared directly on the bark. Principal among the foes caught are the wingless females of the winter moths.

Bands of hay or old sacking are tied around the trees in early summer to provide a shelter for the cocoons of the codling moth (667) and the apple blossom weevil (667). If the bands are removed in mid–autumn, many of these pests will be found and can be destroyed.

179. Fruits for Special Localities
DAMP PLACES. Blackcurrants, quinces.

COOL AND SHADY WALLS. Morello cherries, currants, gooseberries and such plums as Czar, Belgian Purple, Oullin's Golden Gage, Rivers' Early Prolific, and Victoria.

WARM AND SUNNY WALLS. Apricots, peaches, nectarines, figs, grapes, and choice dessert plums, pears, and apples.

APPLES

180. Soil and Situation Apples succeed on a wide variety of soils and in most parts of the country. Fertilization is usually uncertain at altitudes above 200m (700ft). In such places late–flowering varieties such as Crawley Beauty, Edward VII, Court Pendu Plat, Royal Jubilee, and Orleans Reinette usually give best results. Devonshire Quarrendon, Keswick Codlin, and Margil also succeed. Nitrogen and potash are the two most essential foods; phosphates do not show much result and need be supplied only occasionally. Soil must be dug thoroughly. Manure or compost may be incorporated prior to planting at 50kg to 12 square metres (1cwt to 15yd^2). Lime is not essential.

181. Planting This may be done at any time from mid–autumn till early spring; late autumn is the best time if soil is in good condition. Roots should be spread out in wide holes sufficiently deep to allow the uppermost roots to be covered with 7·5–10cm (3–4in) of soil. Make thoroughly firm and stake securely. The union between stock and scion must not be buried. Distance for planting will depend on type of tree (see Table 18). Plant horizontal–trained trees 3·5–4.5m (12–15ft) apart, in rows at least 2m (6ft) apart; dwarf pyramids 1·2m (4ft) apart, in rows at least 8ft apart.

182. Forms of Training Apples are commonly grown as cordons, either single stemmed or double stemmed, dwarf pyramids, horizontal trained, bush, half-standards, and standards. Cordon trees and dwarf pyramids are suitable for confined places or where fruits of very high quality are required. Horizontal-trained trees are suitable for walls and espaliers and give fruit of excellent quality. Bushes may be used in large fruit gardens and orchards; usually ground is cultivated beneath them. Half-standards are for orchard planting or use as specimens. They are frequently grassed under (173).

183. Pollination A few varieties of apples are self-sterile, ie they will not produce fruit with their own pollen, while all set better crops when cross-pollinated. In consequence, it is unwise to plant apples singly. They should be near other varieties of apple blooming at approximately the same time. (See page 69.)

184. Pruning Trained trees and small bushes should be pruned in summer and winter. Large bushes, half-standards and standards are usually pruned in winter only, as summer pruning involves too much labour. SUMMER PRUNING is done during mid- to late summer, when side growths are nearly as thick as lead pencils and starting to get woody at the base. Each is shortened to five well-developed leaves. Leading growths (those extending branches) are not pruned in summer. In late autumn laterals are further cut back to two buds, and leaders are shortened by a quarter or one-third their length. The object of this double pruning is to overcome individual peculiarities of growth and make all trees conform to one type with fruit-bearing spurs closely clustered along the main branches. See also Lorette pruning (175).

Where WINTER PRUNING only is carried out, individual peculiarities must be considered. Some varieties tend to produce fruit buds all along the stems or mainly at the tips. Examples are Allington Pippin, Irish Peach, Cornish Gilli-flower, Gladstone, Lady Sudeley, St Everard, and Worcester Pearmain. These must be pruned lightly. Tip leaders, remove badly placed or crossing branches and those growing inwards but, where possible, retain laterals at full length. Other varieties produce fruit on long spurs. Examples are Bismarck, Blenheim Orange, Bramley's Seedling, Encore, and Newton Wonder. Treat as above, but shorten laterals by one-third. Most other varieties form short spurs readily. These may have leaders shortened by one-third and laterals cut to fruit buds wherever these have formed. Other laterals, unprovided with fruit buds, may be left unpruned for a further year, if there is room for them, or be cut back to three or four growth buds if they are overcrowded. All this work may be done at any time between late autumn and late winter.

In the illustration on page 70 the following buds are shown:
1 (a) Fruit bud on tip of young growth.
  (b) Growth bud.
2 (a) Fruit buds in various positions.
  (b) Growth buds. (c) Stipulary buds (Lorette Pruning. (175)).
3. Old spur in need of reduction.

185. Pruning Young Trees For the first few years growth is more important than fruiting, and pruning must be designed to encourage this. Prune laterals in winter to one or two buds and shorten leaders to the point at which it is desirable they should fork. With bush and standard trees this means that they should be shortened to points at which they are 30-45cm (12-18in) apart, considered laterally, or 60-90cm (2-3ft) apart, considered vertically, these being the correct average spacings for the main branches. Be partic-

183.   POLLINATION TABLE FOR APPLES

Early flowering	Mid-season flowering	Late flowering
Adam's Pearmain	Arthur Turner	Allington Pippin
Astrachan Red	Blenheim Orange★	American Mother
Baumann's Reinette	Bowden's Seedling	Annie Elizabeth
Beauty of Bath	Bramley's Seedling★	Cellini
Belle de Boskoop★	Charles Ross	Court Pendu Plat
Bismarck	Cox's Orange Pippin	Cox's Pomona
Brownlee's Russet	Devonshire Quarrendon	Crawley Beauty
Egremont Russet	Duchess Favourite	(very late)
Golden Spire	Early Victoria	Delicious
Irish Peach	Encore	Edward VII
Keswick Codlin	Epicure	Ellison's Orange
Lord Lambourne	Exquisite	Gala
Manx Codlin	Fiesta	Gascoyne's Scarlet
Margil	Fortune	Heusgen's Golden
Norfolk Beauty	George Carpenter	Reinette
Rev. W. Wilkes	Golden Noble	Lady Sudeley
Ribston Pippin★	Grenadier	Lane's Prince Albert
St. Edmund's Pippin	Howgate Wonder	Laxton's Pearmain
Vista Bella	James Grieve	Lord Derby
Wagener	John Standish	Monarch
Warner's King	King of Tompkins	Newton Wonder
Washington	Country★	Orleans Reinette
White Transparent	King's Acre Pippin	Reinette du Canada★
	Laxton's Superb	Royal Jubilee
	Lord Grosvenor	Winston
	Merton Prolific	Worcester Pearmain
	Merton Worcester	
	Peasgood's Nonsuch	
	Rival	
	St. Cecilia	
	St. Everard	
	Stirling Castle	
	Sturmer Pippin	
	Sunset	
	Tydeman's Early	
	Tydeman's Orange	
	Wealthy	

★ Varieties marked with an asterisk produce little pollen. Pollinator should be chosen from varieties in the same group so that their flowering times may coincide.

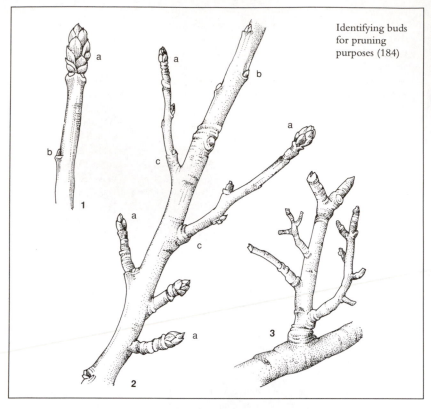

Identifying buds for pruning purposes (184)

ularly careful to remove inward-pointing shoots in bushes and standards and always to cut leaders to strong outward-pointing buds.

186. Forming Espaliers Leading growths of side arms are shortened by only a few inches. The central vertical growth is cut back to within about 40cm (15in) of the uppermost pair of arms. In the spring one shoot from this pruned central stem is trained vertically and two more are tied down to left and right to form a new pair of arms. When sufficient arms have been obtained, the vertical shoot is cut right out and prevented from re-forming. The same treatment is given to the leading shoots of arms when these

have extended far enough.

187. Forming Cordons The leading growth is not pruned at all until the tree has grown to the maximum desired height. It is then cut out and prevented from re-forming. Laterals are summer and winter pruned from the outset (184). Cordons are frequently planted at an angle of 45°, mainly to enable a greater length of stem to be obtained within reach from the ground, but also to check the spring uprush of sap and so obtain more even production of side growths throughout the length of the tree. The pruning of dwarf pyramids is very similar except that side shoots are given more liberty and may eventually be permitted to grow out to a length of approximately 30–60cm (1–2ft).

188. Thinning Fruits This is necessary if the set is heavy. Thinning should start in early summer but not be completed until midsummer, as there is often a natural drop in early summer. Large cooking varieties require more drastic thinning than small dessert kinds. In general, not more than one fruit should remain per spur after final thinning, but frequently this may be exceeded with dessert varieties. Large cookers should be spaced 20cm (8in) apart after final thinning, but this may be deferred until the fruits are large enough to be of service. Always retain the most perfect fruits. Watch carefully for any holed by maggots. Thinning may be done by hand or with pointed vine scissors.

189. Picking This should start as soon as fruits part readily from the branches. Test by lifting and gently pulling a typical fruit. If it breaks away easily, continue to gather; if it can only be dragged or torn away by force, leave the remainder longer. All fruits should be gathered by mid- to late autumn.

190. Storing Only the later varieties are suitable for storing. Early varieties shrivel rapidly and must be used within a few weeks of gathering. The apple store should be cool, moderately ventilated, but with a slightly damp atmosphere. An earthen floor and thatched roof are ideal. Fruits keep best if wrapped singly in waxed paper or tissue paper and placed in three or four layers in boxes. Too much ventilation and too dry an atmosphere encourage early shrivelling.

191. Routine Feeding Each spring, spread well-rotted dung or compost round trees at the rate of 50kg to 12 square metres (1cwt to 15yd²) for full presumed root spread. Each autumn, give sulphate or muriate of potash at the rate of 25–50g per square metre (³/₄–1¹/₂ oz per yd²) over same area. Every second autumn give, in addition, basic slag, at 130g per square metre (4oz per yd²). If growth is poor and fruits undersized, give sulphate of ammonia, nitrate of soda, or Nitro-chalk in mid-spring at 30g m² (1oz per yd²). Alternatively, use fruit tree fertilizer (88).

192. Routine Pest Control Apart from steps taken against pests or diseases which actually occur, it is wise to undertake certain routine measures. In midwinter all trees are sprayed with tar-oil winter wash (664) to destroy eggs, hibernating insects, etc. In spring trees are sprayed with fungicide, such as mancozeb (62), following the manufacturer's instructions, against scab. Insecticide such as fenitrotrion (648) used after flowering controls various pests, including codling moth, apple sawfly, capsid bugs and winter moth. In late autumn grease bands (178) are placed round the trunks of trees to prevent female winter moths, etc, from ascending to lay their eggs. The bands must be kept sticky until they are finally removed in mid-spring.

193. Bordeaux Scorching Beauty of Bath, Cox's Orange Pippin, Lane's Prince Albert and Lord Derby are damaged by copper fungicides. These should be sprayed with captan or other fungicide (638) which does no harm.

194. Propagation By grafting in early and mid-spring or by budding from midsummer until early autumn. Many methods of grafting are employed, but three, whip grafting (196), rind grafting (197) and framework grafting (198), are of most use. New varieties are raised from seed sown outdoors or in frames in early spring.

195. Stocks These are used for grafting and budding and they have a marked effect upon growth and bearing. Stocks

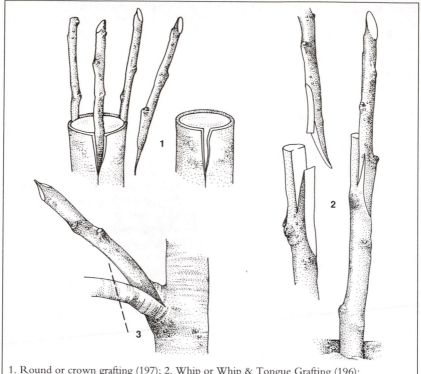

1. Round or crown grafting (197); 2. Whip or Whip & Tongue Grafting (196);
3. Framework or Stub grafting (198)

are of two main types: crabs, raised from seed and in consequence very variable in character, and Paradise stocks, raised from layers and constant to type. Paradise stocks are classified under numbers prefixed by M (for Malling) or MM (for Malling-Merton) indicating where they were developed. M.27, M.9 and M.26 are very dwarfing and encourage very early fruiting. They are excellent for cordons, especially on rich soils or for fairly vigorous varieties. MM.106 is semi-dwarfing and suitable for espaliers, dwarf pyramids and small bushes. MM.111 and M.2 are more vigorous and suitable for large bushes. Vigorous stocks must not be used for trained trees.

196. Whip or Whip and Tongue Grafting This is employed where stock and scion are not far removed in thickness. On both a long, sloping cut is made, with a second smaller, incision in the opposite direction, forming a tongue. All cuts should be of the same length and width. Scion and stock are fitted together by means of the tongues and are bound firmly with polythene tape. The whole wounded area is sealed with grafting wax. This method is shown in Fig 2, on page (72).

197. Rind or Crown Grafting This is used where the stock is much thicker than the scion. A vertical incision is made through the bark at the head of the stock.

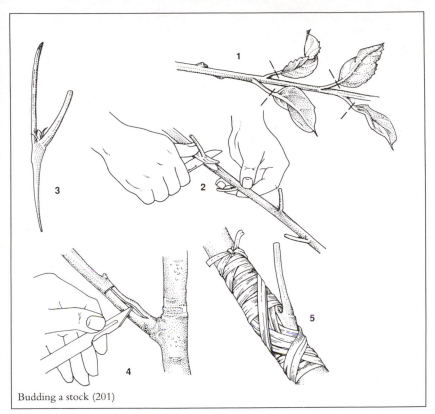

Budding a stock (201)

The bark is lifted with a scalpel. The scion is cut in the form of a long, thin wedge and slipped beneath the raised bark. It is bound in position and waxed. If desired, several scions may be inserted round the head of each stock. This method is shown in Fig 1, on page 72. Top buds of the scions should point outwards.

198. Framework, or Stub Grafting is employed to re-work unprofitable trees and get them back into bearing rapidly. Every side growth that is as thick as, or a little thicker than, a lead pencil is grafted separately and the whole main framework of the tree is retained. Several methods are employed, the simplest being to make a downward incision near the base of each side shoot and on its upper side, bend the shoot down so as to open this cut and then insert in it a scion previously prepared with a short double wedge cut at the base. The shoot is then released so that it springs back and grips the scion in position. Finally the shoot is cut off just beyond the scion and the wounded area covered with wax. No tying is required. This method is shown in Fig 3, on page 72. Several hundred scions may be inserted on one tree.

199. Heading Back Old trees that are to be rind grafted should be headed back in mid-winter. Young stocks are headed back at grafting time.

200. Scions These can be collected

when pruning. Any one-year growths about the thickness of a pencil or slightly less are suitable. Label and heel in under a cool and shady wall or fence to retard growth.

201. Budding This is a quicker operation than grafting, but is suitable only for young stocks in which the bark is still thin and pliable. A T-shaped incision is made in this and the flaps lifted with a scalpel. A dormant growth bud on ripe, young wood is cut with a shield-shaped portion of bark. Any wood contained within this is stripped out. The bud is slipped beneath the flaps of bark and bound in position with polythene tape. No waxing is necessary. Stocks are not headed back till the following late autumn. The illustration on page 73 shows:

1. A suitable shoot from which buds can be cut, also point at which leaves should be severed.
2. The method of cutting out the bud with a shield-shaped portion of bark.
3. The bud ready for insertion.
4. Flap of bark formed by 'T' incision being raised by a scalpel.
5. The finished job with the bud bound in position.

202. Height for Buds and Grafts Insert all buds and grafts on young stocks (22–40cm (9–15in) above soil level. Grafts on old stocks can be inserted at any convenient height.

203. Varieties of Apple *Note – C denotes cooking and D dessert varieties; CD dual-purpose apples. The seasons are those in which the variety is at its prime.*

Adam's Pearmain (D), early winter – early spring; Advance (D), late summer; Allen's Everlasting (D), mid-spring – early summer; Allington Pippin (D), mid-autumn – early winter; American Mother (D), mid – late autumn; Annie Elizabeth (C), early winter – early summer; Arthur Turner (C). early – mid-autumn; Ash-mead's Kernel (D), early winter – early spring; Astrachan Red (D), late summer.

Barnack Beauty (D), early winter – mid-spring; Barnack Orange (D), late autumn – early winter; Baumann's Red Winter Reinette (D), early – late winter; Beauty of Bath (D), late summer; Beauty of Kent (C), late autumn – early spring; Beauty of Stocke (CD), mid-winter – early spring, Belle de Boskoop (CD), mid-winter – mid-spring, Bismarck (C), late autumn – mid-winter, Blenheim Orange (D), late autumn – mid-winter, Bowden's Seedling (D), late autumn – early spring, Bramley's Seedling (C) late autumn – mid-spring; Brownlee Russet (D), mid-winter – mid-spring.

Cellini (D), mid – late autumn; Charles Ross (CD), mid – late autumn; Christmas Pearmain (D), early – mid winter; Claygate Pearmain (D), early – late winter; Cornish Aromatic (D), early – late winter Cornish Gillyflower (D), early winter – late spring; Court Pendu Plat (D), early winter – mid-spring; Cortland (D), late autumn – mid-winter, Cox's Orange Pippin (D), late autumn – late winter, Cox's Pomona (CD), mid – late autumn, Crawley Beauty (C), early winter – mid-spring; Cutler Grieve (D), late autumn – mid-spring.

D'Arcy Spice (D), Early winter – mid-spring; Delicious (D), late autumn – late winter; Devonshire Quarrendon (D), late summer – early autumn; Duchess's Favourite (D), Mid – late autumn; Duke of Devonshire (D), late winter – mid-spring; Dumelow's Seedling (C), late autumn – early spring.

Early Crimson (D), midsummer; Early Victoria (or Emneth Early) (C), mid – late summer; Early Peach (D), late summer; Easter Orange (D), early – mid-spring; Ecklinville Seedling (C), late summer – mid-autumn; Edward VII (C), mid-winter – mid-spring; Egremont Russet (D), mid-autumn – early winter; Ellison's Orange (D), early – mid-autumn; Emperor Alexander (CD), mid – late autumn; Encore (C), early winter – early summer; Epicure (D), early autumn; Exquisite (D), early autumn.

Fortune (D), early autumn; Gascoyne's Scarlet (D), early autumn – mid-winter; George Carpenter (D), mid-autumn – late winter; George Cave (D), late summer – early autumn; George Neal (C), midsummer – early autumn; Golden Delicious (D), early – late winter; Golden Noble (C), mid-autumn – early autumn; Golden Spire (C), early – mid-autumn; Granny Smith (D), early winter – mid-spring; Grenadier (C), late summer – early autumn.

Herring's Pippin (CD), mid – late autumn; Heusgen's Golden Reinette (CD), early winter – mid-spring; Holstein (D), late autumn – early winter; Howgate Wonder (C), mid-autumn – mid-winter.

Imperial (D), mid-autumn – mid-winter; Irish Peach (D), late summer.

James Grieve (D), early – mid-autumn; John Standish (D), mid-winter – early spring; Joy Bells (D), late autumn – early winter.

Keswick Codlin (C), late summer – early autumn; King George V (D), late winter – early spring; King of the Pippins (D), mid – late autumn; King of Tompkins County (D), early winter – mid-spring; King's Acre Pippin (D), midsummer – early spring.

Lady Sudeley (D), late summer – mid-autumn; Lane's Prince Albert (C), late autumn – early spring; Langley Pippin (D), late summer – early autumn; Lord Burghley (D), late winter – mid-spring; Lord Derby (C), late autumn – early winter; Lord Grosvenor (C), late summer – early autumn; Lord Hindlip (D), mid-winter – mid-spring; Lord Lambourne (D), mid-autumn – mid-winter, Lord

Suffield (C), late summer – early autumn.

Margil (D), late autumn – mid-winter; May Queen (D), mid-winter – late spring; McIntosh Red (CD), mid-autumn – mid-winter; Melba (D), late summer; Merton Charm (D), early – mid-autumn; Merton Russet (D), early – late winter; Merton Worcester (D), early – mid-autumn; Miller's Seedling (D), early – mid-autumn; Monarch (C), early winter – mid-spring; Mr Gladstone (D), mid – late summer; Mutsu (D), early – late winter.

Newton Wonder (C), early winter – late spring; Norfolk Royal (D), late autumn – early spring.

Ontario (CD), early winter – late spring; Orleans Reinette (D), early – late winter.

Peasgood's Nonsuch (CD), early – late autumn; Pioneer (D), mid – late autumn; Queen (C), mid – late autumn.

Reinette du Canada (D), mid – late winter; Rev. W. Wilkes (C), mid – late autumn; Ribston Pippin (D), late autumn – mid-winter; Rival (CD), mid-autumn – early winter; Rosemary Russet (D), early – late winter; Roundway Magnum Bonum (CD), late autumn – early spring; Royal Jubilee (C), mid-autumn – early winter; Royal Russet (C), late autumn – mid-spring.

Saltcote Pippin (D), mid-autumn – early winter; Sandringham (C), early – late winter; Scarlet Pimpernel (D), mid – late summer; St Cecilia (D), mid-winter – early spring; St Edmunds Russet (D), early – mid-autumn; St Everard (D), early autumn; Stark (D), mid-spring – early summer; Stark Earlies (D), mid – late summer; Stirling Castle (C), early – mid-autumn; Sturmer Pippin (D), early spring – early summer; Sunset (D), late autumn – early winter; Superb (D), early winter – early spring.

Thos. Rivers (C), early autumn – early

winter; Triumph (D), late autumn – mid-winter; Tydeman's Early (D), early autumn; Tydeman's Late Orange (D), early winter – early spring.

Wagener (C), mid-winter – late spring; Warner's King (C), mid-autumn – early winter, Wealthy (D), mid – late autumn; Wellington (C), late autumn – early spring; White Transparent (CD), mid – late autumn; William Crump (D), early – late winter; Winston (D), early winter – late spring; Worcester Pearmain (D), early – mid-autumn; Wyken Pippin (D), early winter – early spring.

APRICOTS

204. Soil and Situation Apricots require a sheltered, sunny position and rather rich, well-drained soil. Extra drainage, with rubble buried 60cm (2ft) beneath surface, may be necessary. They are usually grown against warm and sunny walls or in sunny greenhouses. Borders are specially prepared. If the natural soil is very heavy or sandy, it is removed and replaced with good loam. In any case, plenty of old mortar rubble or ground chalk is added and a little well-rotted manure.

205. Planting This may be done at any time from mid-autumn until early spring. Late autumn is usually the best time. Trees to be grown in greenhouses should always be planted then. Holes should be wide and rather shallow. Uppermost roots should be covered with 8cm (3in) of soil. All must be made thoroughly firm. Wall trees are spaced 4·5m (15ft) apart.

206. Forms of Training Apricots are almost always grown as fan-trained trees. Details of training and early formation are exactly the same as for fan-trained plums (344).

207. Pruning Most of the work should be done in summer, when all badly placed or unwanted growths are rubbed out early. Other side growths should be shortened to the sixth good leaf reckoning from the base when about as thick as a pencil and commencing to get woody at the base (usually from about the middle of summer outdoors). In winter, leaders are shortened by one-third, or as much as is necessary to confine the tree within bounds. Side growths may be tied in without further pruning if there is room for them. Otherwise they are further shortened to three buds.

208. Routine Feeding As for plums (347). A spring mulch of decayed manure is especially beneficial to trees grown under glass. Such must also be watered freely while in growth.

209. Routine Pest Control As for plums (348).

210. Propagation By budding in mid- to late summer as for plums (349). The plum stocks are also used, especially Mussel, Brompton, and St Julien A, and the dwarfing Pixy.

211. Varieties of Apricot UNDER GLASS Breda, late summer – early autumn; Early Moorpark, midsummer; Frogmore Early, midsummer; Pêche de Nancy, late summer – early autumn; Hemskerke, late summer – early autumn; Kaisha, late summer; Luizet, mid – late summer; Moorpark, late summer – early autumn; New Large Early, midsummer; Royal, late summer; Shipley or Blenheim, midsummer.

OUTDOORS Farmingdale, late summer; Breda, late summer; Hemskerke, late summer.

BLACKBERRIES, LOGANBERRIES, ETC.

212. Soil and Situation All succeed in most ordinary garden soils except those of a very dry, poor nature. They will grow in sunny or partially shaded positions. Soil should be prepared exactly as for raspberries (359).

213. Planting Canes should be spaced (2·5m) (8ft) apart, and if there is more than one row 2·5m (8ft) should be allowed between rows. Very vigorous varieties such as Himalayan Giant should be spaced 3·5m (12ft) apart each way. Planting may be done at any time from mid-autumn to early spring as for raspberries (360).

214. Training Common practice is to grow loganberries, blackberries, and allied fruits against walls or fences. Alternatively they may be grown in the open tied to wires strained between posts as for raspberries (361). The uppermost wire should be 2m (7ft) above ground level.

215. Pollination Most varieties are self-fertile, ie they will produce fruit when pollinated with their own pollen. A few varieties of hybrid berry are self-sterile or produce no pollen and, in consequence, should be planted with other kinds.

216. Pruning After planting, cut all canes back to within 30cm (12in) of ground level. Young canes should not be allowed to bear fruit the first year. In subsequent years, prune as soon as possible after the crop has been gathered. Cut out to ground level all old fruiting canes and train young canes in their place. With very vigorous varieties such as the blackberry Himalayan Giant, two or three old canes per plant may be kept for a second season. Do not retain more than 10 new canes per plant. Select the sturdiest and cut out the remainder early in the summer. It does not matter if those retained are suckers, ie growing direct from the root.

217. Routine Cultivation As for raspberries (363).

218. Routine Pest Control Usually unnecessary, as foes are dealt with as noted. If cane spot (667) is troublesome, cut out and burn all affected canes and spray with fungicide such as Bordeaux mixture (636) or Benomyl (634), following the manufacturers instructions.

219. Propagation May be effected by division of old plants in autumn or winter, but the best method is to tip-root young canes. This is done by bending such canes down in mid- to late summer and pegging the tips to the soil. If kept moist, roots will be formed rapidly and by the autumn the canes can be severed from the parents. A few weeks later they may be lifted and transplanted to a nursery bed.

220. Varieties of Blackberry Bedford Giant, early; Black Satin, early; Himalayan Giant, mid-season; John Innes, late; Merton Thornless, mid-season; Oregon Thornless, mid-season; Parsley-leaved, mid-season.

221. Varieties of Hybrid Berry Boysenberry, Loganberry, Thornless Loganberry, Tayberry, Veitchberry. Newberry and Phenomenal Berry resemble the Loganberry and Youngberry the Boysenberry.

CHERRIES

222. Soil and Situation Well-drained, loamy soils or loam over chalk are most suitable. Cherries do not thrive on badly drained soils, heavy clays, nor on light sands. They bloom early and are subject to frost damage. In consequence, very exposed positions or damp valleys liable to catch frost are unsuitable. Soil preparation is the same as for apples (180), except that manure or compost may be used at 50kg to 10-12 square metres (1cwt to 10-12 yd²), according to the nature of the soil.

223. Planting Season and method are the same as for apples (181). For distances see (20). Fan-trained trees should be spaced 4-5m (15ft) apart.

224. Forms of Trees As a rule these are fan trained, bush, half-standard, and standard. Occasionally cherries are grown as single or double-stemmed cordons, but they are not very suitable for this method of training. Fan-trained trees are planted against walls or fences; bushes, half-standards, and standards in the open, the last two often grassed under.

225. Pruning For this purpose, cherries fall into two distinct groups. Sweet cherries and the Duke cherries form spurs like apples. The sour cherries such as Morello and Amarelles do not form spurs so freely but fruit also on the previous year's growth. Hard pruning is not desirable with any cherries, as it is inclined to encourage gummosis (667). Standards, half-standards, and bushes can be pruned lightly. Only badly placed or crossing branches and shoots need be removed together with damaged or diseased wood. This is best done in early spring, just before the trees come into flower.

Trained trees must be kept in hand. SWEET AND DUKE CHERRIES should be summer and winter pruned in a similar manner to trained apples (184), except that wherever there is room young laterals should be trained in at full length. The summer work should start in early summer and be completed by late summer. Winter pruning is best deferred till late winter or early spring.

With SOUR CHERRIES a process known as 'disbudding' is carried out throughout the summer. Most young side growths are rubbed out at an early stage, but at least two are retained for each fruiting growth, one as near its base as possible, the other at its tip. In autumn the old fruiting growth is cut out and the young shoot, retained near its base, is trained in to take its place.

226. Pruning Young Trees In the early stages rather harder pruning is necessary to form the tree. Leaders may be shortened by a half or two-thirds. All cuts should be made to outward-pointing buds. Fan-trained trees should be prevented from forming a central stem. Cut this back to 45cm (18in) from soil level and so force branching from near the base. Branches should be spread like the ribs of a fan. Training wires or bamboos must be used for this purpose (344).

227. Pollination Most sweet cherries are self-sterile, ie they will not bear fruit if pollinated with their own pollen. In addition, some varieties are inter-sterile, ie their pollen is ineffective when transferred from one to the other. The only varieties which are fully self-fertile are Morello, Stella and Sunburst. The Duke cherries, ie May Duke, Late Duke, Archduke, etc, are partially self-fertile, but set much better crops when interplanted with other sour cherries. Other varieties may be classified in groups. The varieties within any group are infertile one with the other. Any kind may be planted with a variety from any other group. See table opposite.

228. Picking This should start as soon as fruits part readily from the branches. Fruits usually ripen unevenly and on any one tree several pickings should be made. Cherries cannot be stored and should be used as gathered, but they bottle well.

229. Routine Pest Control Apart from dealing with pests or diseases as noted it is customary to spray cherries with tar-oil wash (664) in mid-winter and fix grease bands (178) around the trees in mid-autumn. If cherry slugworm (667) is troublesome, spray with derris (644), fenitrothion (648) or malathion (651), following manufacturer's instructions.

230. Propagation By budding during mid- and late summer on to a suitable

227. POLLINATION TABLE FOR SWEET CHERRIES

1	2	3
Bedford Prolific (e)	Schrecken Bigarreau (e)	Napolean Bigarreau (m)
Early Rivers (e)	Frogmore Early (m)	Emperor Francis (m)
Knights Early Black (e)	Merton Bigarreau (m)	Monstreuse de Mezel (e)
Roundel Heart (m)	Waterloo (e)	
	Black Elton (l)	
4	**5**	**6**
Kentish Bigarreau (m)	Late Black Bigarreau (l)	Elton Heart (m)
Merton Premier (m)	Turkey Black Heart (e)	Governor Wood (m)
		Merton Heart (e)
7	**8**	**9**
Géante d'Hedelfingen (l)	Peggy Rivers (m)	Red Turk (e)
Bigarreau de Mezel (m)		
10	**11**	**12**
Bigarreau Jaboulay (e)	Guigne d'Annonay (e)	Noble (l)

Varieties within any one box are not inter-fertile. All can be successfully cross-pollinated by varieties from any of the other squares. Letters in brackets mean:

(e) early flowering (m) mid-season flowering (l) late flowering

The following varieties will pollinate one another and members of all other groups:
Bigarreau Gaucher (l), Black Tartarian E (e), Florence (l), Merton Glory (m), Noir de Guben (e), Smoky Heart (l).

stock. The process is the same as for apples (201). Colt is the best semi-vigorous stock for all forms. Malling F 12/1 is more vigorous.

231. Varieties of Cherry *Note - The seasons are those in which the fruits normally ripen. C indicates cooking, D dessert.*

Archduke (C), mid-season; Bedford Prolific (D), mid-season; Bigarreau de Mezel (D), mid- late; Bigarreau de Schrecken (D), early; Bigarreau Jaboulay (D), early; ★Black Tartarian (D), mid-season; Early Rivers (D), early; Elton Heart (D), mid-season; Emperor Francis Bigarreau (D), late; Flemish Red (C), mid-season; Florence (D), late; Frogmore Early (D), mid-season; Géante d'Hedelfingen (D), late; Governor Wood (D), mid-season; Guigne D'Annonay (D), early; Kentish Bigarreau (D), mid-season; Kentish Red (C), mid-season; Knight's Early Black (D), early; Ludwig's Bigarreau (D), mid-season; May Duke (CD), early; Merton Bigarreau (D), mid-season; Merton Heart (D), mid-season; Merton Premier (D), mid-season; Morello (C), late; Napoleon Bigarreau (D), late; Noble (Tradescant's Heart), (D), mid-season;

Noir de Guben (D), mid-season; Peggy Rivers (D), mid-season; Roundel Heart (D), mid-season; Royal Duke (CD), mid-season; Stella (D), mid-season; Sunburst (D), early; Turkey Heart (D), very late; Ursula Rivers (D), mid-season, Waterloo (D), early; White Heart (D), mid-season.

★ There are several distinct forms bearing this name and now distinguished by the letters A, B, C, D or E after the name. There are also three distinct varieties of Bigarreau de Mezel but these have not been given distinguishing letters.

COBNUTS AND FILBERTS

232. Soil and Situation Will succeed in a wide variety of positions from full sun to shade and are not particular as regards soil, though they do not crop well on heavy, wet clays. Preparation should be as thorough as possible and a little well-rotted manure may be worked in.

233. Planting From mid-autumn to early spring, as for apples (181). Other details are also the same.

234. Pollination Incompatibility does not exist, but some varieties produce little pollen and so are bad pollinators. These should be interplanted with varieties that produce pollen freely (241).

235. Form of Training Trees are almost invariably grown as open-centred bushes. In the early stages of growth, winter pruning should be directed towards forming the main framework of these. Inward-pointing branches are cut right out. Leading shoots are shortened by about a half and always cut to an outward-pointing bud to keep the centre of the bush open.

236. Pruning Established bushes are pruned in late winter and early spring, while in flower and immediately afterwards. All ingrowing shoots are cut out, also weak or damaged growths. Suckers

are removed from the roots by a sharp twist and pull. Side growths are cut back to the first catkin reckoning from the tip, or, if there are no catkins, to the first female (red) flower. Shoots that have catkins only should be left unpruned till these fade, when they are cut back to two buds from the main stem. All strong side growths are broken to half length in late summer. This is known as brutting.

237. Picking and Storing Cobnuts and filberts are picked in early to mid-autumn. The yellowing of the husks is the signal for this work to start. Nuts may be hung up in nets in a dry place or stored in earthenware jars or crocks between layers of salt.

238. Routine Feeding Well-rotted manure or shoddy may be spread around the trees at 50kg to 12 square metres (1cwt to 15yd²) each spring. Basic slag at 190g per square metre (6oz per yd²), and sulphate of potash at 30g per square metre (1oz per yd²), should be given in mid-autumn each year.

239. Routine Pest Control If nuts are damaged by weevils which bore holes in them, spray each year in late spring with fenitrothion (648) or derris (644). Gather up and burn all damaged nuts.

240. Propagation By suckers, which may be detached at any time during the planting season. Also by layering in autumn, ie bending whippy branches down to soil level, pegging them firmly to the ground and heaping a little soil over them. Layers should be well rooted by the following autumn, when they may be detached and planted on their own.

Nuts are also raised from seeds sown outdoors in early spring, but seedlings are very variable.

241. Varieties ★Cosford, Duke of Edinburgh, Kentish Cob, ★Nottingham Cob, Prolific Filbert, Red Filbert, and White Filbert.

Cobs have short husks, filberts long husks. Kentish Cob is, in fact, a filbert.

★ *Good pollinators.*

CURRANTS (BLACK)

242. Soil and Condition Blackcurrants succeed on a wide variety of soils and do not dislike moist conditions, provided their roots do not stand in stagnant water during winter. Flowers are produced early and are liable to be damaged by frost, so hollows which are likely to be frost traps should be avoided. Soil must be dug thoroughly; manure or compost may be incorporated at 50kg to 7 square metres (1cwt to 8yd²), as blackcurrants like rather rich conditions. Lime is not essential.

243. Planting This may be done at any time from mid-autumn until early spring, provided soil is working freely. Plant two-year old virus-free certified bushes. Roots are fine and fibrous, and soil must be carefully worked round and between them. Growth is vigorous and at least 1·5m (5ft) should be allowed between the bushes (20).

244. Forms of Training Blackcurrants are almost invariably grown as bushes. It is no disadvantage if these are legless, ie without main stems and with many shoots coming through the soil, direct from the roots. Very occasionally the plants are trained in fan formation against fences or espaliers.

245. Pollination All blackcurrants are fully self-fertile and also inter-fertile. It is therefore possible to plant one variety only or any combination of varieties and obtain good crops. Poor fertilization is common, but is due to frost or lack of insects to secure pollination, not to sterility. The trouble is known as 'running off,' as it is usually the end flowers of each truss that fail to set. More bees or hand fertil-

ization with a camel-hair brush and a more sheltered position are the remedies.

246. Pruning All work can be done in winter, between mid-autumn and late winter, or, if preferred, as soon as the crop has been gathered. The object is to eliminate as much as possible of the growth that has just carried fruits without sacrificing strong young shoots on which the following year's crops will be borne. It does not matter if these come right from the roots (244). After planting, all growth should be cut back to within 5-7cm (2-3in) of soil level.

247. Picking Where fruits are required for home use only, it often pays to pick individual berries, as those nearest to the stem ripen before those at the tips of the truss. For exhibition, fruits must be shown on the truss, and so these are picked whole when all berries are black, but before the biggest start to split. Storing is impracticable, but blackcurrants bottle excellently.

248. Feeding Mulch each early spring with well-rotted dung or compost at 50kg to 6-8 square metres (1cwt to 8-12yd²). Give sulphate of potash at 22g per square metre (³/₄ oz per yd²) each mid-autumn. If dung is not available, substitute nitrate of soda, Nitro-chalk, or sulphate of ammonia at 65g per square metre (2oz per yd²), and follow with a mulch of grass clippings.

249. Routine Pest Control Usually unnecessary, as foes are dealt with as noted. If big-bud mite (667) is troublesome, spray with carbendazim (640), following the manufacturer's instructions. The ideal time for application is when the most forward leaves are 2-3cm (1in) across. Examine bushes each midsummer for reversion (629) and burn any affected.

250. Propagation By cuttings from healthy plants only, taken during mid- to late autumn. Cuttings are from 20-35cm

(8–15in) in length and prepared from well-ripened growths of the current year's formation. Trim each immediately below a joint and insert firmly 10cm (4in) deep in any well-drained soil and reasonably sheltered position. Cuttings should be 15cm (6in) apart in rows 45cm (18in) apart. Transplant to permanent positions after one year's growth.

251. Varieties of Blackcurrant *(The seasons are those in which the variety normally ripens.)*

Amos Black, late; Baldwin, very late; Blacksmith (Tinker), late; Boskoop Giant, early; Daniel's September, late; Davison's Eight, mid – late; Goliath (Victoria, Edina), mid – late; Laxtons Giant, early – mid; Mendip Cross, mid season; French Black, mid – late; Wellington XXX, mid – late; Westwick Choice, mid – late; Worcesterberry is an American hybrid and is grown like a gooseberry.

CURRANTS (RED AND WHITE)

252. Soil and Situation As for blackcurrants (242).

253. Planting As for blackcurrants (243), except that slightly less room may be allowed between the bushes, say 120–150cm (4–5ft). After planting, cut back to 20–22cm (8–9in) of soil level.

254. Forms of Training Red- and whitecurrants are almost invariably grown as bushes, but with a short leg or main trunk, not with sucker growths as for blackcurrants (244).

255. Pruning Both summer and winter pruning should be carried out.

SUMMER PRUNING is done in early to midsummer, when all side growths (laterals) should be cut back a few at a time to five well-developed leaves each. Deal with the strongest growths first.

WINTER PRUNING is done at any time from mid-autumn to late winter. Side growths are further cut back to two or three dormant buds each and leaders are shortened by about one-third. Some varieties produce numerous shoots with dead or poorly developed buds. Such should be cut hard back, to strong buds. If necessary, this can be done in the spring, when growth starts, if they are not noted before. Suckers are removed (254).

256. Routine Feeding The same as for blackcurrants (248).

257. Routine Pest Control Usually unnecessary, but if caterpillars (667) or aphids (667) are troublesome, apply tar-oil wash (664) at ordinary strength in mid-winter each year.

258. Propagation By cuttings prepared and inserted in a similar manner to those of blackcurrants (250), except that all buds on the lower half of each cutting should be nicked out with the point of a knife. This is to prevent sucker growth.

259. Varieties of Redcurrant *(The seasons are those in which the fruits normally ripen.)*

Cherry, early; Earliest of Fourlands, early; Fay's Prolific, mid-season; Jonkheer van Tets, early; Laxton's No 1, mid-season; Laxton's Perfection, mid-season; Raby Castle, late; Red Lake, mid-season; Redstart, very late; Rivers's Late Red, very late; Wilson's Long Bunch, late.

260. Varieties of Whitecurrant Transparent, late; White Dutch (White Grape), mid – late, White Versailles, mid-season.

FIGS

261. Soil and Situation Figs require a sheltered, sunny position and well-drained, not over-rich soil. They are more usually grown under glass than outdoors, but will succeed in the open in warm areas. Manure should be used sparingly when preparing the ground. A little ground chalk or mortar rubble may be worked in.

262. Planting This may be done at any time during the dormant period, but is best early. See Apricots (205).

263. Forms of Training Wall trees and those grown under glass are generally trained as fans. Trees in the open are allowed to form large bushes or even make half-standards.

264. Pruning Figs bear on one- and two-year old stems. In spring and early summer rub off badly placed shoots and in early summer pinch those well placed for tying in. These will produce side growths which will carry the next year's crop. Thin overcrowded growth in midsummer and cut out weak shoots the following early spring. In mid- and late summer sturdy side growths are shortened to five or six well-developed leaves each. If trees make excessive growth and are unfruitful they are root pruned in mid-autumn.

265. Thinning Fruits This is very necessary as the trees are liable to overcrop. Under glass two or, occasionally, even three successive crops, on year-old and new growth, may be produced in the year. Outdoors only one is obtained, in summer on well-ripened side growths produced the previous year. Thin out the smaller fruits towards the ends of these shoots and preserve those of larger size towards the base. In autumn remove all fruits above the size of peas as these will not overwinter outdoors. Under glass they crop early.

266. Routine Feeding Apply a light mulch of well-rotted manure each spring, supplemented by basic slag at 180g per square metre (6oz per yd^2) and sulphate of potash at 50g per square metre (1^1/$_2$oz per yd^2), in mid-autumn. Every second autumn give ground chalk at 250g per square metre (8oz per yd^2).

267. Management under Glass Early figs from which it is desired to obtain three crops of fruit are started in early or mid-winter by closing ventilators, watering borders, and raising the temperature to 18°C (65°F). Usually, only two crops are attempted, and the house is closed in late winter. In any case the temperature is gradually allowed to increase to a maximum of 26°C (80°F) as the figs ripen. Paths and walls should be damped and leaves syringed liberally while in growth, except when the fruits are ripening, when a drier atmosphere must be maintained. After the first crop has been gathered, the year-old laterals are thinned out liberally to expose the second-crop fruits to the light, and the borders are well soaked with water or weak liquid manure.

268. Routine Pest Control Usually unnecessary.

269. Propagation By cuttings of well-ripened one-year-old growths taken in the autumn and inserted singly in pots which are filled with a gritty compost. Cuttings are rooted in a frame or cool greenhouse.

270. Varieties Brown Turkey is the best all-round fig for cultivation in temperate climates. Others are Bourgarotte Grise, Brunswick, *Negro Largo, *White Ischia and White Marseilles.

Greenhouse or warm climate only.

GOOSEBERRIES

271 Soil and Situation Gooseberries succeed on most soils that are reasonably rich and well drained. They flower early and are susceptible to spring frost. Nitrogen and potash are the two most essential foods. Preparation of soil should be the same as for apples (180). Lime is not essential.

272. Planting The same as for blackcurrants (243), except that rather less space is required by some of the weaker-growing varieties. Average 120-150cm (4-5ft) between bushes (20). Cordons should be planted in rows 120cm (4ft) apart. In the rows single-stemmed cordons are spaced 30cm (1ft), double-stemmed 60cm (2ft), and triple-stemmed 1m (3ft apart).

273. Forms of Training Gooseberries are usually grown as bushes on a short leg like red- and whitecurrants (254). Occasionally single, double or even triple cordons are grown, especially where fruits of extra quality for exhibition are required.

274. Pruning This should be done in summer and winter, and in the main is the same as for redcurrants (255). It is important to keep the centres of bushes fairly clear or picking becomes difficult. For the same reasons sucker growths must be cut right out. Some varieties have weak or arching leaders. These should be cut back each autumn to a strong, upward-pointing bud near the summit of the arch. A few varieties grow very erect. Leaders of these should be cut to strong outward-pointing buds to keep the centre of the bush open.

275. Picking This should start as soon as the most forward fruits are of useable size; generally in early summer. Do not strip the bushes at first, but thin the fruits, leaving the remainder 2·5cm (1in) or so apart, to continue swelling and ripening. Storing is impracticable, but all varieties are excellent for bottling.

276. Routine Feeding Potash is of particular importance. Its lack is indicated by leaf scorching. To prevent this give sulphate of potash at 50g per square metre (1¹/₂oz per yd²) in mid-autumn each year. Apply well-rotted dung or compost each early spring at the rate of 50kg to 12 square metres (1cwt to 15yd²) or, failing

this, nitrate of soda, Nitro-chalk, or sulphate of ammonia at 22g per square metre (³/₄ oz per yd²), followed by a mulch of grass clippings.

277. Routine Pest Control Usually unnecessary, as foes are dealt with as noted. If greenfly (667), caterpillars (667), or scale insects (667) are troublesome, spray each mid-winter with tar-oil wash (664). If mildew (667), either American or English, is prevalent, use benomyl (634) following the manufacturers instructions.

278. Propagation By cuttings prepared and inserted in exactly the same way as those of blackcurrants (250), except that all buds on the lower half of each cutting should be nicked out with a sharp knife. This is to prevent sucker formation.

279. Varieties of Gooseberry *Note - the seasons are those in which the varieties normally ripen. Colour of ripe fruits in brackets. C, culinary. D, dessert. CD, dual purpose.*

Bedford Yellow (yellow) D, early; Broom Girl (yellow) D, very early; Careless (white) C, early; Cousen's Seedling (yellow) D, very late; Crown Bob (red) CD, mid-season; Dan's Mistake (red) D, mid-season; Early Sulphur (yellow) D, very early; Golden Drop (yellow) D, mid-season; Green Gem (green) CD, late; Gunner (yellow) D, mid – late; Invicta (green) CD, late; Keepsake (green) CD, early – mid; Lancashire Lad (red) C, mid-season; Langley Gage (white) D, mid-season; Leveller (yellow) CD, mid-season; May Duke (red) CD, very early; Warrington (red) CD, very late; Whinham's Industry (red) CD, mid-season; White Lion (white) CD, very late; Whitesmith (white) CD, mid-season.

GRAPE VINES

280. Soil and Situation Grapes can

be grown in a wide variety of soils if well prepared. Heavy loams require adequate drainage. Only sandy soils, wet clays, and solid chalks are unsuitable.

When grown in a glasshouse in temperate climates, it is usual to prepare a special border. This may be surrounded by brick or concrete to prevent roots penetrating to unprepared soil. Such borders may be inside the house, when they usually occupy its whole length and width with the exception of the path, or outside, when they are the length of the house and 3-3·5m (10-12ft) in width. All should be 90cm (3ft) in depth with a slight slope to the front. Holes are left near soil level in the wall of the vinery if the border is outside. The main stems are taken into the house through these.

Place rubble in the bottom for drainage. Over this place a layer of turves grass side downwards. Fill the remainder of the border with a mixture of eight parts of chopped turf (preferably medium yellow loam), one part of old mortar rubble, half a part of wood ashes, and a quarter part of charcoal broken to the size of peas. Add bonemeal at 250g per 35 litres (½lb per bushel) of mixture.

Vines can be grown indoors or out. For the latter purpose only hardy, early varieties should be chosen (293). The position must be warm and sheltered, such as against a sunny wall.

VINERIES may be of any shape and size, but must have ample provision for ventilation at the ridge, along the sides and in the walls near soil level. Lean-to and three-quarter-span houses (483) should face the sun. Span-roofed houses should run from north to south. Vines can be planted on both sides of span-roofed houses.

281. Planting Early winter is the best time to purchase vines. Obtain strong specimens in pots and prune back so that the top eye is level with the bottom panes of glass in the vinery. Do not plant till buds begin to break in late winter or early spring. Tease out roots with a pointed stick and spread them widely in a shallow hole. Cover the topmost with 5cm (2in) of soil. Make thoroughly firm. Water in freely. Vines to be grown on the single-stem system (282) are planted 1·5-2m (5-6ft) apart. If to be grown on multiple-stem system (282), any multiple of 120cm (4ft) may be allowed between the vines.

282. System of Training Each vine may be restricted to a single main steam or 'rod', which is trained direct from the floor to the ridge of the house. Alternatively, the main stem can be trained horizontally at the top of the front or side wall and at every 120cm (4ft) a branch stem can be trained from it to the ridge of the house. This is known as the multiple-stem system. Almost any number of branch stems may be grown, depending upon the vigour of the vine. Examples are known in which one vine fills the whole of a large house. The single-stem system is the better for the amateur. In all methods, training wires should be provided, stretched horizontally 22cm (9in) beneath the glass and about 35cm (15in) apart.

283. Pruning Vines are thinned and stopped periodically during the spring and summer and hard pruned in winter.

Thinning and stopping start as soon as the vine starts into growth. In an established vine there are spurs every 35-45cm (15-18in) on each side of every main rod. Only one new shoot is required from each spur. If more form, the weakest should be rubbed out. That retained is allowed to grow until it produces a flower truss or is 60-90cm (2-3ft) in length. Its point is then pinched out. One leaf must be left beyond the flower truss. If secondary shoots are produced, these should be pinched beyond the first leaf. All young growths are tied down to the training wires. Foliage must not touch the glass. Tying down must be done gradually, as the young shoots are brittle.

In late autumn or early winter, when all leaves have fallen, each lateral (side growth) is cut back to within one dormant bud of the spur on the main rod.

284. Pruning and Training Young Vines When shoots have made six leaves, remove points from all except the leading one which is to form the rod. Stop all secondary laterals above the first leaf. Tie in young growths gradually to avoid breakage. When the leading growth is 2m (6ft) long, pinch out the tip, also any side growths it is producing above the first leaf, except the top one, which may be allowed to grow unchecked. Leave all further shoots on the leading growth until early autumn when they should be pinched. Any later growths that form should be pinched out at once. If vines have grown well, they should have filled available space. In late autumn when all leaves have fallen, cut back all side growths to the main rod and shorten the leading growth to within 90-120cm (3-4ft) of ground level, according to its strength.

The second year, rub out superfluous side growths on the main stem as they form. Retain one strong growth every 35-45cm (15-18in) on each side of the main stem to lay the basis of future spurs. Subsequent treatment of these side growths is as for established vines (283). The leading growth is allowed to grow 2m (7ft), or until it reaches the ridge of the house, when it is stopped. Side growths on this portion are treated as those on the young vine the first year.

285. Starting Vines Vines may be started at any time from mid-winter to early spring, according to the date at which fruits are required. This is done by closing the ventilators, raising the temperature to a minimum of 10°C (50°F) at night, rising to 15°C (60°F) by day, watering the border, mulching with 7-8cm (3in) of rotted manure and maintaining a moister atmosphere by syringing with tepid water in the morning, and filling troughs over soil-warming cables with water. Vines are lowered from training wires to check uprush of sap and ensure even growth from bottom to top. Later, when growth starts, they are retied.

286. Vines in Flower When vines come into flower, syringing should be discontinued and temperature raised by 2°C (5°F). Soak the border occasionally with very weak liquid manure. Tap the rods daily or dust flowers lightly with a camel-hair brush to assist pollination.

287. Thinning the Fruits The bunches must be thinned a little at a time from about a fortnight after berries first start to form. Use a pair of pointed grape scissors. Begin thinning at the bottom of the bunch. Leave the extreme point of the bunch, but remove all berries within 2cm (³/₄in) of it. Berries at the top of the bunch can be left almost twice as thick. Those between should be given intermediate spacing. Do not touch berries by hand. Use a small pointed stick to turn them if necessary.

288. General Management Ventilation throughout should be as free as possible consistent with maintenance of necessary temperatures. Keep water trays filled or damp paths and walls every morning until berries start to colour. Then empty trays or discontinue damping and allow temperature to rise slightly. Water when soil appears dry on surface. Give sufficient to soak border thoroughly. Feed in winter and spring with vine fertilizers (89), (90).

289. Picking and Storing Early grapes should be gathered as soon as they are well coloured or have a full, sweet flavour. No attempt should be made to keep them for any length of time. They are cut with a short length of lateral to serve as a handle for the bunch. Later varieties may be allowed to hang on the vine for a considerable time if the house is well ventilated and there is plenty of foliage to shade the berries. Later, when the foliage has fallen, each bunch may be cut with about 30cm (1ft) of lateral. The lower end of this is slipped into a bottle nearly filled with water, and this is stood, at an angle of 45° in a cool, dark, but dry room.

290. Outdoor Culture This follows the same general lines as for vines under glass, except that growth is allowed to start naturally in the spring, no syringing is practised and a rather freer growth is permitted. Outdoor vines are generally permitted to form several main rods. Overcrowding must be prevented or berries may be shaded excessively by foliage.

291. Routine Pest Control Each winter, when vines are dormant, loose bark is rubbed off and the rods are sprayed with tar-oil winter wash (664). If red spider (667) or mildew (667) appears in summer, give increased top ventilation and avoid cold draughts. For red spider mite, spray with malathion (651) or dimethoate (646) following the manufacturer's instructions. Under glass, biological control can be used (626). For mildew spray with benomyl (634) or sulphur (663) following the manufacturer's instructions. Scalding of foliage and berries is caused by too hot and dry an atmosphere. Shanking, ie withering of the footstalk of the berry with consequent collapse of the berry itself, is an indication of impoverished soil or lack of water.

292. Propagation May be effected by eyes, cuttings, layers, grafting, inarching and seed. The first named is the best for the amateur. Eyes (dormant growth buds) are secured in autumn or winter from sturdy, well-ripened laterals. They are either scooped out with a shield-shaped portion of bark and wood or else are cut complete with a short section, about 2cm (3/4in) long of stem. They are inserted singly in small pots filled with a light compost and are started into growth in a propagating box or frame, placed over soil-warming cables in the greenhouse. The buds should be just level with the surface of the soil.

293. Varieties of Grape UNDER GLASS Alicante, mid-autumn - late winter; Appley Towers, late autumn; Black Hamburgh, late summer mid-autumn; Black Prince, early autumn; Buckland Sweetwater, mid – late summer; Canon Hall Muscat, late autumn – mid-winter; Gros Colmar, mid-autumn – mid-winter; Guillaume, late autumn – early spring; Lady Downe's Seedling, late autumn – early spring; Lady Hasting, mid-autumn – early winter; Lady Hutt, late autumn – early winter; Madresfield Court, late summer – early autumn; Muscat Hamburgh, mid-autumn; Mrs Pearson, late autumn – early spring; Mrs Pince, late autumn – late spring; Muscat of Alexandria, late autumn – early spring; Prince of Wales, late autumn – late spring.

OUTDOORS Brandt, early – mid-autumn; Buckland Sweetwater, early autumn; Chasselas Rose, early autumn; Foster's Seedling, early autumn; Muscat Hamburgh, early autumn; Perle de Czaba, early autumn; Reine Olga, early autumn; Royal Muscadine, early – mid-autumn.

Loganberry See **Blackberry (212).**

MEDLARS

294. Soil and Situation Succeed in sunny places and rather rich soils, such as those that suit plums (339).

295. Planting From mid- to late autumn until early spring as for apples (181). Other details are also the same. Trees should be spaced at least 6m (20ft) apart.

296. Form of Training Usually grown as a standard but occasionally seen as a bush.

297. Pruning Early treatment is the same as for apples (185). Established trees that are in bearing do not as a rule require much pruning.

298. Picking This should be done in mid- to late autumn. The fruits are placed in single layers, eyes downwards, on a shelf in a dry store or room, until they turn dark and become soft, a condition known as bletted. Bletting may take several weeks.

299. Routine Feeding As for apples (191).

300. Routine Pest Control Unnecessary.

301. Propagation By budding mid- to late summer, or grafting in early to mid-spring, on to pear stocks (337).

302. Varieties Dutch, Nottingham, Royal, Stoneless.

MELONS

303. Raising and Planting From the cultural standpoint melons closely resemble cucumbers (136). They must be grown in greenhouses or frames as they are not sufficiently hardy for outdoor culture in temperate climates. Seed should be sown and germinated exactly as for cucumbers. For an early crop, seed may be sown in a heated greenhouse at 18°-21°C (65°-70°F) in mid-winter, but most amateurs will prefer to wait until early or even mid-spring. The preparation of the bed is as for cucumbers and the plants are put in their fruiting quarters in the same way when they have made three or four

rough leaves each. Water freely and maintain a damp atmosphere by frequent syringing and wetting of the path and walls. During the summer, shading may be required to prevent scorching, but should be as unobtrusive as possible, as exposure to sunlight is necessary for ripening the fruits.

304. Training and Fertilizing In a glasshouse, the main stem is allowed to grow unstopped till it is 1·8m (6ft) long, when the tip is pinched out. Flowers are produced on the side growths and female flowers may be recognised by the embryo fruits immediately beneath them. They must be fertilized by shaking male flowers with ripe, dry pollen over them. Four fruits are sufficient for one strong plant, and four female flowers to produce these should be fertilized at the same time; all other flowers must then be removed. Side growths should be stopped as soon as they start to interfere with those of other neighbouring plants. Fruits are weighty and must be supported by nets slung from the training wires. From the time fruits set, the plants should be fed liberally with weak liquid manure. Top dress with well-broken manure or compost when white rootlets appear on the surface.

305. Cultivation in Frames This is similar, except that the plants are pinched as soon as they have made four leaves. The three or four growths produced as a result of this pinching are trained around the plant and stopped again when they reach the confines of the frame. They are pegged to the surface of the soil. As the fruits ripen they are propped above the leaves on inverted flower pots to catch the sun.

306. Varieties of Melon Hero of Lockinge, King George, Superlative. For frames, Cantaloupe varieties such as Charantais, Dutch Net, Sweetheart and Tiger.

MULBERRIES

307. Soil and Situation Succeed best in rich, rather moist, but not waterlogged soil. Should be given a sunny position.

308. Planting From mid-autumn to early spring as for apples (190). Trees should be spaced at least 10m (30ft) apart.

309. Form of Training Almost always grown as a standard.

310. Pruning In the early stages of growth the trees are shaped in the same way as young apples (185). Later, when mature, little or no pruning is required.

311. Routine Feeding Usually unnecessary.

312. Routine Pest Control Unnecessary.

313. Propagation By seeds sown under glass in early spring or outdoors in late spring. Also by cuttings, partly of current and partly of two-year-old wood inserted half their depth in sandy soil in autumn. By layering (478) whippy branches in autumn and by grafting on to seedlings in early spring.

314. Varieties The Black Mulberry is the variety usually planted for fruiting.

PEACHES AND NECTARINES

315. Soil and Situation Both fruits require a warm, sunny position and good, well-drained soil. In these respects they resemble apricots, and the same general treatment should be observed (204). They are equally suitable for sunny greenhouses or walls and fences.

316. Planting This may be done at any time during the dormant period as for apricots. The same particulars apply (205).

317. Training Outdoors sometimes as bushes; against walls and under glass in fan formation. The details of training and early pruning are the same as for plums (344).

318. Pollination So far as is known, all varieties will set fruit with their own pollen. To ensure pollination it is advisable to dust pollen from flower to flower with a ball of cottonwool or a soft paint brush when these are fully open and the atmosphere is dry. This is especially necessary under glass. An alternative is to rap the tree smartly every day while in flower.

319. Pruning This is the same as for Morello cherries (225), as the fruit is borne on year-old side growths.

320. Thinning Fruits This should begin as soon as the fruits are as large as marbles but must not be completed until the stones are formed. This can be ascertained by cutting a typical fruit in half. At first the fruits should be reduced to one per cluster. Later they may be further spaced out 22-30cm (9in-1ft) apart for peaches, a little closer for nectarines. Select healthy, well-formed fruits that are placed where they will get the maximum amount of sunshine. Later, a few leaves that are shading fruits may be removed and the latter propped forward to catch the sun.

321. Routine Feeding and Watering Mulch with strawy, well-rotted manure each early spring. This is especially necessary with greenhouse trees. Give Nitro-chalk, nitrate of soda, or sulphate of ammonia in early spring and again in late spring, 30g per square metre (1oz per yd^2) at each application. Give sulphate of potash 30g per square metre (1oz per yd^2) each mid-autumn, with basic slag, 200g per square metre (6oz per yd^2), one year, hydrated lime, 250g per square metre (8oz per yd^2), the following year. Borders against walls and fences must be soaked thoroughly with water at frequent intervals while the fruits are swelling.

322. Routine Pest Control Spray with tar-oil wash (664), in early winter. At the end of winter spray with Bordeaux mixture (636), captan (638) or mancozeb (652) following the manufacturer's instructions, or try biological control (626).

323. Greenhouse Management Early trees can be started into growth in mid-winter by closing ventilators, watering border, and raising the temperature to 8°C (45°F) at night, 10°-13°C (50°-55°F) by day. Most houses are not started until about a month later. Peaches and nectarines in unheated houses should not be hurried unduly and ventilation must be given freely until early spring. All plants under glass must be well watered while in growth. Never encourage temperatures above 16°C (60°F) at night and 24°C (75°F) by day, and these only when fruit is set. Maintain a moist atmosphere by damping the paths and syringing the trees daily with tepid water, except while in flower and after fruit starts to ripen, when syringing should be discontinued.

324. Propagation By budding during mid- to late summer in the same manner as for apples (201), Brompton, Common Mussel and St Julien A are used for the purpose, although Mussel tends to form suckers.

325. Varieties of Peach Advance, mid-season; Alexander, early; ★Amsden, early; ★Barrington, late; ★Bellegarde, late; Bonanza, early; ★Crimson Galande, mid-season; ★Duke of York, early; ★Dymond, late; Early Grosse Mignonne, mid – late; Goshawk, mid – late; Golden Eagle, very late; ★Hale's Early, early – mid; Lady Palmerston, late; Late Devonian, late; Noblesse, mid – late; ★Peregrine, mid-season; Prince of Wales, late; Princess of Wales, very late; Rochester, mid-season, ★Royal George, late; ★Sea Eagle, very late; Stirling Castle, late; Thomas Rivers,

late; Violette Hâtive, late; ★Walburton Admirable, late; ★Waterloo, early.

326. Varieties of Nectarine Cardinal, early; Darwin, late; ★Dryden, mid-season, ★Early Rivers, early; ★Elruge, mid-season; Garden Delight, mid-season; ★Hardwick, mid-season; ★Humboldt, mid-season; John Rivers, early; Lord Napier, mid-season; Pine Apple, late; River's Orange, late; Spenser, late; ★Stanwick Elruge, late; Victoria, late; ★Violette Hâtive, mid-season.

★ *May be planted outdoors in temperate climates.*

PEARS

327. Soil and Situation Pears require a warmer position and better drainage than apples, but in other respects are similar in their requirements. The preparation of the ground should be, within these limits, the same (180). If of a heavy nature, plenty of lightening material such as strawy manure, grit, or sand should be added, or it may be necessary to install land drains (32). Choice dessert varieties do best when planted against a warm and sunny wall.

328. Planting Times and methods are the same as for apples (181).

329. Forms of Training The same as for apples (182), but standards and half-standards are not usually very satisfactory except for certain vigorous varieties, such as Beurré Clairgeau, Hessle, and Jargonelle. Choice dessert varieties are excellent as horizontal-trained or single-cordon trees.

330. Pollination As with apples, very few varieties of pear crop satisfactorily when planted alone, but require other pears to provide pollen. The table overleaf gives more details.

331. Pruning Young trees are formed in exactly the same way as apples of the

330.	POLLINATION TABLE FOR PEARS	
Early flowering	**Mid-season flowering**	**Late flowering**
Beurré Clairgeau	Beurré d'Amanlis★	Beurré Bedford★
Beurré Diel★	Beurré Superfin	Beurré Hardy
Beurré Gillard	Conference	Bristol Cross★
Easter Beurré	Dr Jules Guyot	Catillac★
Emile d'Heyst	Doyenné Bussoch★	Clapp's Favourite
Louise Bonne of Jersey	Durondeau	Doyenné du Comice
Marguerite Marillat★	Fertility	Glou Morceau
Princess	Fondante d'Automme	Gorham
Seckle	Jargonelle★	Hessle
Uvedale's St Germain★	Merton Pride	Marie Louise
Vicar of Winkfield	Packham's Triumph	Pitmaston Duchess★
	Souvenir de Congrès	Winter Nèlis
	Triomphe de Vienne	
	Thompson's	
	Williams's Bon Chrétien	

★ Varieties marked with an asterisk should not be planted alone or as pollinators for other pears. So far as possible, pollinators should be chosen from the same group so that their flowering periods coincide. Beurré d'Amanlis and Conference are incompatible with one another. Fondante d'Automme, Louise Bonne of Jersey, Seckle and Williams's Bon Chrétien are also mutually incompatible varieties.

same type (185), (186), (187). As the trees become older and start to bear, summer and winter pruning should be practised as for apples (184), except that treatment on the whole can be slightly more severe as most varieties form spurs readily. A few kinds, notably Jargonelle and Joséphine de Malines, produce fruit buds at the tips of side growths.

332. Thinning This is necessary, especially with the larger-fruited varieties and the best dessert pears. The details are the same as for apples (188), except that final distance apart for best dessert varieties should be 12cm (5in); large cooking varieties slightly more.

333. Picking Early pears such as Doyenné d Eté, Jargonelle, and William's Bon Chrétien must be picked as soon as they are ripe and part from the tree readily. They will not keep. Later varieties can be left hanging until mid-autumn.

334. Storing Pears require a drier and slightly warmer atmosphere than apples (190). They keep well in a spare room or airy, concrete-floored shed and are best laid in single layers on open-slat shelves, not placed in several layers in a box. They must be used as soon as ripe, which is indicated by softening of the flesh near the stem. Pears must be watched very closely, as some varieties go sleepy, ie rotten in the centre, within a few days of ripening.

335. Routine Feeding The same as for apples (191), except that rather heavier dressings of well-rotted manure can be given in the spring, say 50kg to 8-10 square metres (1cwt to 10-12yd²), as pears require more nitrogen than apples.

336. Routine Pest Control Spray in mid-winter with tar-oil wash (664). Spray with fungicide such as captan (638), benomyl (634) or carbendazim (640) against scab, following the manufacturer's instructions. Spray with insecticide such as fenitrothion (648) for caterpillars or dimethoate (646) against aphids (667), following the manufacturer's instructions. Place grease bands (178) round the trunks of the trees in early autumn and keep them sticky until the following mid-spring.

337. Propagation By grafting or budding at the same time and in the same manner as for apples (196), (201). The stock used is usually pear and quince which is best for all trained trees and bushes. Selected forms of quince have been obtained and are known under letter. Quince A is fairly vigorous and suitable for large bushes. Quince C is moderately dwarfing and encourages early bearing. It is good for cordons and other trained trees. These stocks can be raised vegetatively by layering.

Old pears can be re-worked by rind grafting, or stub grafting, as described for apples (197), (198), (199).

338. Varieties of Pear Admiral Gervis (D), early winter; Bellissime d'Hiver (C), late autumn – early spring; Bergamotte Esperen (D), late winter – mid-spring; Beurré d'Amanlis (D), early autumn; Beurré d'Anjou (D), late autumn – mid-winter; Beurré Bosc (D), early – mid-autumn; Beurré Clairgeau (C), late autumn – early winter; Beurré Diel (D), mid – late autumn; Beurré Easter (D), mid-winter – early spring; Beurré Giffard (D), late summer; Beurré Hardy (D), mid-autumn; Beurré Six (D), early winter; Beurré Superfin (D), mid –

late autumn; Blickling (D), early – mid-winter; Bristol Cross (D), mid-autumn;

Catillac (C), early winter – mid-spring; Charles Ernest (D), mid – late autumn; Clapp's Favourite (D), late summer; Colmar d'Été (D), early autumn; Comte de Lamy (D), mid-autumn; Conference (D), mid – late autumn;

Directeur Hardy (D), early autumn; Dr Jules Guyot (D), early autumn; Doyenné Bussoch (D), early autumn; Doyenné d'Été (D), mid – late summer; Doyenné du Comice (D), late autumn; Durondeau (D), mid – late autumn;

Easter Beurré (D), late winter – mid spring; Emile d'Heyst (D), mid – late autumn; Fertility (D), mid-autumn; Fondante d'Automme (D), mid-autumn; Forelle (Trout Pear) (D), late autumn – mid-winter;

Glou Morceau (D), early – mid-winter; Gorham (D), early autumn;

Hessle (D), early autumn;

Jargonelle (D), late summer; Jersey Gratioli (D), mid-autumn; Joséphine de Malines (D), early – late winter;

Knight's Monarch (D), early – late winter;

Le Lectier (D), early – mid-winter; Louise Bonne of Jersey (D), mid-autumn; Malling Concorde (D), mid – late autumn;

Maréchal de la Cour (D), mid – late autumn; Marguérite Marrilat (D), early autumn; Marie Louise (D), mid – late autumn;

Nouvelle Fulvie (D), late autumn – late winter;

Olivier de Serres (D), late winter – early spring;

Packham's Triumph (D), mid – late autumn; Pitmaston Duchess (CD), late autumn; Princess (D), late autumn – early winter;

Record (D), mid – late autumn; Roosevelt (D), mid-autumn;

Santa Claus (D), early winter; Satisfaction (D), mid-autumn; Seckle (D), mid-autumn; Souvenir de Congrés (D), early autumn;

Thompson's (D), mid – late autumn; Triomphe de Vienne (D), early autumn;

Uvedale's St Germain (C), mid-winter – mid-spring;

Verulam (C), mid-autumn; Vicar of Winkfield (C), mid-winter; Victor (D), late autumn;

William's Bon Chrêtien (D), early autumn; Winter Nelis (D), early winter – early spring; Winter Orange (C), late winter – early spring; Wonderful (D), late autumn.

PLUMS AND DAMSONS

339. Soil and Situation Succeed best on rather rich, loamy land. Plums and damsons require more nitrogen than apples and are therefore less suitable for grass orchards, though certain vigorous varieties, such as Blaisden Red and Pershore Egg, succeed. Lime is beneficial. Sour, poor, and dry, sandy soils are unsuitable.

Plums flower early and are, in consequence, unsuitable for very exposed places in which the blossom is usually destroyed or fails to set. Choice dessert varieties may be trained against sunny walls. Some kinds, such as Belgian Purple, Czar, Oullin's Golden Gage, Early Rivers, and Victoria, are also suitable for shady walls.

340. Planting This may be done at any time from mid autumn to early spring. Details are the same as for apples (181). For correct distances see table (20). Fan-trained trees should be 4·5m (15ft) apart.

341. Forms of Training Plums are grown as cordons, fan-trained trees, bushes, half-standards, and standards.

Cordons are not recommended as the very restrictive pruning necessary may cause bacterial canker (667). Choice dessert varieties, and particularly gages, should be fan trained against walls. The more vigorous, free-fruiting varieties, especially cooking plums and damsons, make excellent standards.

342. Pollination Many varieties are completely self-sterile, while others set a very poor crop with their own pollen. Such should be planted with another variety of plum or damson that flowers at the same time. Self-fertile varieties may be planted alone. See page 94.

343. Pruning Bushes and half- and full standards are treated very lightly after the first few years, during which the framework of the tree is built up in the same manner as that of an apple (185). Subsequently, all dead wood and any large branches that have been damaged, or are diseased, should be cut out in early summer. Further thinning of poor or ill-placed branchlets is done in late summer after the crop has been gathered. Leaders are shortened a little in early spring, to an upward-pointing bud for drooping varieties and an outward-pointing bud for those of upright habit.

All large wounds should be covered at once with a proprietary wound dressing.

Trained plums must be treated rather more severely. From early to late summer the tips of young side shoots are pinched out when they have made six to eight leaves. In early autumn older shoots are shortened to fruit buds where these have formed. Leaders are shortened each early autumn by about one-third of their length until the wall space is filled, after which they are cut right out.

344. Forming Fan-trained Trees Maiden (ie one-year-old) trees are cut back in late autumn to within 35cm (15in) of ground level. The following

342.   POLLINATION TABLE FOR PLUMS

Early flowering	Mid-season flowering	Late flowering
Allgrove's Superb	Bountiful★	Belle de Louvain★
Black Prince	Byanston Gage	Blaisdon Red
Coe's Golden Drop	Czar★	Bradley's King
Denniston's Superb★	Early Laxton	Damson★
Diamond	Goldfinch★	Cambridge Gage
Early Rivers	Kirke's Blue	Comte D'Althann's
Farleigh Damson	Late Orange	Gage
Golden Tranparent	Laxton's Gage★	Cox's Emperor
Jefferson	Merryweather Damson★	Early Orleans
Late Orleans	Pershore (yellow)★	Early Transparent
Monarch★	Purple Gage	Frogmore Damson
President	Purple Pershore★	Giant Prune★
Prince of Wales★	Severn Cross★	Gisborne's★
Reine Claude de Bavay★	Transparent Gage	Green Gage
Utility	Victoria★	Late Transparent
Warwickshire Drooper★		Marjorie's Seedling
		Oullin's Golden Gage
		Pond's Seedling
		Red Magnum Bonum
		Shropshire Damson★
		Wyedale

★ Varieties marked with an asterisk are fully self-fertile, and may be planted alone if desired. All others require cross pollination. So far as possible pollinators should be chosen from the same group, so that their flowering periods may coincide. Incompatibility occurs only in the following cases with the varieites mentioned: Allgrove's Superb, Coe's Golden Drop, and Jefferson fail to pollinate one another. Late Orange and President fail both ways; either may be pollinated by Cambridge Gage or Greengage, but the reverse cross is not satisfactory.

spring about four new shoots are retained and trained equidistantly like the main ribs of a fan. The following late autumn these main branches are shortened to about 35-45cm (15-18in) each, and the thinning and training process repeated in the spring, with the result that the tree is provided with anything up to 16 principal branches evenly spaced in one plane. The process may be repeated indefinitely until the whole available space is covered.

Thereafter, pruning is the same as for established trees.

345. Thinning Fruits This is usually unnecessary, except with choice dessert varieties against walls. Fruits on these may be reduced to one every 5-8cm (2-3in) after stones are formed. A preliminary thinning to half distance may be given three or four weeks after flowering.

346. Picking Should start as soon as the fruits are well coloured and juicy.

Culinary varieties may be picked over several times, first when the fruits are sizeable but still green. These can be used for cooking or bottling, leaving more space for the remainder to grow. Plums cannot be stored but may be bottled or dried.

347. Routine Feeding Nitrogen and potash are the two important elements but with more emphasis on the former than with apples. Give a good dressing of rotted dung at 50kg to 10 square metres (1cwt to 12yd²) each early spring, lightly forked in, followed by sulphate of ammonia, nitrate of soda, or Nitro-chalk, at 50g per square metre (1½ oz per yd²) in late spring, and sulphate of potash at 30g per square metre (1 oz per yd²) in mid-autumn. Every alternate autumn give, in addition, basic slag at 200g per square metre (6oz per yd²), or instead use fruit-tree fertilizer (88).

348. Routine Pest Control Spray early each winter with tar-oil wash. Cut out all dead wood or branches carrying silvered leaves (667) in midsummer and paint wounds with fungicidal paint. Sterilize tools after use. Spray with an insecticide such as malathion (651) or dimethoate (646) against aphids (667).

349. Propagation By budding in mid- to late summer exactly as for apples (201). A number of stocks are used. Brompton is vigorous, suitable for standards and large bushes and is compatible with all varieties. Myrobalan B is vigorous and one of the most popular stocks for large trees but a few varieties such as Count Althann's Gage and Oullins Golden Gage will not grow on it. Common Mussel is semi-dwarfing and suitable for small trees and fan-trained plums but some varieties will not grow on it. St Julien A is moderately dwarfing and suitable for small trees. It is compatible with all varieties. Pixy is a dwarfing rootstock, but less suitable for cold areas.

A few varieties of plum are best propagated by suckers, a method usually too slow for nurserymen. These are Blaisdon Red, Pershore, and Warwickshire Drooper.

350. Varieties of Plum Belgian Purple (CD), mid-season; Belle de Louvain (C), mid – late; Blackbird (CD), mid-season; Black Prince (C), early; Blaisdon Red (C), mid-season; Blue Rock (D), mid-season; Blue Tit (D), mid-season; Bountiful (D), mid-season; Bradley's King (Damson) (CD), late; Bryanston Gage (D), late;

Cambridge Gage (D), mid-season; Coe's Golden Drop (D), late; Count Althann's Gage (D), late; Cox's Emperor (CD), late; Cropper (CD), late; Czar (CD), mid-season;

Denniston's Superb (D), mid-season; Diamond (C), late;

Early Laxton (C), early – mid; Early Orleans (C), early; Early Rivers (C), early; Early Transparent Gage (D), mid-season; Evesham Wonder (C), mid-season;

Farleigh Damson (Cluster or Crittenden) (C), late; Frogmore Damson (C), late;

Gisborne's (C), mid-season; Giant Prune (C), late; Golden Transparent Gage (D), late; Goldfinch (D), late; Green Gage (D), mid-season;

Jefferson (D), late; Jubilee (D), mid-season;

Kirke's Blue (D), late;

Langley Bullace (C), very late; Late Orange (C), very late; Late Transparent Gage (D), late; Laxton's Gage (D), mid-season;

Marjorie's Seedling (C), very late; Merryweather Damson (C), late; Mirabelle (C), mid-season; Monarch (C), late;

Oullin's Golden Gage (CD), mid-season

Pershore (C), mid-season; Pond's Seedling (C), late; President (C), late; Purple Gage (Reine-Claude Violette) (D), late; Purple Pershore (C), mid-season;

Reine Claude de Bavay (D), late; Red Magnum Bonum (C), late;

Severn Cross (C or D), late; Shepherd's Bullace (C), very late; Shropshire Damson (CD), late;

Transparent Gage (D), late; Utility (D), mid-season; Victoria (CD), mid – late;

Warwickshire Drooper (CD), late; White Bullace (CD), very late; Wyedale (C), very late.

QUINCE

351. Soil and Situation Likes a sunny position and rich, rather moist soil. Well-rotted manure may be dug in freely before planting, especially on light, sandy soils.

352. Planting As for apples (181).

353. Form of Training Usually grown as bushes, but occasionally seen as small standards.

354. Pruning As for pears (331).

355. Picking Gather fruits towards mid-autumn and store as for pears (334). Very valuable for making into conserve or jelly.

356. Routine Feeding As for pears (335).

357. Routine Pest Control Usually unnecessary.

358. Varieties of Quince Apple-shaped: Champion, Meech's Prolific. Pear-shaped: Portugal, Vranja.

RASPBERRIES

359. Soil and Situation Raspberries succeed in most soils except those of a very light, dry nature. They appreciate moisture while in growth. Soil must be dug deeply and should be dressed with well-rotted manure at the rate of 50kg to 10 square metres (1cwt to 12yd²), and sulphate of potash at 30g per square metre (1oz per yd²). The addition of lime is not essential.

360. Planting Plants must be certified virus-free and bought from a reputable supplier. This may be done at any time from mid-autumn until early to mid-spring. Autumn planting is best, but spring planting gives excellent results in some seasons. Canes should not be allowed to fruit the first year. They are spaced 45cm (18in) apart in rows 1·8m (6ft) apart (20). The uppermost roots should be covered with about 2cm (1in) of soil.

361. Training Wires strained between posts, or a fence or trellis, must be provided to support the canes. The uppermost wire should be 1.5m (5-5½ft) from ground level. Each plant should be allowed to form five or six canes and these are trained to spread out fanwise on the support.

362. Pruning After planting, cut all canes back to within 20cm (9in) of ground level. In subsequent years summer-fruiting varieties are pruned as soon as the crop has been gathered. All canes that have borne fruit are cut out to ground level; strong young canes are trained in their places. Very long young canes are tipped in late winter, when they should be cut back to within about 2m (6½ft) of ground level. Autumn-fruiting varieties are pruned in late winter. All old canes are cut to within 15cm (6in) of ground level. Perpetual-fruiting raspberries, such as Lloyd George, are pruned in both ways. Summer-fruiting canes are removed immediately after fruiting and autumn-fruiting canes cut back the following late winter.

NEW CANES, or suckers, are produced direct from the roots. Usually there are far more than are required. Retain five or six of the strongest nearest to the parent root. Canes appearing far from these should be cut out early in the summer or they become a nuisance. A few may be retained for propagation if necessary (365).

363. Routine Cultivation Raspberry plantations become very weedy unless regularly hoed. Take care not to disturb the soil deeply, as most roots are near the surface. Forking and digging should not be attempted. Each late spring spread a mulch of well-rotted manure over the roots; each early spring give sulphate of potash at 30g (1oz) and sulphate of ammonia at 15g ($\frac{1}{2}$ oz) per square metre (per yd^2).

364. Routine Pest Control When raspberry beetle (667) is troublesome, dust or spray with derris (644), malathion (651) or fentrothion (648), following the manufacturer's instructions, when the first fruits are seen. Keep a sharp watch for mozaic (667) and remove and burn any plants showing signs of this disease.

365. Propagation Effected by digging up young canes (suckers) in mid- to late autumn. Canes at some distance from the parent plants are most suitable, as they can be dug up with roots without injury to these plants. Replant at once in the ordinary manner. Do not propagate from diseased plants.

366. Varieties of Raspberry Autumn Bliss, late summer – mid-autumn; Lloyd George, early summer – mid-autumn; Malling Enterprise, early-midsummer; Malling Exploit, early – midsummer; Malling Jewel, mid summer; Malling Landmark, midsummer; Malling Promise, early – midsummer; Norfolk Giant, midsummer.

STRAWBERRIES

367. Soil and Situation Strawberries succeed best in rich soils. They will grow well in heavy loam if good winter drainage can be assured. Phosphates have a marked effect on growth. Soil should be deeply dug, enriched with manure or compost at 50kg to 10-12 square metres (1cwt to 12-15yd^2), and dusted with basic slag at 200g per square metre (6oz per yd^2), and sulphate of potash at 45g per square metre (1$\frac{1}{2}$oz per yd^2). Lime is not essential.

ALPINE STRAWBERRIES do not as a rule make runners and are increased by seed. These are sown in early spring in a cool greenhouse with an average temperature of 13°C (55°F) in ordinary seed compost (493). The seedlings are pricked off (494) into boxes as soon as they can be handled conveniently and then transferred to a frame and gradually hardened off for planting outdoors in early summer.

368. Planting Buy only certified virus free plants. The best season is late summer and early autumn. Failing this, pot-grown runners (572) can be planted in early spring. These should not be allowed to fruit the first season. Space plants 45cm (1$\frac{1}{2}$ft) apart in rows 75-90cm (2$\frac{1}{2}$-3ft) apart (20). On heavy land, draw the soil into low ridges 60cm (2ft) apart and plant along the summits of these. Be careful not to bury the crowns below the surface. Roots should be just covered and crowns on the surface.

369. Pollination A few varieties produce no pollen and consequently no fruits unless other pollen-bearing varieties are planted with them. Others are self-sterile, ie they produce pollen, but this is not effective for their own pollination. All these must be interplanted with other varieties. Few such varieties are cultivated in gardens nowadays, having been discarded in favour of self-fertile varieties.

370. Routine Cultivation All runners must be cut off during the summer months unless required for propagation (372). Soil should be kept clean by frequent hoeing, but digging or forking must not be attempted, because many roots are produced near the surface. Clean straw can be spread between plants in late spring to conserve moisture and preserve fruits from mud splashes, or strawberry mats may be used. Alternatively the ridges can be covered with black polythene in which slits are cut to allow planting.

Each early spring, top dress with a mixture of six parts by weight of superphosphate of lime, three parts of sulphate of potash, and two parts of sulphate of ammonia, at 100g per square metre (3oz per yd^2).

371. Routine Pest Control Usually unnecessary, as foes are dealt with as noted. Spray with fungicide such as benomyl (634) or carbendazim (640) if mildew or grey mould (667) appear; burn off straw on the beds when the crop has been gathered to destroy old foliage together with possible pests and fungi. This should be done on a dry, breezy day, so that the straw burns quickly. If red spider (667) is troublesome, spray with malathion (651) or dimethoate (646), following the manufacturer's instructions.

372. Propagation Strawberries soon deteriorate, and beds are rarely worth keeping after their third year. Usual practice is to remake one-third of the bed each year, so that the whole plantation is renewed every three years. Propagation is effected by runners produced throughout the summer. These should be selected from the best plants only, chosen for health and good cropping. Do not use plants that show any sign of virus. Retain five or six runners per plant. Pinch the tip out of each just beyond the first plantlet

formed on it. Peg this plantlet firmly to the soil or fill a small flower pot with loamy soil, plunge to its rim near the parent plant and peg the runner into this. Propagation should be done in early to midsummer. If kept moist, each plantlet will produce roots by late summer, when the runner joining it to the parent plant may be severed. A week or so later lift and replant in fruiting quarters, or, alternatively, pot and winter in a frame for spring planting. Replace the stock with new certified plants every four to five years.

The Alpine varieties of strawberry, which produce small fruits during most of the summer and early autumn, do not make runners and are usually raised from seed. The large-fruited perpetual strawberries produced by crossing Alpine varieties with normal large-fruited strawberries do make runners but not always very freely.

373. Forcing Strawberries can be gently forced to fruit a month or more ahead of normal time. Strong runners should be rooted in early summer (372) and potted singly in 10 or 12·5cm (4 or 5in) pots in late summer. Use an ordinary potting compost (497), place pots on ash base in a frame, shade for a week, but give no further protection till mid-autumn. Then use lights to ward off extreme wet and snow, but ventilate freely whenever possible. Remove pots to a cool greenhouse maintaining a temperature of 5°-10°C (40°-50°F) from mid-winter to early spring according to the time at which fruit is required. Water with increasing freedom as growth proceeds. Hand fertilize flowers with camel-hair brush. From the time plants come into flower, temperature may be increased gradually to a maximum of 21°C (70°F) to be reached as the fruit swells. Drop to 16°-18°C (60°-65°F) for the last few days. Cooler conditions may be maintained throughout if it is not desired to hurry ripening unduly.

Cloches of the continuous barn type (512) may also be used to cover strawberry plants growing in the open. They should be placed in position in late winter and may need to be lightly shaded with whitewash for the last few weeks if the weather is very sunny. Remove cloches as soon as crop has been gathered.

374. Varieties Cambridge Favourite, mid-season; Cambridge Prizewinner, early; Cambridge Rival, early; Cambridge Vigour, mid-season; Elsanta, mid-season; Elvira, early; Gorella, early; Pantagruella, early; Redgauntlet, mid-season; Royal Sovereign, early; Talisman, late; Ostara, Aromel, Gento and Rapella are perpetual-fruiting varieties.

WALNUTS

375. Soil and Situation Will succeed in most soils that are not waterlogged, or very poor and liable to dry out severely in summer. Prefer open, sunny places.

376. Planting As for apples (181). Space trees at least 10m (30ft) apart.

377. Forms of Training Almost invariably grown as standards. Often planted for ornament as well as utility.

378. Pollination Male catkins and female flowers appear on the same tree and are compatible (174). Unfortunately, some varieties produce female flowers years before the male catkins start to appear, and are therefore unfruitful for an unnecessarily long period. Other kinds bear catkins early and are useful for pollination. Most walnuts grown in this country are seedlings and, in consequence, very variable. It is not possible to say in

advance to which type they will belong. Where possible, selected varieties chosen for their early production of catkins should be planted.

379. Pruning Practically unnecessary except for the removal of badly placed branches to improve the balance of the head. This may be done in late autumn.

380. Picking and Storing Leave the nuts to fall naturally or shake them from the tree. Remove outer skins, wipe with damp cloth and store in earthenware jars or crocks with a layer of salt over each layer of nuts. If desired, dry coconut fibre or peat may be mixed in equal bulk with the salt.

381. Routine Feeding and Pest Control Unnecessary.

382. Propagation Usually by seeds sown outdoors in early spring. Better results are obtained by budding or grafting seedling walnuts with selected varieties. Budding is done outdoors in late spring to early summer, using a special method known as patch budding. The bud is cut out with a circle or rectangle of bark and a similar piece of bark is removed from the stock to receive it. Alternatively, young seedlings potted for the purpose may be grafted in the greenhouse, usually in late winter to early spring. A temperature of 16°-18°C (60°-65°F) must be maintained. Quicker results are obtained in a propagating case, temperature 22°-24°C (70°-75°F). The grafted plants must be carefully hardened off for transference to a frame in late spring to early summer and planting in a nursery bed in the autumn.

383. Varieties Franquette, Leeds Castle, Mayette, Northdown Clawnut and Stutton Seedling.

THE ORNAMENTAL GARDEN

ALPINES

384. Description Strictly a plant from a mountainous region but used loosely to cover all plants of dwarf habit suitable for planting in rock gardens. Most are hardy herbaceous perennials (443), some are biennials (421), others annuals (402), and a few are shrubs (473). There are evergreen and deciduous kinds (473).

385. Soil and Situation Most alpines delight in a sunny situation and a rather gritty, well-drained soil. A few like shade and moisture. Detailed requirements, however, are very varied and some of the choicest varieties are difficult to grow. The moraine and scree are designed to meet the needs of these. These are beds, usually on a slope, filled with extremely gritty or stony compost. The moraine has an underground water supply; the scree has not. Specimen composts are for ordinary alpines – loam 6 parts, leaf-mould or peat 3 parts, stone chippings 1 part, sharp sand $\frac{1}{2}$ part. For peat lovers – lime-free loam 4 parts, leaf-mould and peat 3 parts, lime-free sand or grit 2 parts. For moraine or scree – loam 2 parts, leaf-mould or peat 2 parts, sand or grit 1 part, stone chippings 4 parts.

Contrary to popular belief, few alpines will grow on rocks with little soil. They are mostly deep-rooting plants and should have at least 45cm (18in) of good soil. Sempervivums and a few sedums are practically the only kinds that will grow on roofs and similar bare places. Dry walls must have a core of soil in contact with the soil below so that plants can root through.

Good bottom drainage is most impor-

tant. It is usually advisable to spread a thick layer of brick ends or clinkers under the whole of the selected site. On top of this place the soil, which may be worked into irregular mounds to give a natural effect if so desired, though good results can be obtained from flat beds. The stone chosen should be fairly porous yet reasonably durable. Limestone and sandstone are most suitable, and the former can be obtained from hillside workings with natural weather and water marks on them. It is desirable to bed the stone well down into the soil, usually on its broadest face rather than to rear it up on the surface. Several rocks can be built together to form large spurs or outcrops. Crevices between such rocks can be suitably planted provided the crevice has an outlet to an ample body of soil behind or below. A good effect can often be obtained by arranging the stones to simulate a natural outcrop of rock such as may be seen on many hillsides.

386. Planting Most nurserymen grow alpines in small containers. They can be transplanted from these with little or no root disturbance at any time of the year except when ground is frozen. Plants that are to be lifted from the open ground should be transplanted in early to mid-spring or, if they are in flower at that time, as soon as the flowers fade. Water freely until established. In general, small plants are to be preferred. When planting in the moraine or scree, shake all soil from the roots, spread these out and work the gritty compost around them. All alpines should be planted firmly.

387. Cultural Routine Most varieties will benefit from the removal of faded flowers. With aubretias, helianthemums, and iberis, this can be extended to a thorough trimming up with scissors or shears after flowering. A few plants may be left to carry seed if this is required for propagation (388). Apart from this the only cultural attentions required are to remove weeds, to cut back rampant plants which tend to smother others in their path, to remove fallen leaves, particularly tree leaves in the autumn, and to top dress with gritty soil in winter or early spring. This may consist of equal parts of coarse sand, stone chippings and loam, and should be worked between and among the shoots. In spite of the fact that most alpines grow in rocky places, they appreciate liberal watering in hot weather.

388. Propagation Most alpines can be increased by division in similar manner to herbaceous perennials (446). This is best done in early to mid-spring or, if they are in flower at that time, immediately after flowering. Many varieties, particularly those of shrubby habit, can be increased by cuttings taken in mid- to late summer and treated in the same manner as summer shrub cuttings (478). The cuttings are naturally smaller, usually 1–5cm ($^{1}/_{2}$–2in) in length. Seed provides a cheap method of increasing most kinds and should be sown in early spring in a frame or outdoors in late spring. (In other respects, treatment is the same as for seed of hardy perennials (446).

389. Alpines for Shady Situations *Anemone appenina, A. blanda, Arenaria balearica, Calceolaria polyrrhiza*, hardy cyclamen in variety, *Daphne blagayana, Gaultheria procumbens, Gentiana asclepiadea, Haberlea rhodopensis, Hepatica angulosa, Hutchinsia alpina, Iberis sempervirens, Linnaea borealis, Omphalodes verna, Oxalis enneaphylla, Primula denticulata* and varieties, *P. japonica, P. juliae, P. juliana* varieties, *Ramonda pyrenaica, Sanguinaria canadensis*, saxifraga (mossy varieties), *S. primuloides, Synthyris reniformis, Tiarella cordifolia, Viola cornuta* and varieties, *V. gracilis*.

390. Autumn- and Winter-flowering Alpines Colchicums, *Crocus imperati, C. sieberi, C. speciosus, C. zonatus, Erica carnea* and varieties, *E. vulgaris* and varieties, *Galanthus byzantinus, G. cilicicus, Gentiana farreri, G. sino-ornata, G. macaulayi, Iris histrio, I. reticulata, Primula winteri, Sternbergia lutea*.

391. Alpines for Planting between Paving Stones Acaenas, *Ajuga reptans* in variety, antennarias, *Arenaria balearica, Armeria maritima, Asperula gussonii, Calamintha alpina*, cotulas, *Frankenia laevis, Geranium pylzowianum, Herniaria glabra, Hypsela longiflora, Linaria aequitriloba, Mazus pumilio, M. reptans, Mentha requienii, Mimulus radicans, Nierembergia repens, Raoulia australis, Saxifraga muscoides*, sedums, *Silene alpestris, Thymus serpyllum* in variety, *Veronica rupestris*.

392. Scree Plants *Androsace arachnoidea superba, A. sempervivoides, Armeria caespitosa, Asperula suberosa, Calandrinia umbellata, Campanula allionii, C. arvatica, C. aucheri, C. senisea, C. excisa, C. raineri, C.rupestris, C.stansfieldii, C.tommasiniana, C. wockii, Chrysanthemum alpinum, Dianthus alpinus, D. neglectus, Douglasia vitaliana, Draba imbricata, D. polytricha, D. pyrenaica, Erigeron leiomerus, E. trifidus, Erinus alpinus* (all varieties), *Erodium corsicum rubrum, Gentiana farreri, G. verna, Globularia incanescens, Gypsophila cerastioides, Helichrysum frigidum, Linaria alpina, Lychnis pyrenaica, Myosotis rupicola, Omphalodes lucilliae, Papaver alpinum, Penstemon rupicola, Phyteuma comosum, Polygala calcarea, Potentilla nitida, Ranunculus alpestris, R. glacialis, Raoulia australis*, saxifraga (all varities of cushion and porphyrion types), *S. cochlearis minor, S. valdensis, Silene acaulis,*

Teucrium montanum, Wahlenbergia pumilio, W. serpyllifolia major. All can also be grown in the moraine.

393. Easily Grown Alpine Plants
Achillea tomentosa, Aethionema 'Warley Rose', *Alyssum saxatile, Androsace lanuginosa, A. sarmentosa, Aquilegia caerulea, Arabis albida flore pleno, Arenaria montana, Armeria laucheana,* aubrietas, *Campanula carpatica, C. portenschlagiana, C. pusilla, Cotyledon simplicifolia, Dianthus caesius, D. deltoides, Erinus alpinus, Erodium hybridum roseum, Gentiana acaulis, G. lagodechiana, G. septemfida, Geranium sanguineum lancastriense, Gypsophila repens subcaulescens,* helianthemums, *Hypericum olympicum, Iberis sempervirens, I. saxatilis, Linum perenne, Oenothera missouriensis, Penstemon scouleri, Phlox divaricata, P. subulata, Potentilla tonguei, Primula denticulata, P. frondosa, P. juliana, P. marginata, P. rosea, Rosa roulettii, Saponaria ocymoides, Saxifraga aizoon, S. apiculata, S. cotyledon, S. elizabethae, S. granulata* 'Plena', *S. haagii, S. lingulata albertii, S. oppositifolia, S. primuloides* Elliott's variety, all mossy saxifrages, sedums, sempervivums, *Silene alpestris, S. schafta, Sisyrinchium angustifolium, Thymus nitidus, T. serpyllum, Tunica saxifra, Veronica prostrata, Viola cornula, V. gracilis.*

ANNUALS (HALF-HARDY)

394. Description These complete their cycle of growth in one year, but they cannot be sown outdoors in temperate climates in early spring because of the danger of frost. Most must be raised under glass, but there are borderline varieties, nearly but not fully hardy, that may be sown outdoors in mid – late spring. All can be grown outdoors without protection during the summer. Half-hardy annuals are also grown as pot plants for greenhouse decoration.

395. Soil and Situation The same as for hardy annuals (403) with, if anything, more emphasis on good drainage and a sunny position. Nicotiana is one of the few exceptions which likes shade.

396. Sowing Seed of most varieties can be sown in a warm greenhouse in late winter or in an unheated greenhouse or frame in early – mid spring. Temperature of about 15°C (60°F) is required for germination. Seed is sown in well-drained pots, pans, or boxes in any good seed compost (493). It should be scattered very thinly, covered lightly with a sprinkling of finely sifted soil and then each receptacle covered with a sheet of glass and another of brown paper. The paper must be removed at the first signs of germination. A day later tilt the glass slightly with a pebble or stick, and two or three days after this remove altogether.

Soil must be kept moist. This is best done by holding each pan for a few moments almost to its rim in a bucket of water with the chill off. When the rising water darkens the surface of the soil, remove the pan and allow it to drain.

397. Pricking off When the seedlings have made two or three leaves each, they must be transferred carefully to other trays or pans prepared in a similar manner (496). Lift carefully with a pointed stick, divide into single plants with as little injury to the roots as possible and replant with a round-ended dibber about as thick as an ordinary pencil. The seedlings should be planted about 5cm (2in) apart each way. Make the soil firm round the roots, water freely overhead through a fine rose and return to the greenhouse or frame. Shade from strong sunlight for a day or so until growth resumes. Subsequently, give full exposure to sun and ventilate as freely as possible, consistent with a minimum temperature of 13°C (55°F) by day, 10°C (50°F) by night.

398. Hardening off The seedlings

must be gradually accustomed to the out-door temperature. Those raised in the warm greenhouse should be transferred to a frame about mid-spring. Ventilation must be further increased as weather permits until by late spring lights are removed entirely except when frost threatens, as it may on clear, calm nights.

399. Planting In some sheltered gardens half-hardy annuals can be planted out in mid – late spring, but in most localities it is not safe until late spring or early summer. Remove seedlings from the boxes or pans with as little soil disturbance as possible. This is most readily done if they have been well watered a few hours previously. Divide into separate plants and replant with a trowel. Make the soil thoroughly firm around the roots and water in freely. Small varieties should be 15cm (6in) apart; those of medium height 22-30cm (9 or 12in), large-growing kinds 45-60cm (1½to 2ft) (401).

400. Culture The same as for hardy annuals (406). The trailing growths of *Phlox drummondii* should be pegged to the soil. Floppy varieties can be supported with bushy twigs (448).

401. See overleaf.

ANNUALS (HARDY)

402. Description An annual completes its whole cycle of life, including the production of flowers and seed, within one year, and then dies. A hardy annual is, in addition, sufficiently resistant to cold to be sown outdoors without protection in the spring. Some hardy annuals can also be sown outdoors in the autumn and wintered without protection, but this does not apply to all (407).

403. Soil and Situation Hardy annuals are extremely adaptable and there are few soils or places in which they will not grow. They prefer soils that are well drained and positions that are open and sunny, but godetias do tolerably well in shade also. Little preparation is required, beyond thorough forking to prepare a fine seed bed. Manure as a rule does more harm than good, tending to produce leaves at the expense of flowers.

404. Sowing Seed may be sown at any time from early to late spring and, in the case of particularly hardy varieties, again in early autumn. Autumn-sown plants will winter without thinning outdoors and start to flower in early summer the following year. Early and mid-spring-sown annuals flower from midsummer to early autumn, while those sown in late spring flower from late summer to mid-autumn. Seeds are sown where the plants are to flower. Some seedlings may be transplanted elsewhere later on if overcrowded, but the majority are left undisturbed. Taprooted annuals, such as godetias, eschscholzias, and Shirley poppies, do not transplant well. Seed may be sown broadcast or in drills and should be covered very lightly with finely broken soil. Water if the soil is dry, not otherwise, Germination takes from one to three weeks according to variety and weather.

405. Thinning Seedlings must be thinned as soon as they can be handled, except autumn-sown annuals, which are not thinned until the following spring. Small varieties should be thinned to 10-12cm (4-5in) apart, kinds of medium growth to 20-30cm (8-12in) and tall varieties to 45cm (18in) or more (407).

406. Culture Faded flowers should be removed before seed is formed unless it is intended to save some seed for the following year. If it is desired to save seed, a few good plants should be marked for the purpose early in the summer and all flowers retained. The seed pods are cut with a length of stem as soon as they turn yellow and start to split open or, with daisy-type

401. Table of Half-hardy Annuals

Name	Colour	Height cm/in	Planting distance cm/in
Ageratum★	mauve	15-30/6-12	15-20/6-8
Antirrhinum★	white, yellow, pink to crimson	15-90/6-36	15-30/6-12
Arctotis	white, yellow, orange, red, purple	30-60/1-2ft	30/12
Aster	blue, purple, pink, red, white	30-75/12-30	30/12
Begonia semperflorens★	white, pink to crimson	15-30/6-12	22/9
Celosia	red, yellow	30-75/12-30	30/12
Cleome	pink	90/3ft	45/18
Cosmea★	white, pink to crimson, orange	60-90/2-3ft	30/12
Dianthus sinensis	white to crimson	15-30/6-12	15/6
Helichrysum	yellow, orange, red, white	45-75/18-30	22-30/9-12
Heliotrophe★	purple	45-60/18-24	30/12
Impatiens	red, pink, white	15-60/6-24	22-30/9-12
Kochia (summer cypress)	green foliage, turning crimson	60-90/2-3ft	60/2ft
Lobelia★	blue	15-20/6-8	15/6
Marigolds (African and French)	yellow, orange and crimson	15-60/6-24	15-30/6-12
Mesembryanthemum criniflorum	white, buff, pink to crimson	15/6	15/6
Nemesia	various	22-30/9-12	15-20/6-8
Nicotiana	white, pink to crimson	30-90/1-3ft	30/12
Petunia★	white, blue, pink to purple	30-45/12-18	20-30/8-12
Phlox drummondii	white, scarlet to purple, etc	15-45/6-18	22/9
Rudbeckia hirta	yellow, red	45-90/18-36	30-45/12-18
Salpiglossis	various	45-60/18-24	30/12
Salvia splendens★	scarlet, purple	15-60/6-24	15-30/6-12
Statice sinuata	blue, red, yellow, white	45/18	30/12
Stocks (ten weeks)	white, pink, red, purple	30-45/12-18	30/12
Ursinia	orange	30-35/12-15	22-30/9-12
Venidium	orange	60-90/2-3ft	45/18
Zinnia	red, pink, orange, yellow	15-90/6-36	15-30/6-12

★ Strictly speaking, half-hardy perennials but usually treated as half-hardy annuals.

flowers, as soon as the heads turn yellow and show signs of shedding their seeds. Ripening should be completed in clean, paper-lined trays in a sunny window or greenhouse. Different varieties of the same kind of annual, eg different colours of eschscholzias, cross readily and unless special precautions are taken seed will be mixed, ie the seedlings will produce flowers of many different colours.

Feeding is usually unnecessary. The only other routine measure is to keep

407. Table of Hardy Annuals for Summer Borders

Name	Colour	Height cm/in	Distance to thin cm/in
Alyssum (Sweet)	white	10–15/4–6	10–15/4–6
Amaranthus caudatus	crimson and green	75/30	30/12
Bartonia	yellow	45/18	30/12
Calandrinia†	rose, crimson	22–45/9–18	15–22/6–9
Calendula★	yellow and orange	30–45/12–18	30/12
Calliopsis (coreopsis)	yellow and crimson	45–60/18–24	30/12
Candytuft★	white, lilac and purple	15–30/6–12	15–22/6–9
Chrysanthemum (annual)★	white, yellow, scarlet to maroon	30–60/12–24	30–45/12–18
Clarkia	white, pink to crimson	45–60/18–24	30/12
Collinsia	white and purple	30/12	15–22/6–9
Convolvulus	purple, crimson and white	30–35/12–15	22–45/9–18
Cornflower★	white, blue and rose	30–90/12–36	22–30/9–12
Dimorphotheca	orange, salmon, etc	30/12	30/12
Echium	blue, lavender, pink and white	30/12	22/9
Eschscholzia	yellow, orange, carmine and rose	22–30/9–12	22/9
Godetia	pink to crimson and white	15–60/6–24	22–30/9–12
Gypsophila elegans	white, pink, and carmine	45/18	22–30/9–12
Helipterum roseum	pink and white	45/18	15/6
Ipomoea purpurea	blue, purple, pink and white	Climbing	30/60/1–2ft
Jacobaea†	white, mauve, pink and purple	45/18	22–30/9–12
Larkspur★	white, blue, pink and scarlet	60–90/2–3ft	45/18
Lavatera	white and rose	90–120/3–4ft	45–60/18–24
Layia†	yellow and white	30/12	22/9
Leptosiphon†	various	8–15/3–6	7–10/3–4
Limnanthes	pale yellow	15/6	15/6
Linum (scarlet flax)	scarlet	22–30/9–12	15/6
Love-in-a-mist (nigella)	blue and white	45/18	30/12
Lupin	white, blue, pink to crimson	60/2ft	30/12
Malope	purple, white, etc	60–90/2–3ft	45/18
Matthiola bicornis	purple	22–30/9–12	7–15/3–6
Mignonette	greenish yellow, white and red	30/12	15–22/6–9
Nasturtium†	yellow, scarlet, etc	22–30/9–12 also climbing	22–35/9–15
Nemophila	blue	15/6	10–15/4–6
Phacelia	blue	20/8	22/9

Most of these can be sown outdoors from early to late spring. Those marked with an asterisk (★) may also be sown in early autumn. Do not sow those marked † until mid-spring.

Name	Colour	Height cm/in	Distance to thin cm/in
Poppy (Shirley and Cardinal)	white, pink, crimson, heliotrope, etc	60-90/2-3ft	30-35/12-15
Salvia horminum	blue, pink and white	45-60/18-24	22/9
Saponaria	rose	60/2ft	15/6
Scabious (Sweet)	white, lavender, pink to maroon	45-60/18-24	30-35/12-15
Sunflower (Annual)	yellow and orange	1-3m/3-10ft	60-90/2-3ft
Sweet pea★	white, pink, blue, scarlet, etc	2-3m/6-10ft	10-22/4-9
Sweet sultan†	white, rose and purple	45/18	22/9
Tagetes signata pumila†	yellow	22-30/9-12	15/6
Tropaeolum canariense† (Canary creeper)	yellow	climbing	22-30/9-12
Virginia stock	white, yellow, pink to crimson	15/6	7-10/3-4
Viscaria	white, blue, pink to crimson	30/12	15/6

Most of these can be sown outdoors from early to late spring. Those marked with an asterisk (★) may also be sown in early autumn. Do not sow those marked † until mid-spring.

beds free of weeks, by hoeing until the plants cover the ground, and then by hand weeding.

407. See pages 105-106.

AQUATICS

408. Description Any plants that grow wholly or mainly in water. Almost all are herbaceous perennials (443). There are hardy, half-hardy, and tender varieties. The first can be grown outdoors all the year; the second should have protection from frost in the winter; the third are suitable for cultivation only in indoor aquariums with warm water.

409. Soil and Situation Most aquatics are sun-loving plants and for this reason ornamental pools should, if possible, be in the open, not under the shade of large trees. A few plants will grow in the water alone without soil, but the majority must have suitable compost. Medium to heavy loam is best. Manure and fertilizers should not be used for fear of polluting the water and increasing the growth of algae. Spread soil to a depth of about 15cm (6in) (more if possible) over the bottom of the pool and cover with 2-3cm (1in) of clean sand or gravel. Less depth is required in an aquarium. Alternatively, place compost in mounds with fine-meshed wire netting to hold it in place, or in plastic baskets or pots. Depth of water varies from 1m (3ft) for some of the strongest-growing water lilies to 8cm (3in) for many marginal plants (413).

410. Planting Plants with normal roots and crowns, eg water lilies, rushes, reed maces, etc, can be planted exactly like herbaceous perennials (445), if water can be emptied from the pool. If not, they are best planted in plastic baskets or pots and sunk in position. A simple way of planting oxygenating plants, ie plants which supply oxygen to the water, is to tie a stone to the bottom of each, and sink in position. No plants should be put into ice-cold water or water drawn direct from the main. It should be allowed to stand for a while to be warmed by the sun and acted upon by the atmosphere. It is better to fill pools gradually as plants grow than to plant in the maximum depth of water straight away. Mid- and late spring are the best times for planting outdoors. Indoor aquariums may be planted a little earlier.

Fishes, water snails, etc, should be introduced a few weeks after planting, when the water clears. It is always a little muddy at first.

411. Cultural Routine All dead leaves must be removed in the autumn. Pond weed, etc, can be raked out from time to time. Algae (green scum on the surface) is removed by drawing a sack across the surface. In small quantity these weeds do no harm, but rather good. Excess growth is a sign that the pond is not balanced. Ensure that there are enough oxygenating plants and provide some shade by introducing water lilies or floating plants.

It is not necessary or desirable to change the water frequently, nor vital to grow plants in running water. Pools and aquariums properly stocked with water plants, including oxygenating plants (414), fish, water snails, etc, maintain a balance of life and do not become unpleasant. Water lost by evaporation should be made good with water at the same temperature as that of the pool or aquarium.

412. Propagation Most water plants can be increased by division at the ordinary planting season (410), exactly like herbaceous perennials (446). As a rule they benefit from such division at intervals of five or six years, as this prevents overcrowding.

Some kinds can also be raised from seed sown in ordinary seed compost (493) in well-drained pans, which should then be supported on inverted flower pots or bricks at the edge of the pool so that their rims are about 1cm ($\frac{1}{2}$in) below water level. Seed is sown in the spring.

Most of the submerged oxygenating plants (414) can be increased by cuttings. Pieces 5-10cm (2-4in) long will root readily in a sandy compost.

413. See overleaf.

414. Useful Oxygenating Plants In all these the foliage is submerged and supplies oxygen to the water. Those preceded by an asterisk are tender and must be protected in winter. Apium (Marshwort), ★Cabomba (Washington grass), Callitriche (Water starwort), Ceratophyllum (Hornwort), Chara, Elatine (Waterwort), Eleocharis (Needle spike rush), Elodea, Fontinalis (Willow moss), Hottonia (Water violet), ★*Myriophyllum hippuroides*, *Myriophyllum verticillatum* (Water millfoil), Oenanthe (Water dropwort), Pilularia (Pillwort), Potamogeton (Pondweed), *Ramunculas aquatilis* (Water crowfoot), Utricularia (Bladderwort), ★Vallisneria (Tape grass).

BEDDING PLANTS (SUMMER)

415. Description This is purely a garden term with no botanical significance. Some summer bedding plants are half-hardy annuals (394), some half-hardy perennials, ie plants which continue to live for many years, but may be damaged by frost, so cannot be left outdoors for the winter. Their sole link is that all may be planted out at the end of spring or early in summer to fill the garden with flowers in the summer. They are either thrown away in the autumn or lifted and wintered in a greenhouse, frame, or other frost-

413. Table of Aquatic Plants

Botanical name	Popular name	Ornamental Value	Depth of water cm/in
Acorus	Sweet flag	sword-like foliage	8-12/3-5
Alisma	Water plantain	broad foliage, pink flowers	8-12/3-5
Aponogeton	Water hawthorn	pink flowers, floating leaves	15-45/6-18
Butomus	Flowering rush	pink flowers	2-8/1-3
Caltha	Marsh marigold	yellow flowers	Bog
Carex	Sedge grass	grassy foliage	Bog
Cyperus	Umbrella grass	rush-like foliage	Bog
Eriophorum	Cotton grass	rush-like foliage, cotton-like seeds	2-8/1-3
Hydrocleis (Limnocharis)	Water poppy	yellow flowers	22-30/9-12
Iris pseudacorus	Water flag	yellow flowers	8-12/3-5
Juncus	Bog rush	narrow foliage	Bog
Limnanthemum (Villarsia)	Floating heart	yellow flowers	15-45/6-18
Mentha	Water mint	aromatic foliage	Bog
Menyanthes	Buckbean	floating foliage, white flowers	8-12/3-5
Mimulus	Water musk	yellow flowers	Bog
Myosotis palustris	Water forget-me-not	blue flowers	Bog
Nuphar	Yellow water lily	yellow flowers	60-90/2-3ft
Nymphaea	Water lily	flowers of many colours	15-90/½-3ft
Orontium	Golden club	glaucous foliage, yellow flowers	8-45/3-18
Pontederia	Pickerel weed	heart-shaped leaves, blue flowers	2-8/1-3
Sagittaria	Arrowhead	foliage and white flowers	8-12/3-5
Scirpus	Bulrush	rush foliage	2-8/1-3
Typha	Reed mace	rush foliage, cigar-like flower heads	2-8/1-3

NOTE The depth of water is that which should cover the crowns.

proof place. Treatment of half-hardy annuals has already been described (394–401); here only perennials are dealt with.

416. Soil and Situation With few exceptions bedding plants thrive in well-dug but not over-rich soils and sunny positions. A few kinds, notably calceolarias and tuberous-rooted begonis, will succeed in shade.

417. Culture This will vary according to the nature of the plant, and further particulars are given in a table (420). Summer treatment is similar to that of annuals except that it is rarely wise to save seeds, as these may give very disappointing results. Trailing plants, such as ivy-leaved geraniums, may be pegged to the soil or tied up to short stakes. Tall plants, eg standard fuchsias, heliotropes, abutilons, etc, are often spaced at regular intervals (dot plants) among dwarf kinds (ground plants) to give an attractive effect.

418. Propagation Some kinds, such as geraniums (zonal and ivy-leaved pelargoniums), calceolarias, gazanias, fuchsias, marguerites, and penstemons, are increased by cuttings. These must be prepared from firm, non-flowering shoots. They should be 2·5-10cm (1-4in) in length accoding to the nature of the growth, severed immediately beneath a joint, and the lower leaves must be removed. Cuttings are inserted firmly 1-2cm (½-1in) deep in sandy soil round the edge of a well-drained flower pot or in a propagating frame (492). Spring cuttings root best with bottom heat; summer and autumn cuttings in an unheated frame or greenhouse. When well rooted, cuttings must be potted singly in 7·5cm (3in) pots in an ordinary compost (497). Later it may be necessary to remove to 10cm (4in) pots of a similar compost if the smaller pots become filled with roots before planting-out time arrives.

Other kinds, eg heliotrope, verbenas, etc, may be raised from seed as well as from cuttings. The seed should be treated in the same way as for half-hardy annuals (396).

Tuberous-rooted begonias can be raised from seed as above, or old tubers can be divided after starting into growth in spring (419). Cannas can be raised from seed in a temperature of 21°C (70°F) but are usually increased by division in spring.

419. Lifting and Wintering If they are to be kept over the winter, either for replanting the following year or to supply cuttings in spring, bedding plants must be lifted and brought into a frost-proof place before cold becomes too intense. With all except tuberous-rooted plants this lifting should be done in early or mid-autumn, before foliage is damaged by frost. They are then potted in the smallest pots that will contain the roots and placed in a greenhouse. Water should be given sparingly throughout the winter, but soil must never become absolutely dry. Frost protection is sufficient for calceolarias, marguerites, and fuchsias. A slightly higher temperture is preferable for geraniums and heliotropes.

Tuberous-rooted plants such as begonias, cannas, dahlias, and *Salvia patens* are lifted as soon as foliage is blackened by frost. The tops are cut off, and the tubers stored in dry sand, peat or peat substitute in any dry, cool, but frost-proof place. They are re-started into growth from mid-winter to mid-spring in moist soil, peat or peat substitute in a temperature of 16-18°C (60°-65°F).

420. See pages 110 and 111.

BIENNIALS (HARDY)

421. Description Plants which complete their cycle of life within two years, ie are sown one year, flower the next year, produce seed, and then die. A few biennials can be induced to behave as annuals (402) if sown very early in a warm greenhouse. Monocarpic plants are those which die in the same way as biennials and annuals after having flowered and produced seed, but complete their cycle in an indefinite number of years. The most important true hardy biennials are Canterbury bells, foxgloves, and some verbascums, but wallflowers, forget-me-nots, double daisies, hollyhocks, and sweet williams are often treated as such. (There are also half-hardy and tender kinds for the greenhouse, such as *Campanula pyramidalis* and *Humea elegans*) (526).

422. Soil and Situation Most are adaptable plants, thriving in ordinary soils and sunny or partially shady positions. Soil should be prepared by thorough digging. A general garden fertilizer (95) can

420. Table of Summer Bedding Plants

Name	Colour	Height cm	Height ft
Abutilons	variegated leaves	60-120	2-4
Alternanthera	ornamental foliage	creeping	
Begonia (tuberous rooted)	various late winter – early spring	22-30	9-12in
Calceolaria (shrubby)	yellow, bronze	30-45	1-1½
Calocephalus	silvery leaves	60-90	2-3
Canna	various	60-90	2-3
Cordyline	ornamental foliage	60 and upwards	2 and upwards
Dahlia	various	45-200	18in-7ft
Echevaria	blue-grey rosettes	5-8	2-3in
Fuchsia	pink, red, purple, etc	30-120	1-4
Gazania	yellow, orange, etc	trailing	
Heliotrope	blue	22-90	9in-3ft
Marguerite	white, yellow	45-60	18in-2ft
Mesembryanthemum (various)	various	trailing	
Pansies	various	10-15	4-6in
Pelargonium (bedding geranium)	pink, red, white, etc	30-60 and trailing	1-2
Penstemon	various	45-60	1½-2
Salvia (blue)	blue	45-60	1½-2
Senecio cineraria	silver leaves	45-60	1½-2
Verbena★	various	trailing	
Violas	various	10-15	4-6in

★ Note that these plants are often treated as half-hardy annuals (394).

be used in the spring as a top dressing. Animal manure is not desirable.

423. Sowing and Planting Seed must be sown every year to maintain a supply of flowering plants. The best time for sowing is late spring. Brompton stocks and forget-me-nots may be left until early to midsummer. Seed may be sown outdoors in a sheltered border of finely broken soil, but the choicer kinds, such as Canterbury bell and Brompton stock, are best reared in an unheated frame in a semi-shady position. Transplant seedlings 8-10cm (3-4in) apart in rows 20cm (8in) apart into a bed of similar character as soon as they can be handled conveniently, usually between mid- and late summer. Plants can be transferred to flowering quarters in mid- to late autumn or early spring. Details of planting are exactly the same as for herbaceous perennials (445).

Distance apart for planting		Method of propagation
cm	ft	
1–1·2m	3–4	cuttings in spring
10–15	4–6in	cuttings in spring
22–30	9–1ft	seed in late winter or division of tubers after starting in
22	9in	cuttings in early autumn or spring
30–45	1–1½	cuttings in spring
30–60	1–2	division in spring or seed in mid – late winter
90–180	3–6	cuttings in spring, seed in late winter
30–90	1–3	cuttings in spring, seed in late winter – early spring
15–22	6–9	division in spring
30–90	1–3	cuttings in spring or late summer
15–22	6–9in	cuttings in early autumn or spring
22–120	9in–4ft	cuttings in spring
30–45	1–1½	cuttings in early autumn or spring
30–60	1–2	cuttings in spring or late summer
15–22	6–9in	seed in spring or early summer
30–60	1–2	cuttings in late summer or spring
30	1	cuttings in early autumn
30	1	cuttings in spring or division in spring
60	2	cuttings in early autumn or spring
22–30	9in–1ft	cuttings in spring or seed in mid – late winter
15–22	6–9in	seed in spring or early summer or cuttings in late summer

424. Propagation By seed as above.

425. Cultural Routine Practically non-existent except for hoeing and removal of weeds. If desired, some plants may be retained after flowering to ripen seeds. These are handled in the same way as annuals retained for seed (406). Other plants should be removed and burnt or placed on the compost heap as they have finished flowering.

BULBS (HARDY)

426. Description Botanically a bulb is built up of many fleshy or scaly segments, such as those of a lily. In this work the term is used more loosely to include many plants with thickened root stocks storing food to carry the plants over a dormant period. These plants are all perennials. There are also half-hardy and tender kinds (526).

427. Soil and Situation Like hardy herbaceous perennials (443), bulbs are of many kinds and have varying requirements. Some thrive in shade, others in full sun, but in general most prefer open, well-drained, reasonably rich soils. Ground should be dug deeply and, if believed to be poor, should be enriched with manures such as bonemeal (57), basic slag (55), and hoof and horn (60), plus moderate dressings of well-rotted animal manure well worked in.

428. Planting Spring-flowering bulbs are planted in late summer and autumn; summer-flowering bulbs in spring, and autumn-flowering bulbs in mid- and late summer. Of the spring-flowering varieties, snowdrops and narcissi (daffodils) should receive first attention (late summer – early autumn), while tulips and hyacinths may be left until last (mid- late autumn). For depths and distances see table (432). Planting may be done with a trowel, stout blunt-ended dibber, or spade. Never plant with a pointed dibber, as this may leave an air space beneath the bulb. A special tool (38) can be obtained for planting bulbs in grass.

Most lilies may be planted in autumn when dormant or they may be moved in early or mid-spring like herbaceous perennials (445). Exception must be made for *Lilium candidum* (the Madonna lily) and *L. testaceum*, which should be planted in mid- or late summer. Moreover, these lilies and also *L. giganteum* are only just covered with soil. Stem-rooting lilies are planted most deeply, though often the holes are only half filled at first, more soil being added as the stems grow (429).

Gladioli should be put in successionally during early and mid-spring to prolong the flowering season.

429. Cultural Routine Beyond hoeing and weeding there is little that can be done while bulbous plants are in growth. Tall-growing kinds, eg lilies, or those with heavy spikes of blooms, eg gladioli, will require staking and tying. This should be done early. Some lilies form roots from the stems as well as from the bulbs. Soil may be drawn towards these while in growth or, better still, a mixture of soil and leaf-mould or peat can be spread around them in the spring to encourage formation of stem roots. Most bulbs can be fed with weak liquid manure (49) or a general fertilizer (95) applied during the spring for spring-flowering kinds and during the early summer months for gladioli.

430. Lifting and Storing Spring-flowering bulbs may be lifted after the foliage has died down in summer. This will be in early or midsummer for narcissi (daffodils) and early tulips, and in midsummer for late tulips, hyacinths and Spanish, English and Dutch irises. In no case should foliage be removed before these times. If bulbs must be lifted earlier, they should be replanted (heeled in) at once, close together in trenches, to complete their growth.

After lifting, pull or cut off the dead leaves, sort the bulbs into sizes, place in shallow boxes, and store in a cool airy place, but not in full sunshine, until planting time. Small bulbs will not as a rule flower the following year but may be planted in a reserve bed to grow on.

Gladioli are lifted in mid – late autumn, about six weeks after flowering. Cut off the leaves at once about 2-3cm (1in) above the corms (bulbs). Then remove and discard the old withered corms at the base of the new plump corms. Remove tiny cormlets which can be grown on to flowering size if desired. All are stored in shallow trays in an airy, frost-proof place.

Montbretias may be treated in the same way as gladioli, but it is better not to allow them to become fully dormant. Instead, lift in late autumn and replant close together in a frame, watering very moderately during the winter.

It is not necessary or desirable to lift and store all bulbs every year. Gladioli must come up because they are tender; tulips and hyacinths usually benefit from lifting. Lilies should be left undisturbed unless overcrowded, diseased, or in other ways in need of removal. Crocuses, snowdrops, muscari, bulbous irises, and narcissi (daffodils) can generally be left for several years undisturbed until a falling off in quality and quantity of bloom indicates overcrowding.

431. Propagation Most bulbs can be increased by removing offsets or young bulbs which are formed alongside or above the old ones. This should be done at the usual lifting season (430) and the small bulbs should be replanted exactly like the large ones but at about two-thirds the depth and in a separate bed, as they will not flower the first year. Some kinds also make tiny bulbils or cormels; certain lilies have these bulbils in the axils of the leaves, while gladioli carry them round the new flowering corm. Like small bulbs, they must be grown on to flowering size but will take longer to attain this, possibly two to four years. Treatment is the same as for bulbs except that they must be covered with approximately their own depth of soil.

Bulbs can also be raised from seed sown in a frame or sheltered position outdoors in early spring. Choice varieties of lily, etc, are best sown in pans and germinated in a cool greenhouse. The seedlings are left undisturbed until they die down, when the tiny bulbs are unearthed and treated like bulblets or cormels. See above.

Most lilies can also be propagated by scales. These should be pulled from mature bulbs from midsummer to early autumn, and laid fairly closely in trays half filled with seed compost, peat moss or leaf-mould and sand. Cover with 1cm ($1/2$in) of the same mixture, moisten and keep in a cool place. Bulbs form on the scales and can be treated like bulblets or formels. See above.

432. See pages 114 and 115.

CARNATIONS (BORDER)

433. Types For exhibition purposes these are classified as selfs (flowers of one colour only); white-ground fancies (flowers with coloured markings on a white base); yellow-ground fancies (similar but with a yellow base); fancies, with markings on a base other than white or yellow; and picotees, flowers of one main colour with a narrow band of a contrasting colour round the margin of each petal. Cloves are distinguished by their rich clove fragrance.

434. Soil and Situation A fairly rich, rather limy or chalky, well-drained soil is most suitable. Digging should be thorough; only small quantities of animal manure or compost should be employed, but bonemeal (57) or basic slag (55) and hoof and horn meal (60) may be used. If lime is deficient, ground chalk or limestone should be forked in at 520g per square metre (1lb per yd²). Situation should be open and sunny.

435. Planting Can be done in early or mid-autumn, or early spring. For autumn planting, rooted layers (437) can be lifted direct from the ground; for spring planting, potted layers wintered in a frame are best. Just cover topmost roots with soil and make very firm. Plant 30cms (1ft) apart each way, but rather more space will be needed for exhibition plants.

432. Table of Hardy Bulbs

Botanical name	Popular name	Colour	Season
Acidanthera		white and maroon	late spr – early aut
Allium		various	late spr – mid sum
Amaryllis belladonna	Belladonna lily	pink	early aut – mid aut
Anemone (St Brigid, De Caen, fulgens)	Windflower	various	mid spr – mid sum
Antholyza		orange	late spr – early aut
Calochortus	Butterfly tulip	various	late spr – early sum
Chionodoxa	Glory of the snow	blue	early spr – mid spr
Colchicum	Autumn crocus	various	early aut – mid aut
Convallaria	Lily of the valley	white	mid spr – late spr
Crinum		white pink	late sum – early aut
Crocus		various	mid aut – early spr
Cyclamen		white to crimson	mid aut – late spr
Eranthis	Winter aconite	yellow	mid win – late win
Erythronium	Dog's-tooth violet	various	early spr – late spr
Fritillaria imperialis	Crown imperial	yellow, red	late spr
Fritillaria meleagris	Snakeshead fritillary	various	mid spr – late spr
Galanthus	Snowdrop	white	late aut – late win
Galtonia	Spire lily	white	mid spr – late spr
Gladiolus		various	early spr – early aut
Hyacinthus	Hyacinth	various	mid spr – late spr
Iris (bulbous rooted)		various	mid win – mid sum
Ixia		various	early sum
Leucojum	Snowflake	white	mid win – late spr, late a
Lilium	Lily	various	early sum – early aut
Montbretia		yellow to crimson	late sum – early aut
Muscari	Grape hyacinth	blue	mid spr – late spr
Narcissus	Daffodil	white, yellow, orange	late win – late spr
Ornithogalum	Star of Bethlehem	white	late spr – early sum
Puschkinia		blue and white	mid spr
Ranunculus (Turban, French)		various	late spr – early sum
Schizostylis	Kaffir lily	pink, scarlet	mid aut – late aut
Scilla	Squill, Bluebell	blue, white, pink	early spr – early sum
Sparaxis	Harlequin flower	various	late spr – early sum
Sternbergia	Lily-of-the-field	yellow	mid aut – late aut
Tigridia	Tiger flower	various	mid sum – late sum
Tulipa	Tulip	various	early spr – late spr
Watsonia	Bugle lily	various	late sum – early aut

Height cm	Height ft	Planting Depth cm	Planting Depth in	Planting Time
90	3	8	3	mid spr – late spr
30–120	1–4	10	4	aut
60–90	2–3	10–15	4–6	late sum
22–30	9–12in	5–8	2–3	mid aut – mid spr
90	3	8	3	early spr – mid spr
15–60	½–2	8	3	mid aut – late aut
10–15	4–6in	8	3	aut
8–20	7–8in	2	1	late sum
15	6in	2–5	1–2	late aut – early spr
90–120	3–4	22	9	early spr
7–15	3–6in	8–10	3–4	late sum – mid aut
10–15	4–6in	1	½	late sum – early aut
5	2in	5	2	aut
15–30	6–12in	8	3	aut
60–90	2–3	10–12	4–5	aut
15–30	6–12in	5–8	2–3	aut
10–20	4–8in	10	4	aut
60–90	2–3	15	6	aut
60–150	2–5	10	4	early spr – mid spr
22–35	9–15in	12–15	5–6	mid aut – late aut
15–75	½–2½	8	3	aut
60	2	5	2	aut
10–45	4–18in	8	3	late spr – early aut
45–350	1½–12	2–20	1–8	aut
60–90	2–3	5–8	2–3	early spr – mid spr
10–20	4–8in	5–8	2–3	aut
10–60	4–24in	8–15	3–6	aut
30–45	1–1½	10	4	aut
15	6in	8	3	aut
22	9in	5	2	late aut – early spr
45	18in	8	3	early spr – mid spr
8–35	3–15in	8–15	3–6	aut
30	1	5	2	aut
10	4in	10	4	late sum
45	18in	5	2	mid spr – late spr
15–75	6–30in	10–12	4–5	aut
90–120	3–4	8	3	mid spr

436. Cultural Routine Keep beds regularly hoed throughout the spring and summer; top dress with carnation fertilizer (93) in mid-spring. Tie flower stems to bamboo canes, making uppermost tie 10-12cm (4-5in) below flower bud so that this arches over in a natural manner and does not collect rain as it opens. Remove from half to two-thirds the number of side flower buds that form below the terminal (tip) bud. Usually plants are not worth keeping after their second year and should be replaced by young rooted layers. Spray occasionally during the summer with a good systemic insecticide to keep down greenfly. For other foes, see Section 8.

437. Propagation By layering in mid-summer. Layers are prepared from young, non-flowering growths. An upward-sloping incision is made through a joint at a point 5-8cm (2-3in) from the base where the shoot can be bent readily to soil level. The incision is then opened and the stem pressed into the soil. It is fixed in position with a wire or wooden pin and more soil is heaped over it. The extremity of the shoot is tied to a small stake. A number of layers may be pegged down round each parent plant. If kept moist, roots will be formed in a few weeks. Layers can be severed from the parent in early autumn and planted a week or so later.

DAHLIAS

438. Types The principal types grown today are decorative, sub-divided into giant, large, medium, small and miniature flowered; cactus, with the same divisions, single flowered, anemone, collerette, peony, ball, pompon and bedding.

439. Soil and Situation Dahlias require a deep, rich, well-watered soil.

Digging should be thorough. Animal manure or compost may be added at 50kg to 7 square metres (1cwt to 8yd²). Lime is not necessary. The situation should be sunny but not too exposed.

440. Planting Dahlias are very tender and must not be planted out until all danger of frost is past. Plant all except bedding varieties 90cm (3ft) apart each way. Bedding kinds may be 35-45cm (15-18in) apart. Tubers should be covered with about 5cm (2in) of soil and this made moderately firm.

441. Cultural Routine Staking is necessary for all except bedding kinds. Stakes must be strong and driven well into the ground, as growth is heavy. For exhibition purposes growths of large-flowered decoratives and large cactus varieties are reduced to one to three per plant according to strength. All flower buds except the main terminal buds on each stem are removed. Water freely during dry weather, mulch with strawy manure or grass clippings and feed every ten days or so with weak liquid manure (49). Sprinkle leaves with pepper dust during August and September and place inverted flower pots stuffed with hay on dahlia stakes to drive off or trap earwigs. For other foes, see Section 8.

442. Propagation Best results are obtained from cuttings. Tubers stored as above are placed in boxes or large pots in late winter – mid-spring and covered with old potting soil. They are watered moderately, placed in a greenhouse or frame with average temperature 16°-18°C (60°-65°F). Shoots appear freely and are severed nearly to the tuber when 5cm (2in) long. Remove lower leaves, trim each cutting cleanly just below a joint and insert 1cm (½in) deep in sandy soil in a propagating frame (492) within the greenhouse, preferably with bottom heat. Water freely and shade from direct sun. Pot singly in ordinary potting compost (497) as soon as each cutting has rooted. Remove to a frame in late spring and harden them off for planting out.

POT-TUBERS, ie small tubers for planting out from pots in early summer are produced from late cuttings taken in late spring or early summer and inserted singly in 7·5cm (3in) pots. The rooted cuttings are grown in the same small pots all summer and are gradually dried off in early – mid-autumn. The following spring they are watered again and kept in a sunny greenhouse or frame till planting-out time.

Alternatively, old tubers can be started into growth in a frame in mid–spring, split into several pieces when shoots appear and be planted out in early summer. Yet another method is to plant tubers in late spring where they are to flower, covering shoots with cloches or inverted flower pots at night if they appear too early in the season and there is likely to be danger from frost.

HERBACEOUS PERENNIALS (HARDY)

443. Description Plants which continue to live for a number of years irrespective of whether they flower or not, have a comparatively soft, as distinct from woody, growth, and are hardy enough to be grown outdoors all the year round.

444. Soil and Situation There are hardy herbaceous perennials suitable for every imaginable soil and situation from light sands to heavy clays, and from full sun to dense shade. Many are extremely adaptable (450). Ground should be prepared by thorough digging and all weeds of a perennial nature (31) should be removed, as little further cultivation will be possible for some years. For the same reason, if soil is believed to be poor,

organic manure (42), compost (43), or slow-acting fertilizers, such as bone meal (57), basic slag (55), or hoof and horn meal (63) should be worked in prior to planting.

445. Planting All can be planted in the spring, from early to mid-spring. Many kinds can also be planted in early and mid-autumn, especially if the soil is warm and well drained. It is not advisable to transplant *Scabiosa caucasica, Aster amellus*, pyrethrums, or *Leucanthemum vulgare* in the autumn. Bearded (German) irises can, in addition, be transplanted immediately after flowering, in early to midsummer. Planting should be done with a trowel or spade, not a dibber. Holes must be wide enough to allow roots to be spread out naturally; deep enough to permit crowns to be just covered with soil. The rhizomes of flag irises should be barely covered; later they will work out on top, their natural position. The soil mark on the plant, or the difference in colour (green above ground, whitish below), usually gives a reliable guide to planting depth. Distance will vary according to habit and height, ranging from 15cm (6in) for low-growing plants to 90cm (3ft) for the tallest varieties. See table (450).

Plant very firmly. Water in freely if the soil is dry, and continue to water until growth recommences.

446. Propagation Almost all can be increased by division, ie by pulling the roots and crowns to pieces, either by hand or with the aid of pointed sticks or small forks thrust back to back through the plant and levered apart. A knife may be required to cut through hard pieces, but should be used as little as possible. When dividing old plants the younger, outside portions are to be preferred; old woody centres should be discarded unless stock is short. Each piece of growth must have roots attached. It is no use planting shoots without roots or vice versa. Division can be done at the usual planting season, but in general the best time is spring, when growth is just beginning.

Some herbaceous perennials can be increased by cuttings, eg anthemis, delphiniums, lupins, *Scabiosa caucasica*, and *Coreopsis grandiflora*. These are prepared from firm young shoots 8-12cm (3-5in) in length taken in spring as growth begins. They should be severed as low down as possible. Trim just below a joint, remove lower leaves and insert firmly in sandy soil in a frame or under a handlight (510), (512). Water moderately and shade from strong sunshine until growth recommences, when discontinue shading and gradually increase ventilation. Rooted cuttings may be planted out in early or midsummer and should be watered freely until established.

A few kinds, eg anchusas, gaillardias, oriental poppies, phloxes, romneyas, and verbascums can be increased by root cuttings. These are taken at any time during the winter. The thicker roots are cut into pieces 2-5cm (1-2in) in length, strewn thinly on ordinary potting compost (497) in well-drained pots or boxes, and covered with 1cm (½in) of the same material. An alternative method is to dibble them in 3cm (1in) apart right way up with the tops just beneath soil level. They are placed in an unheated greenhouse or frame and watered moderately. Shoots will be formed in the spring and the plants can be planted out in early or midsummer.

Most herbaceous perennials can be increased by seed, but seedlings of highly developed garden races (eg delphiniums, phloxes, lupins) are liable to vary considerably from their parents. Seed may be sown in a greenhouse or frame in early spring or outdoors in late spring or early summer. Seed beds should be as fine as possible with extra peat and sand if needed. If sown in frames, prick off (397) as soon as possible and harden off (398) for planting out during mid- or late summer. If sown outdoors, prick off into another similar bed, placing the seedlings 8-10cm (3-4in) apart, in rows 15-20cm (6-8in) apart, so that they can grow into sturdy plants for removal to their permanent flowering quarters the following spring. Germination of some perennials is extremely slow and such are best sown in pots, pans or boxes. These should not be discarded as failures for two or three years.

The double-flowered forms of *Gypsophila paniculata* are propagated by grafting young shoots in spring or early summer on to seedling roots of the single gypsophila. The shoot is cut to form a wedge, the root is slit vertically, the wedge is inserted in this, bound in position and the whole potted and placed in a propagating frame (492).

Most perennials are improved by division or renewal from cuttings every four or five years, some even more frequently, but this does not apply to paeonies or Christmas roses (helleborus), which resent root disturbance.

447. Thinning Better results are often obtained by thinning the shoots in the spring. This is particularly true with delphiniums and Michaelmas daisies. Thinning should be done early and the best shoots only retained. The number will depend upon the age of the plant and the purpose for which flowers are required. Thus with young delphiniums needed for exhibition, only one shoot will be kept per plant; two-year-old plants might carry two or three shoots; three-year-old, five or six shoots.

448. Staking Most tall herbaceous perennials require staking. So far as possible, allow one stake to each main growth; thrust into the ground firmly near the base of the plant and allow the stakes to lean outwards at the top like a shuttlecock to open growth rather than crowd it together. Plants of medium height that are liable to flop about, eg gaillardias, erigerons, etc, are most readily supported by thrusting bushy twigs into the ground round them while still young; they will grow up through the twigs and find their own support.

449. Cultural Routine Most herbaceous perennials will benefit from annual feeding. This may be done by spreading animal manure (42) or compost (43) around them in mid- or late spring, and by sprinkling a good compound fertilizer (95) around them occasionally during the spring or summer and hoeing in. Watering of established plants is usually unnecessary unless the weather is exceptionally dry, or special results, eg exhibition flowers, are required. When flowers fade they should be cut off, but leaves should not be removed unnecessarily until the autumn, when growth dies down. Then all shoots can be removed down to 2-3cm (1in) or so above ground level, except from plants with evergreen leaves, eg kniphofias, bearded irises, etc, which must be allowed to retain all healthy foliage. Dead or diseased leaves may be removed at any time.

A few hardy perennials require some winter protection especially if the soil is wet and heavy. The two most important are *Gunnera manicata* and all kinds of eremurus. The first can be protected by placing a low tunnel of fine-mesh wire netting over the crowns, after the dead leaves have been removed in late autumn, piling dead leaves, straw or bracken on top and pegging more netting on top to keep in position. The leaves, etc, must not be heaped directly on the crowns or they may cause decay. Eremuri can be protected by heaping sharp sand or boiler ashes over the crowns in late autumn.

This can be left in position till the shoots grow through the following spring. Christmas roses (helleborus) may be protected in late autumn and early winter with cloches (512) or frames, but solely to protect the blooms from mud splashes, not because the plants lack hardiness.

450. See pages 120-123.

LAWNS

451. Soil Preparation Ground should be dug at least one spit deep and may be enriched with animal manure (42) or compost (43) in moderate quantity if believed to be poor. Bonemeal (57) may also be applied, but lime should not be used unless ground is really acid. It tends to produce growth of clover and the coarser grasses at the expense of fine grass. Drainage (32) must be improved if ground tends to lie waterlogged in the winter. It is a great advantage to leave ground fallow for a month or so prior to sowing so that weed seeds may germinate and the weed seedlings be destroyed by hoeing before the grass is sown. Break the surface down as finely as possible with fork and rake prior to sowing or turfing. Either tread or roll to secure even firmness throughout. A fairly firm seed bed is essential.

452. Sowing This can be done in mid-spring or early autumn. Seed is sown broadcast at 30-65g per square metre (1-2oz per yd²), and is either raked in or covered with a light sprinkling of soil. If seeds are properly covered, no further protection from birds is necessary; small birds do not scratch but simply pick up the seeds from the surface. Proprietary dressings can be obtained to make seeds unpalatable for birds and ready dressed seed is also available. Do not sow when ground is very dry or wet; it should be slightly moist.

The finest lawns are formed from

450. Table of Hardy Perennials

Name	Height cm	Height ft	Colour
Acanthus	90–120	3–4	orange, pink
Achillea	10–60	4–24in	white, yellow, crimson
Alstroemeria	90	3	orange, pink
Anchusa	90–150	3–5	blue
Anemone japonica	60–120	2–4	white, pink
Anthemis	90	3	yellow
Aquilegia	45–90	1½–3	various
Artemisia lactifloria	150	5	white
Aster (Michaelmas daisy)	15–180	6in–6ft	various
Astilbe	30–90	1–3	white, pink to crimson
Auricula	15	6in	various
Bergenia	30	1	pink, crimson
Campanula	15–120	6in–4ft	blue, white
Carnations (border)	60	2	various
Centaurea	45–120	1½–4	yellow, pink, blue
Centranthus	60	2	pink, red, white
Chrysanthemum maximum	75–90	2½–3	white
Coreopsis	60–90	2–3	yellow
Delphiniums	90–180	3–6	blue, white
Dicentra	30–60	1–2	pink, red
Dictamnus	75	2½	purple, white
Echinacea	90	3	purple
Echinops	90–150	3–5	blue
Eremurus	90–220	3–8	white, pink, yellow
Erigeron	30–60	1–2	blue
Eryngium	60–90	2–3	blue, white
Euphorbia	30–60	1–2	yellow, orange
Gaillardia	60	2	yellow and scarlet
Geranium	30–90	1–3	crimson, pink, blue
Geum	30–60	1–2	red, yellow, orange
Gypsophila paniculata	60–90	2–3	white
Helenium	60–150	2–5	yellow, crimson
Helianthus	1·2–2m	4–7	yellow
Heliopsis	90–120	3–4	yellow, orange
Helleborus	30–45	12–18in	white, pink to crimson
Hemerocallis	60–90	2–3	yellow
Heuchera	45–75	1½–2½	pink, scarlet
Hollyhock	1·5–2·3m	5–8	various
Hosta	45–90	1½–3	white, mauve
Incarvillea	45–90	1½–3	pink, carmine
Iris	15–150	½–5	various
Kniphofia	60–22	2–8	yellow to scarlet
Liatris	45–90	1½–3	purple

Distance apart for planting cm	ft	Position to plant	Flowering period
22	9in	sun	mid sum
15–30	6in–1ft	sun	late spr – early aut
22	9in	sun	mid sum
60	2	sun	early sum
45–60	1½–2	sun or shade	late sum – mid aut
45	18in	sun	early sum – early aut
30	1	sun or semi-shade	late spr – early sum
75	2½	sun or semi-shade	late sum – early aut
30–90	1–3	sun or shade	late sum – mid aut
45	18in	sun or shade	mid sum – late sum
15	6in	sun	late spr – early sum
30	1	sun or shade	early spr – late spr
15–60	6in–2ft	sun or semi-shade	late spr – mid sum
30	1	sun	mid sum
30–60	1–2	sun	early sum - early aut
30	1	sun	early sum – mid sum
45	18in	sun	early sum – late sum
45	18in	sun	early sum – early aut
60–90	2–3	sun	early sum – mid sum
22–30	9–12in	sun or shade	late spr – early sum
45	18in	sun or shade	mid sum – late sum
60	2	sun	late sum – early aut
60	2	sun	mid sum – late sum
90	3	sun	late spr – early sum
30	1	sun	early sum – mid sum
45	18in	sun	mid sum – early aut
30	1	sun	mid spr – late spr
30	1	sun	early sum – mid aut
30	1	sun	early sum – early aut
1	30	sun	late spr – mid aut
75	2½	sun	mid sum – late sum
45–90	1½–3	sun	mid sum – early aut
60–120	2–4	sun	mid sum – mid aut
60	2	sun or semi-shade	mid sum – late sum
30	1	sun or shade	late aut – mid spr
60	2	sun or semi-shade	early sum – mid sum
30	1	sun	early sum – late sum
90	3	sun	mid sum
30–45	12–18in	sun or shade	mid sum
30	1	sun	late spr – early sum
15–60	6in–2ft	sun	late spr – early sum
45–90	1½–3	sun	early sum – mid aut
22–30	9–12	sun or semi-shade	mid sum – late sum

Name	Height cm	Height ft	Colour
Ligularia	1·2-1·5m	4-5	yellow
Limonium	30-60	1-2	blue, pink
Lupinus	90-120	3-4	various
Lychnis	30-90	1-3	scarlet, crimson
Lysimachia	90-120	3-4	yellow
Meconopsis	30-150	1-5	blue, yellow, orange
Monarda	90	3	scarlet
Nepeta	30	1	blue
Oenothera	45-90	1½-3	yellow
Paeonia	60-90	2-3	white, pink-crimson
Papaver orientale	60-90	2-3	scarlet, pink, white
Phlox	30-120	1-4	white, pink to scarlet, purple
Phygelius	90	3	orange
Physalis	45	1½	orange pods
Physostegia	45-90	1½-3	pink, white
Pinks	22-45	9-18in	white, pink-crimson
Platycodon	30-45	12-18in	blue, white
Polemonium	45	1½	blue, white
Polyanthus	15-22	6-9in	various
Polygonatum	60-90	2-3	white and green
Potentilla	15-60	6-24in	yellow, scarlet, crimson
Primrose	15	6in	various
Pulmonaria	15-45	6-18in	blue, purple, red
Pyrethrum	90	3	white, pink-crimson
Rodgersia	90	3	pink, white
Romneya	1·5-1·8m	5-6	white
Rudbeckia	60-200	2-7	yellow
Salvia superba	90	3	blue
Santolina	30	1	yellow
Scabiosa caucasica	60-90	2-3	blue, white
Sedum spectabile	45	18in	pink to crimson
Sidalcea	60-120	2-4	white, pink-crimson
Solidago	60-150	2-5	yellow
Spiraea	60-150	2-5	white, pink-crimson
Sweet william	60	2	various
Thalictrum	90-180	3-6	yellow, mauve, white
Trollius	30-60	1-2	yellow
Verbascum	90-230	3-8	white, yellow, pink
Veronica	30-180	1-6	blue, pink, white
Viola	15	6in	various

Distance apart for planting		Position to plant	Flowering period
cm	ft		
90	3	sun or semi-shade	mid sum − early aut
45	18in	sun	late sum − early aut
60	2	sun	early sum
30	1	sun	mid sum − late sum
45	18in	sun or shade	mid sum − late sum
22−45	9−18in	semi-shade	late spr − late sum
60	2	sun or semi-shade	mid sum − late sum
22	9in	sun	early sum − early aut
30−45	1−1½	sun	early sum − mid aut
60	2	sun	late spr − early sum
45	18in	sun	early sum
30−45	12−18in	sun or semi-shade	mid sum − early aut
60	2	sun	mid sum − early aut
22−30	9−12in	sun	mid sum − mid aut
22−30	9−12in	sun or semi-shade	late sum − mid aut
15−30	6in−1	sun	early sum − late sum
22	9in	sun	mid sum − late sum
22	9in	sun or shade	late spr − early sum
22	9in	sun or shade	early spr − mid spr
22	9in	shade	late spr − early sum
15−30	½−1	sun	early sum − early aut
15−22	6−9in	sun or shade	early spr − mid spr
22	9in	shade	early spr − mid spr
45	1½	sun	early sum
60	2	sun or shade	mid sum − late sum
90	3	sun	mid sum − early aut
45−90	1½−3	sun	mid sum − early aut
60	2	sun	mid sum − late spr
30	1	sun	mid sum − late sum
30	1	sun	mid sum − mid aut
30	1	sun	early aut − mid aut
45	18in	sun	mid sum − late sum
60−90	2−3	sun or semi-shade	late sum − mid aut
45−90	1½−3	sun or shade	mid sum − late sum
30	1	sun or semi-shade	early sum − late sum
60	2	sun	early sum − late sum
30	1	semi-shade	late spr − early sum
30−90	1−3	sun or shade	mid sum − late sum
30−90	1−3	sun	mid sum - late sum
15	6in	sun or shade	late spr − late sum

certain species of agrostis and festuca, particularly New Zealand brown top (Agrostis tenuis) and Chewing's fescue (Festuca rubra fallax). A drawback to these is that they germinate slowly and take a considerable time to give a good cover to the ground. In consequence, unless the lawn site has been well fallowed to get rid of weeds, there is a danger that these will get the upper hand. Perennial rye grass grows quickly at the outset and smothers weeds well but tends to die out after a few years of close mowing. A mixture of several fine grasses but without rye grass is best for most purposes. The wood meadowgrass (Poa nemoralis) may be used in shady places.

453. Aftercare of Seedling Lawns Seedling grass should be cut for the first time when 8cm (3in) high. Cut with a sharp scythe or a sharp mower, with blades set high at first but gradually lowered at each subsequent cutting. Roll lightly before the first cutting, but never use the roller when the surface of the ground is very wet.

454. Turfing Turves may be laid at any time from mid-autumn to mid-spring, when the ground is not frozen or waterlogged. Turves are cut in two sizes, 30cm by 90cm (1ft by 3ft), (supplied rolled up), and 30cm (1ft) square (supplied flat). The latter make a more even lawn, but are usually more expensive and take longer to lay. Plantains, dandelions, etc, should first be cut out with a knife. Lay lengthwise in straight rows but stagger joints in alternate rows like bricks in a wall. Bed turves evenly and beat them down gently with the back of a spade or a wooden turf beater. Scatter fine soil lightly on the surface and brush into crevices with a stiff besom.

Never lay small portions of turf at the edge of a lawn either when making new lawns or repairing old ones. If pieces are required to complete a row, lay a whole turf on the edge and use the pieces inside. When repairing worn patches, first remove a rectangle of old turf to the thickness of new turf, then rake bottom level and lay turves in the ordinary way.

455. Cultural Routine Established lawns, whether formed from seed or turf, require the same treatment. Mow regularly throughout the year, but at less frequent intervals during autumn and winter than in spring and summer and with blades set higher. Very close mowing and heavy rolling are undesirable except for lawns used for sport. For ordinary purposes, set the cutting edge about 1·5cm ($\frac{1}{2}$in) off the ground. Use the roller only when the surface is moist, not when sodden or quite dry. Lawns which get heavy wear may be aerated each autumn by pricking all over with a fork, special perforating tool or spiked roller. Brush in sharp sand or flint grit to improve drainage.

In spring and early summer give occasional top dressings of peat or leaf-mould mixed with equal parts of well-decayed manure and loam, all passed through a 0·5cm ($\frac{1}{4}$in) mesh sieve. No top dressing must exceed 0·5cm ($\frac{1}{4}$in) in depth. Lawn fertilizer (98) is best used in mid – late spring. Weeds can be killed either by watering with selective lawn week-killer (see Section 8) or by dusting with lawn sand (100). Both treatments are most effective in spring or when growth is strong.

Moss on lawns can be dragged out with a spring-toothed rake or killed with sulphate of iron (685). The growth of moss is usually an indication of bad drainage or poor soil, which should be rectified.

456. Cumberland Turf This is obtained from coastal regions and is actually washed by sea water at high tide. It is exceptionally fine and valued for bowling greens, etc, but is not recommended for lawns generally as it is difficult to maintain in inland gardens. An early spring application of agricultural salt, 16g per square metre ($\frac{1}{2}$oz per yd^2), is beneficial, otherwise treatment is as for ordinary lawns.

PANSIES AND VIOLAS

457. Description Pansies and violas are closely allied but differ in habit and type of colouring. Violas are in the main more tufted and flowers are either of one colour or else, if of two colours, these are not so clearly defined and strongly contrasted as those of pansies. Both pansies and violas are subdivided into two groups - exhibition and bedding. The former are characterized by the size and quality of the flowers, while the latter are freer flowering and of more compact habit.

458. Soil and Situation All delight in a deep, cool, rather rich soil. Dig thoroughly and work in animal manure (42) or compost (43) freely. Peat or leafmould can be employed to improve moisture-holding qualities of light soil. A partially shaded position, but not beneath large trees, gives the best results, but all are adaptable.

459. Planting This is done in mid- and late spring. For bedding, plants are set 15-22cm (6-9in) apart; for exhibition 30cm (1ft) apart. Other details are the same as for herbaceous plants (445).

460. Cultural Routine For bedding, it is only necessary to remove faded flowers and keep down weeds. For exhibition, each plant is restricted to one or two main stems at a time. These are replaced, when old, with young shoots. Selected growths are tied to short stakes, and plants are fed freely during the summer months with weak liquid manure (49) or a general garden fertilizer (96). Syringe with a good systematic insecticide to keep down greenfly. For other foes, see Section 8.

461. Propagation Bedding violas and pansies are usually raised from seed sown in a warm greenhouse in late winter, in a frame in early spring or outdoors in late spring. Early seedlings will flower the same year, late seedlings the following year. When grown in this way the plants are generally discarded after flowering as many may die from soil-borne diseases in winter and those that survive are apt to get straggly. However, this does not apply to *Viola cornuta, V. gracilis* and their varieties which will usually survive for years.

Specially selected exhibition varieties are increased by cuttings taken from late summer to mid-autumn. A few selected plants are cut back almost to the roots in mid – late summer and a little sifted potting compost (497) worked around them. Young shoots form freely, and these are severed to the base when about 5cms (2in) in length and inserted 1cm ($\frac{1}{2}$in) deep and 5cm (2in) apart in sandy soil in a frame. Once rooted, the frame lights will be required only during frosty weather or heavy rain.

VIOLETS

462. Types of Violet There are two main groups, the Parma violets, with double flowers, and the singles. These latter may be further split up into 'hardy' for flowering outdoors in winter, and 'large flowered' for flowering in frames. A few singles have petaloid centres to the blooms and are termed 'semi-double'.

463. Soil and Situation A cool, rich, rather heavy soil suits all violets best and they like a sheltered position shaded from the noonday sun. Manure or compost can be used freely in the preparation of the summer quarters (42), (43).

464. Propagation New stock should be raised every year, either from cuttings, taken in late summer to early autumn or by offsets (young rooted pieces) pulled from old clumps in early – mid-spring. Violet cuttings are prepared from the ends of runners, but in other ways are made, inserted, and treated in exactly the same manner as those of violas or pansies (461).

465. Cultural Routine Rooted cuttings or offsets are planted out in early – mid-spring, singles 30cm (1ft) apart in rows 45cm (18in) apart, doubles 16cm (6in) apart in rows 30cm (1ft) apart. Water in freely if weather is dry. Subsequently keep hoed, feed with dilute liquid manure (49) frequently during the summer and spray with derris (644) or malathion (651) occasionally to keep down red spider.

466. Frame Culture Make up beds of loamy soil, with plenty of leaf-mould or peat and a little sharp sand, to within 15-22cm (6-9in) of the glass. Transfer clumps to these in early autumn with large balls of roots and soil and plant so that leaves are just touching. Ventilate freely at first, more sparingly as weather becomes cold. Water moderately. Stir soil occasionally with a pointed stick.

ROSES

467. Types The principal types of roses grown for garden display are large-flowered, cluster-flowered, shrub, climber and rambler. Large-flowered bush roses, formerly called hybrid teas, produce the finest individual flowers but cluster-flowered bush roses, formerly called floribundas, produce the greatest quantity of bloom. These and the so-called perpetual-flowering climbers flower in flushes from early summer to early autumn. Most ramblers and some shrub roses flower only once each sum-

mer. There are also polyantha pompon roses of bushy habit with large clusters of small rosette flowers like those of ramblers, and miniature roses, which may be anything from 15-35cm (6-15in) high with small leaves and flowers.

Bush roses branch from ground level. Standard roses have a head of branches on a bare main stem 90-120cm (3-4ft) in height. These are especially useful in giving a second tier of flowers above bush roses. Climbers and ramblers have long, whippy stems which need to be tied to supports such as wires, trellis work, arches, pergolas, pillars, screens or walls. Ramblers produce small to medium-sized flowers in large clusters and most have a rather short flowering season in mid- and late summer. Climbers have flowers of various types and sizes. Some are more or less continuous flowering and some flower once only each summer. Shrub roses branch from ground level but are bigger than large- or cluster-flowered bush roses and more suitable for planting as individual specimens or for mixing with other shrubs than for massing in beds together.

468. Soil and Situation All like an open situation, though most will tolerate some shade. They like a well-cultivated, rich soil. Animal manure or compost may be dug in at 50kg to 6·5 square metres (1cwt to 8yd^2) and bonemeal at 130-200g per square metre (4-6oz per yd^2). Turves, dug in grass side downwards, are very useful. Lime is not required; excess lime causes yellowing of the foliage (known as chlorosis).

469. Planting Mid – late autumn is the best planting time, though work can be continued during any open weather until early – mid-spring. Container-grown roses can be planted at any time. Plant in wide, rather deep holes with roots spread outwards and downwards.

The soil mark on the stems gives best indication as to correct depth; it should be just covered. Other planting details are the same as for trees and shrubs (475). All standards must be securely staked.

470. Pruning After planting, all roses, except climbing 'sports', must be pruned severely. Cut strong growths to within three dormant growth buds of soil level (or the main stem in standards of all types), weaker growths to one or two buds and remove thin shoots altogether. Climbing 'sports' which always have the word 'Climbing' before their name, eg Climbing Etoile de Hollande, should have strong growths shortened by one-third, medium growths by two-thirds, weak growths removed. In subsequent years, pruning will vary according to type and requirements. These 'sports' arise spontaneously from bush varieties which they resemble in size and colour of flowers. They differ in their much more vigorous growth and most do not flower as freely as their parent varieties.

LARGE-FLOWERED BUSH ROSES are pruned most severely. First of all old, diseased, damaged, very thin, or worn-out branches are removed completely. Then strong young growths are shortened to between two and four dormant buds and medium growths to one or two buds. This work is best done during early spring or early – mid-spring in very cold gardens. The severest pruning is required for exhibition work; lighter pruning for garden decoration. After first flowering in summer, faded blooms are removed with two-thirds of their stems.

CLUSTER-FLOWERED BUSH ROSES are pruned at the same time and in a similar manner to large-flowered types, etc, but less severely. Strong growths may be left with six or eight buds, medium three or four beds, weak one or two.

POLYANTHA POMPONS AND MINIA-TURES are also pruned in early spring. Remove thin, weak, and worn-out growths and then shorten remaining stems by about half.

CLIMBING SPORTS are so known because they have been derived as 'sports' (ie chance variations from the normal type) from bush roses. They are pruned at the same time as large-flowered types. Shorten strong growths by almost one-quarter, medium growths by one-half, weak by two-thirds or more. An occasional sturdy shoot may be cut back to within 30cm (1ft) of ground level to maintain basal growth.

RAMBLERS make a great deal of new growth from the base and are pruned as soon as possible after flowering, when the old flowering stems are cut right out to make way for young growth.

Weeping standards are produced by growing rambler roses on a long base stem so that their flexible stems hang down all round. They are pruned like other ramblers, but rather more severely. Growths retained are tied spirally downwards on crinoline-like wire trainers fixed to stakes.

CLIMBERS other than climbing sports are pruned moderately in late winter or early spring when all old, diseased and worn-out stems are removed and good young stems shortened from a third to two-thirds according to the room available.

SHRUB ROSES can be pruned at any time from mid-autumn to early spring. They only require thinning, and particularly the removal of old, diseased and worn-out stems.

Make all cuts cleanly just above growth buds. On bushes and standards these should point outwards, away from the centre of the tree. Suckers must be cut out as soon as noted from roses budded on a stock (472), but not from those raised from cuttings. Note that in standard and half-standard roses the main stem is formed by the stock and therefore any growths which appear on this below the head of branches will be suckers. Note also that some ramblers produce strong basal growths which must not be mistaken for suckers.

471. Cultural Routine Mulch with well-rotted manure (42) or compost (43) each spring at about 50kg to 10 square metres (1cwt to 12yd^2) and fork in later. A mulch of long grass clippings may be maintained throughout the summer; it assists growth and keeps down black spot. Use a good rose fertilizer (94) or a general garden fertilizer (95) in mid-spring. Garden roses will require no further feeding, but exhibition roses may be fed with liquid manure (49) or a general garden fertilizer (95) occasionally during the summer. Exhibition roses are also disbudded, ie side flower buds are removed at an early stage and only the terminal bud on each stem is allowed to mature.

It is advisable to spray occasionally between late spring and early autumn with a fungicide and an insecticide to keep pests and diseases under control. For further information on this subject, see Section 8, 'Pests, Diseases and Weeds'.

472. Propagation Rambler roses, shrubs, and some vigorous bushes can be increased by cuttings 30-35cm (1ft-15in) in length prepared from well-ripened young growths in mid- or late autumn. Sever each beneath a joint and insert 10cm (4in) deep in rather sandy soil and sheltered position outdoors. Cuttings should be rooted and ready for removal to flowering quarters by the following autumn.

Most choice varieties of other types are propagated by budding. In the main, details are the same as for budding apples (201), but for bush roses buds are inserted just below soil level where stem and root join. Soil is scraped away immediately before budding to allow this to be done.

Brier stems which are intended for use as root stocks for standards are allowed to form side growths at the height desired for the head of branches, about 100cm (3$\frac{1}{2}$ft) for full standards, 75cm (2$\frac{1}{2}$ft) for half-standards, and one bud is inserted near the base of each such shoot. Buds are inserted direct on to the main stem of rugosa standard stocks at the required height. Whichever stock is used, it is usual to have three buds per standard.

Budding is carried out from early summer until early autumn while the bark peels readily from the wood. Buds are cut from half-ripened young shoots. A test is to break off the thorns. They should snap off cleanly but have a moist scar. Stocks are left unpruned until early spring following budding, when all growth is cut off about 8cm (3in) above the bud. This final 8cm (3in) is cut off a month or so later when the bud has started into growth.

Numerous stocks are used, including brier, rugosa, Manetti, laxa, and multiflora. The two first are the commonest. Brier gives long life, but rugosa makes a big plant more rapidly. Briers for bush stocks are usually raised from seed sown outdoors in early spring, but can also be reared from cuttings treated like those of garden roses. Rugosa should always be raised from cuttings. Standard brier stems are cut with roots attached from hedgerows and thickets in autumn.

Roses can also be raised from seed, but in practice this method is adopted only for the 'fairy' roses (*Rosa lawranceana*) species and when raising new varieties. Ripe hips are gathered in the autumn and placed in shallow seed trays filled with sand. These are stood in the open and exposed to frost. In early spring the hips and sand are rubbed between the palms of the hand, to separate the seeds, and then the whole contents of the tray are sown thinly in drills 1cm ($^1/_2$in) deep and 60cm (2ft) apart in the open. Seedlings are not disturbed until they have flowered.

TREES, SHRUBS, AND CLIMBERS (HARDY)

473. Description All plants of fully woody character that can be grown outdoors summer and winter. Some varieties are evergreen, ie retain their foliage throughout the winter, others are deciduous, ie lose their foliage in autumn. There are also half-hardy and tender kinds which can be grown by enthusiasts in a greenhouse (526), (527).

474. Soil and Situation Requirements are very varied. Kinds may be found for practically every conceivable soil and position. (See tables 479, 480, 481). Ground must always be well dug prior to planting. If believed to be poor, it may be enriched with moderate quantities of organic manure (42), compost (43) and slow-acting fertilizers such as bonemeal (57) and hoof and horn meal (60). Little beyond surface cultivation will be possible once trees and shrubs are established.

475. Planting Deciduous trees and shrubs, with one exception, may be planted at any time while bare of leaves, roughly from late autumn to early spring. The exception is magnolia, deciduous forms of which are best planted in mid – late spring. Evergreen conifers, eg pines, firs, spruces, cedars, junipers, cypresses, etc, may be planted at the same time as deciduous shrubs. Late autumn and early spring are usually the most favourable months. Other evergreen trees and shrubs should be transplanted in mid-autumn, or mid – late spring, not in winter, though container-grown trees and shrubs can be planted at any time provided the ground is not frozen or waterlogged.

Plant in wide, rather shallow holes so that roots can be spread out fully and the uppermost covered with 5-8cm (2-3in) of soil. Work fine soil between the roots and make thoroughly firm. Stake and tie all newly planted trees securely, also large bushes. Water freely if the soil is dry. Evergreens moved in the spring should be syringed nightly with water if the weather is hot. Screens of plastic, mesh or sacking, hurdles, or evergreen boughs will help if the weather is windy. Roots must not be damaged unnecessarily, nor allowed to dry.

Certain shrubs, eg brooms, *Berberis darwinii*, and *Cupressus macrocarpa*, resent root disturbance at any time and are usually supplied in containers. From these they may be planted at any time, early autumn and spring being the most favourable. Similar remarks apply to most climbing shrubs such as clematis, jasmine, and honeysuckle. Remove the container carefully and plant with ball of soil and roots intact.

Edging box is sold by the metre or yard as measured along the rows in the nursery beds. The plants are divided and replanted 10cm (4in) apart so that they occupy approximately three times the room, ie 1 metre of purchased box edging will plant 3 metres.

476. Cultural Routine Surface hoeing to keep down weeds and light forking in the autumn or winter are the only attentions required by established trees and shrubs. For the first few years grass should not be allowed to grow over the roots. Later the ground may be grassed over if desired. Trees and shrubs can be fed with a good compound fertilizer (95) or a mulch of organic manure (42), or compost (43), either applied in spring.

For treatment of suckers see (478).

477. Pruning Most trees, shrubs, and climbers require little regular pruning, but sometimes it is essential to check growth to keep plants within bounds or prevent overcrowding. All diseased or damaged branches must be removed. In general, trees and shrubs which flower before midsummer are best pruned immediately the flowers fade; those which bloom after that date are pruned in late winter or early spring. All cuts should be made cleanly either close to a main branch or just above a growth bud or side branch. Large wounds should be coated with a proprietary wound dressing.

Established wisterias are summer and winter pruned. Side growths are cut back to five leaves in midsummer and further shortened to one or two buds in late autumn.

Evergreen shrubs grown for their foliage, also evergreen hedges, should not be cut in winter. Hard pruning and topping, when necessary, is best done in late spring. Trimming may be carried out at any time during the summer. Deciduous hedges may be trimmed during the summer but any hard cutting is best left until winter.

For further details see tables (479), (480), (481), and (482).

478. Propagation Many kinds can be increased by cuttings prepared during mid – late summer from half-ripened young shoots, and autumn cuttings prepared during mid – late autumn from fully ripened young shoots. Both types may either be severed immediately beneath a joint or be pulled off with a heel of older wood which is then trimmed up closely. Clematis cuttings are severed between joints.

SUMMER CUTTINGS must be rooted quickly or they will flag and die. They are smaller than autumn cuttings, varying from 3–10cm (1–4in) in length according to the nature of growth. Insert in very sandy soil or pure silver sand in a frame or under mist, and give no ventilation until they are rooted, except that the light is lifted and wiped daily, and returned immediately. Water freely and dispense with shading so far as possible, but do not allow severe flagging. Root-forming hormones (102) may be used to hasten rooting. When the cuttings start to grow, ventilation is given, and a few weeks later they are potted singly in ordinary potting compost (497) and slowly accustomed to normal atmospheric conditions.

AUTUMN CUTTINGS do not flag so readily and can root comparatively slowly. They will be from 10–35cm (4–15in) in length and are treated exactly like cuttings of blackcurrants or other fruit bushes (250). Choice varieties, particularly evergreens, may be inserted in a frame, but should be ventilated fairly freely except during severe weather.

Many shrubs and climbers, especially those with pliable branches that can be bent to soil level, can be increased by LAYERING. This is done in the spring or autumn. One- or two-year-old branches or vines are most suitable. Slit half-way through at a joint (with clematis between joints) where the shoot touches the ground, and peg this portion firmly to the soil or weight with a stone. Cover with more soil and water thoroughly if dry. Tie the extremity of the shoot to a stake. Roots will be formed in anything from three to fifteen months, after which the layer can be severed from the parent plant and transferred to new quarters at the normal planting season (475).

AIR LAYERING is another form of layering and is done without bringing the shoots to ground level. An incision is made in the branch or stem to be layered and the cut is dusted with hormone rooting powder. Moist sphagnum moss is placed around the cut and enclosed in a sleeve of polythene film, tightly tied at each end. Roots are formed into the moss and when there are plenty of these the layer is severed and, after removal of the polythene, is potted or planted. Air layering can be done at any time but is usually most effective in spring or early summer.

Some choice varieties of trees and shrubs, notably ornamental cherries, plums, crab apples, double-flowered hawthorns, lilacs, and rhododendrons, are GRAFTED or BUDDED on to suitable stocks. The methods in general are the same as those for fruit trees (196), (197), (200), (201), but rhododendrons are usually grafted in a warm greenhouse. Clematises are raised commercially in the same way, but cuttings or layers produce sturdier plants.

SUCKERS can be detached with roots attached at the normal planting season (475), provided the shrub is not grafted or budded (see above). If it is, the sucker will be from the stock and will not reproduce

the garden shrub grafted upon it. Such suckers must be traced to their source and removed or they may choke the plant. This can be done at any time of the year.

Almost all trees and shrubs can be raised from SEED, but results are sometimes unreliable, especially with choice garden forms and hybrids, as seedlings may differ considerably from their parents. Seeds of the choicest kinds should be sown in well-drained pans filled with ordinary seed compost (493), and germinated in a cool greenhouse or frame. Seeds can be covered with their own depth of soil. The commoner varieties can be sown in drills 0·5-2·5cm ($\frac{1}{4}$-1in) deep made outdoors in early – mid-spring. Seedlings are transplanted, when large enough to handle, at the normal planting season (475). They should be placed 10 or 15cm apart each way in a nursery bed to grow on until big enough for removal to permanent quarters. Kinds that are difficult to transplant (475) should be potted. Berries and other fleshy fruits should be treated like rose hips (472).

Layering. If the tips of young branches are pegged into the soil as shown they will soon form roots and can be detached from the parent plant.

479. Table of Hardy Deciduous Trees and Shrubs

Pruning key

1 No regular pruning required. Remove badly placed, damaged or diseased branches in late winter.

2 Cut back severely in late winter.
3 Cut back severely in mid-spring.
4 Shorten flowering branches to growth buds or side growths after flowering.

Name	Height m	Height ft	Ornamental value
Acer (Maple)	1·8–1·2	6–40	foliage
Aesculus (Horse chestnut)	9–12	30–40	white or pink flowers
Ailanthus	18	60	foliage
Amelanchier	7	25	white flowers
Artemisia abrotanum	1	3	silver foliage
Azalea (except *amoena* and *indica*)	1·2–2·2	4–8	flowers of many colours
Berberis	1–2·2	3–8	flowers and foliage
Betula (Silver birch)	12	40	foliage and silver bark
Buddleia globosa	3–3·5	10–12	orange flowers
Buddleia davidii	1·8–3·5	6–12	purple flowers
Caryopteris	0·6–1	2–3	lavender flowers
Catalpa	9	30	foliage
Ceanothus azureus and hybrids	1·5–2·2	5–8	blue or pink flowers
Ceratostigma (Plumbago)	0·6–1	2–3	blue flowers
Cercis (Judas tree)	4·5–6	15–20	purple flowers
Chaenomeles	1·8–3·5	6–10	scarlet, pink, or white flowers
Chimonanthus (Winter sweet)	2–2·7	7–9	yellow flowers
Colutea	2·7	9	yellow flowers, inflated pods
Cornus alba spaethii	1·5–2	5–7	foliage and bark
Cornus kousa	3·5–5	12–16	cream flowers
Corylus	3	10	foliage
Cotoneaster (some are evergreen)	0·15–4·5	½–15	scarlet or black berries
Crataegus (Hawthorn)	4·5–6	15–20	flowers and berries
Cytisus (Broom)	0·3–3·5	1–12	flowers of various colours
Daphne mezereum	1	3	purple flowers
Deutzia	1·2–2·2	4–8	white or purple flowers
Enkianthus	1·5–2	5–7	creamy flowers
Eucryphia	3·5–6	12–20	white flowers
Euonymus europaeus	1·8–2·2	6–8	orange and red fruits
Exochorda	1·8–2	6–7	white flowers
Fagus (Beech)	18	60	foliage
Forsythia	1·8–2·2	6–8	yellow flowers
Fuschsia (hardy varieties)	0·3–1·5	1–5	variously coloured flowers
Genista	0·6–3	2–10	yellow flowers
Ginkgo	9–18	30–60	foliage
Gleditschia	4·5–6	15–20	foliage
Hamamelis	1·8–3·5	6–12	yellow flowers

5 Shorten flowering branches nearly to base after flowering.

6 Remove faded flower trusses.

7 Thin out oldest growths every third or fourth year.

8 Thin out moderately and shorten young growths a little in late winter.

Flowering or fruiting seasons	Position to plant	Soil	Pruning
	sun	ordinary	1
late spr – mid-sum	sun	ordinary	1
	sun	ordinary	1 or 2
mid-spr	sun	ordinary	1
	sun	light	1
late spr – early sum	sun or shade	peaty	6
late spr – early sum	sun	ordinary	7
	sun or semi-shade	ordinary	1
late spr – early sum	sun	ordinary	1
mid-sum – early aut	sun	ordinary	3
early aut – mid-aut	sun	light	3
	sun	ordinary	1 or 2
mid-sum – early aut	sun	ordinary	3
late sum – early aut	sun	light	3
late spr	sun	light	1
early spr – late spr	sun or shade	ordinary	5
mid-win – late win	sun or semi-shade	ordinary	5
early sum – early aut	sun	light	1
	sun or shade	ordinary	1 or 2
late spr – early sum	sun	ordinary	1
	sun or shade	ordinary	1
mid-aut – early win	sun or semi-shade	ordinary	1
late spr – early sum/ mid-aut – early win	sun	ordinary	1
late spr	sun	light	5
late win – early spr	sun or semi-shade	ordinary, moist	1
late spr – mid-sum	sun	ordinary	4
mid-spr – late spr	shade	peaty	1
	semi-shade	peaty	1
early aut – late aut	sun	ordinary	1
late spr	sun	ordinary	1
	sun	ordinary	1
early spr – mid-spr	sun or shade	ordinary	5
early sum – mid-aut	sun or semi-shade	ordinary	3
late spr – early sum	sun	light	1
	sun	ordinary	1
	sun	light	1
early win – late win	sun or shade	ordinary	1

▶

Name	Height m	Height ft	Ornamental value
Hedysarum	1·2	4	magenta flowers
Hibiscus	2·2	8	flowers of various colours
Hippophaë (Sea buckthorn)	4·5	15	orange berries (on female)
Hydrangea macrophylla	1–1·8	3–6	blue, pink, or white flowers
Hydrangea paniculata	1–1·8	3–6	white flowers
Hypericum patulum	1–1·5	3–5	yellow flowers
Kerria	1·8–2·2	6–8	yellow flowers
Koelreuteria	4·5–6	15–20	yellow flowers
Kolkwitzia	1·8–2·2	6–8	pink flowers
Laburnum	4·5–6	15–20	yellow flowers
Leycesteria	1·8	6	claret flowers
Liquidambar	9–15	30–50	autumn foliage
Magnolia (except grandiflora)	1·8–6	6–20	white to purple flowers
Malus (Crab apple)	4·5–8	15–25	white to crimson flowers, followed by fruits
Metasequoia	12–18	40–60	foliage
Perowskia	1·2	4	blue flowers
Philadelphus (Mock orange)	1–3·5	3–12	white flowers
Populus (Poplar)	12–18	40–60	foliage
Potentilla fruticosa	0·6–1·2	2–4	yellow flowers
Prunus (Almond, Cherry, Plum, Peach)	4·5–9	15–30	pink or white flowers
Pyrus salicifolia	4·5–6	15–20	foliage
Quercus (Oak)	6–18	20–60	foliage
Rhus (Sumach)	1·8–3	6–10	autumn foliage
Ribes sanguineum (Flowering currant)	2	7	pink to carmine
Robinia (False acacia)	9–12	30–40	white flowers
Rubus	1·2–2·3	4–8	white or rose flowers
Salix (Willow)	2·3–12	8–40	catkins and foliage
Sambucus	2·3–3·5	8–12	foliage
Sorbaria	1·8–3	6–10	white flowers
Sorbus (Mountain ash, Whitebeam etc)	4·5–9	15–30	flowers and berries
Spartium (Spanish broom)	2·7	9	yellow flowers
Spiraea (early flowering)	1·2–1·8	4–6	white
Spiraea (summer flowering)	1–2·3	3–8	cream to crimson
Symphoricarpos (Snowberry)	1·8	6	white berries
Syringa (Lilac)	1·8–4·5	6–15	white to purple flowers
Tamarix	1·5–3	5–10	white or pink flowers
Taxodium	9–12	30–40	foliage
Tilia (Lime)	18–24	60–80	foliage
Ulmus (Elm)	6–18	20–60	foliage
Viburnum	1·5–3	5–10	white or pink flowers
Weigela (Diervilla)	2	7	white to crimson flowers

Flowering or fruiting seasons	Position to plant	Soil	Pruning
early sum – early aut	sun	light	1
early aut – mid aut	sun	ordinary	1
early aut – late aut	sun	light	1
mid sum – late sum	sun or shade	ordinary	6
late sum – early aut	sun or shade	ordinary	2
mid sum – early aut	sun or semi-shade	ordinary	8
mid spr – late spr	sun or shade	ordinary	5
mid sum – late sum	sun	ordinary	1
early sum	sun	ordinary	4
late spr – early sum	sun	ordinary	1
mid sum – early aut	sun or shade	ordinary	5
early aut – late aut	sun	ordinary	1
early spr – mid spr mid spr – late spr	sun	peaty	1
early aut – late aut	sun	ordinary	1
	sun	ordinary, moist	1
late sum – early aut	sun	light	3
early sum	sun or semi-shade	ordinary	4
	sun	ordinary	1
mid sum – early aut	sun	light	1 or 2
early spr – mid spr	sun	ordinary	1
	sun	ordinary	1
	sun	ordinary	1
	sun	light	1
early spr – mid spr	sun or shade	ordinary	4
late spr – early sum	sun	light	1
mid sum – early aut	sun or shade	ordinary	5
late win – early spr	sun	ordinary, moist	1 or 2
	sun or shade	ordinary, moist	2
mid sum – early aut	sun	ordinary	2 or 8
late spr – early sum, early aut – mid aut	sun	ordinary	1
early sum – early aut	sun	light	5
mid spr – late spr	sun or semi-shade	ordinary	8
early sum – late sum	sun or semi-shade	ordinary	2
early aut – early win	sun or shade	ordinary	8
late spr – early sum	sun	ordinary	6
mid sum – early aut	sun	ordinary	1 or 2
	sun	ordinary, moist	1
	sun	ordinary	1
	sun	ordinary	1
mid spr – early sum	sun	ordinary	1
late spr – early sum	sun	ordinary	4

480. Table of Hardy Climbing Plants

Name	Ornamental value	Flowering or fruiting months
Ampelopsis (Parthenocissus)	foliage	
Azara★	yellow flowers	late win
Campsis	orange-scarlet flowers	late sum − early aut
Ceanothus★ (evergreen vars)	blue flowers	late spr − early sum
Celastrus	yellow and scarlet fruits	early aut − late aut
Clematis	flowers of various colours	mid spr − early aut
Cotoneaster horizontalis	scarlet berries	early aut − early win
Cotoneaster microphylla★	scarlet berries	early aut − early win
Chaenomeles speciosa japonica	scarlet, pink or white flowers	late win − mid-spr
Escallonia★	white to crimson flowers	early spr − mid-spr
Forsythia suspensa	yellow flowers	early spr − late spr
Hedera★ (Ivy)	foliage	
Humulus (Hop)	foliage	
Hydrangea petiolaris	white flowers	early sum − mid-spr
Jasminum nudiflorum (Winter jasmine)	yellow flowers	late aut − late win
Jasminum officinale (Summer jasmine)	white flowers	early sum − early aut
Kerria	yellow flowers	mid-spr − late spr
Lonicera (Honeysuckle)	yellow or red flowers	early sum − late sum
Magnolia grandiflora★	white flowers	mid-sum − early aut
Polygonum baldschuanicum (Russian vine)	pinkish-white flowers	mid-sum − early aut
Pyracantha★	orange or scarlet berries	early aut − late aut
Solanum crispum	lavender flowers	mid-sum − early aut
Vitis (Vine, Virginian creeper)	foliage	
Wisteria	mauve flowers	late spr − early sum

★ Evergreen foliage

Position	Support	Pruning
sun or shade	wall	Thin in late winter when overcrowded.
sun or shade	wall	No regular pruning. Shorten straggly growths in mid – late spring.
sun	wall	Thin in late winter when overcrowded.
sun	wall	Shorten flowering growths when flowers fade.
sun	screen, low roof	Thin in late winter when overcrowded.
sun	trellis, pole, arch, etc	*Clematis jackmannii* and varieties, cut back young vines to one pair of eyes of main vines in late winter; or cut to within 30cm/1ft of ground level. *C. montana*, thin lightly after flowering. Other kinds, thin out oldest vines and shorten young vines a little in late winter.
sun or shade	wall	Thin in late winter when overcrowded.
sun or shade	wall	No regular pruning. Shorten straggly growths in mid – late spring.
sun or shade	wall	Shorten flowering growths when flowers fade.
sun	wall	Shorten flowering growths when flowers fade.
sun or shade	wall	Shorten flowering growths when flowers fade.
sun or shade	wall	No regular pruning. Shorten straggly growths in mid – late spring.
sun	trellis, pole, arch, etc	Thin in late winter when overcrowded.
sun	wall	Thin in late winter when overcrowded.
sun or shade	wall	Shorten flowering growths when flowers fade.
sun	trellis, arch, etc	Thin in late winter when overcrowded.
sun or shade	wall	Shorten flowering growths when flowers fade.
sun	trellis, pole, arch, etc	Thin in late winter when overcrowded.
sun	wall	No regular pruning. Shorten straggly growths in mid – late spring.
sun	trellis, pergola, tree	Thin in late winter when overcrowded.
sun or shade	wall	Shorten flowering growths when flowers fade.
sun	wall or trellis	Thin in late winter when overcrowded.
sun or shade	pergola, trellis	Thin in late winter when overcrowded.
sun	wall	Shorten side growths to five leaves in mid-summer; two dormant buds in late autumn.

481. Table of Hardy Evergreen Trees and Shrubs

Name	Height m	Height ft	Ornamental value
Andromeda	0·5	1½	pink flowers
Arbutus unedo	4·5-8	15-25	white flowers, orange fruits
Aucuba	2	7	foliage and scarlet berries
Azalea (evergreen vars)	1	3	flowers of various colours
Azara	2·5-6	8-20	yellow flowers
Berberis (some species) are deciduous)	1-3	3-10	yellow or orange flowers
Buxus (Box)	0·3-4·5	1-15	foliage
Calluna (Ling)	0·5-1	1½-3	white to crimson flowers
Ceanothus (evergreen vars)	1·8-3	6-10	blue flowers
Cedrus (Cedar)	18-20	60-70	foliage
Chamaecyparis	0·15-16	½-50	foliage
Choisya	1·5-1·8	5-6	white flowers
Cistus	0·6-1·2	2-4	flowers of various colours
Cotoneaster (some are deciduous)	1·8	6	scarlet berries
Cryptomeria	4·5-16	15-50	foliage
Cupressus	18	60	foliage
Daboëcia	0·6	2	purple or white flowers
Elaeagnus	2·3-3·5	8-12	foliage
Erica (Heather)	0·15-1·8	½-6	white to crimson flowers
Escallonia	1·5-3	5-10	white to crimson flowers
Euonymus	0·3-3	1-10	foliage
Garrya	1·8-2·3	6-8	green catkins
Gaultheria	0·15-1	½-3	white flowers, red berries
Hypericum calycinum	0·15-0·3	½-1	yellow flowers
Ilex (Holly)	12	40	foliage and berries (on female)
Juniperus	0·3-4·5	1-15	foliage
Kalmia	1·8	6	pink flowers
Lavandula (Lavender)	0·3-1	1-3	lavender flowers
Mahonia	1-1·5	3-5	yellow flowers
Magnolia grandiflora	6	20	white flowers
Olearia	1·2-2·3	4-8	white flowers
Osmanthus	1·8-2·3	6-8	white flowers
Pernettya	1-1·2	3-4	coloured berries
Phlomis fruticosa	1	3	yellow flowers
Picea (Spruce)	0·6-18	2-60	foliage
Pieris	1·8-2·3	6-8	white flowers
Pinus (Pine)	1·8-18	6-60	foliage
Prunus laurocerasus (Laurel)	6	20	white flowers
Prunus lusitanica (Portugal laurel)	4·5-6	15-20	white flowers

Season of interest	Position to plant	Soil
late spr	sun or semi-shade	peaty, moist
mid–aut – late spr	sun or shade	ordinary
all year	sun or shade	ordinary
late spr – early sum	sun or semi-shade	lime free
late win	sun or shade, sheltered	ordinary
mid–spr – early sum	sun or shade	ordinary
all year	sun or shade	ordinary
late spr – early aut	sun	lime free
late spr – mid–sum	sun, sheltered	ordinary
all year	sun	ordinary
all year	sun or semi-shade	ordinary
mid–spr – late spr, early aut	sun, sheltered	ordinary
early sum – mid–sum	sun, sheltered	ordinary
aut	sun or semi-shade	ordinary
all year	sun	ordinary
all year	sun or semi-shade	ordinary
mid–sum – mid–aut	sun or semi-shade	lime free
all year	sun	ordinary
all year	sun	lime free
early spr – mid–sum	sun	ordinary
all year	sun or shade	ordinary
late aut – late win	sun, sheltered	ordinary
late spr and late sum	shade	lime free
mid–sum – early aut	sun or shade	ordinary
all year	sun or shade	ordinary
all year	sun	ordinary
early sum	sun or semi-shade	lime free
mid–sum – late sum	sun	light
late win – mid–spr	sun or shade	ordinary
mid–sum – early aut	sun	lime free, sheltered
mid–sum – late sum	sun	ordinary, sheltered
mid–spr	sun	ordinary
aut	sun	peaty
early sum – mid–sum	sun	light
all year	sun	ordinary
early spr – mid–spr	sun or semi-shade	peaty
all year	sun	light
mid spr – late spr	sun or shade	ordinary
early sum	sun or shade	ordinary

Name	Height m	Height ft	Ornamental value
Pyracantha	1·8-2·3	6-8	orange or scarlet berries
Rhododendron	0·3-6	1-20	flowers of various colours
Rosmarinus (Rosemary)	0·3-1·5	1-5	blue flowers
Ruscus (Butcher's broom)	0·6-1	2-3	red berries
Santolina	0·6	2	grey foliage, yellow flowers
Senecio	0·6-1	2-3	yellow flowers
Sequoiadendron (Wellingtonia)	16-32	50-100	foliage
Skimmia	0·3-1	1-3	scarlet berries (on female in *S. japonica*)
Taxus (Yew)	1-4·5	3-15	foliage
Thuja	1-18	3-60	foliage
Ulex (Gorse)	1·2-1·8	4-6	yellow flowers
Viburnum tinus	2·3-3	8-10	white flowers
Vinca	0·15-0·3	½-1	blue flowers
Yucca	1-2·3	3-8	white flowers

NOTE When grown as bushes in the open none of the above requires regular pruning. If they become too large or overcrowded, they may be thinned in late spring or, if in flower then, as

482. Table of Shrubs for Hedges

Name	Height m	Height ft	Distance apart for planting m	ft
Beech	1·8-3	6-10	0·3-0·5	1-1½
Berberis darwinii and *B. stenophylla*	1·8-2·3	6-8	0·5-0·6	1½-2
Box	0·6-1·8	1-6	0·3-0·5	1-1½
Chamaecyparis	1·8-3	6-10	0·6-0·8	2-2½
Cotoneaster simonsii	1·5-2·3	5-8	0·5	1½
Cupressocyparis	1·8-3·5	6-12	0·6-1	2-3
Escallonia	1·2-1·8	4-6	0·5-0·8	1½-2½
Euonymus japonicus	1-2·3	3-8	0·5	1½
Holly	1·2-3·5	4-12	0·5-0·6	1½-2
Hornbeam	1·8-3	6-10	0·5-0·6	1½-2
Laurel (cherry)	1·8-3	6-10	0·5-0·6	1½-2
Laurel (Portugal)	1·8-3·5	6-12	0·6-1	2-3
Lonicera nitida	1-1·5	3-5	0·3-0·5	1-1½
Myrobalan plum	1·5-3	5-10	0·3-0·6	1-2
Privet (golden)	1-1·5	3-5	0·3-0·5	1-1½
Privet (green)	1-2·3	3-8	0·3-0·5	1-1½
Quick (hawthorn)	1·2-2·3	4-8	0·2	¾
Thuja	1·8-3·5	6-12	0·6-1	2-3
Yew	1-3·5	3-12	0·5-0·6	1½-2

Season of interest	Position to plant	Soil
aut	sun or semi-shade	ordinary
mid-spr – mid-sum	sun or shade	lime free
late spr	sun	light
aut	shade	ordinary
mid-sum – late sum	sun	light
mid-sum	sun, sheltered	ordinary
all year	sun	ordinary
aut	sun or shade	lime free
all year	sun or shade	ordinary
all year	sun or semi-shade	ordinary
mid-spr – late spr	sun	light
late aut – late spr	sun or semi-shade	ordinary
early spr – late spr	sun or shade	ordinary
mid-sum – late sum	sun	light

soon as flowers fade. For pruning when trained against walls, etc, see 'Table of Hardy Climbers' (480).

Pruning	Remarks
Trim in summer. Head back in late winter if necessary	Retains autumn foliage.
Trim after flowering	Orange or yellow flowers.
Trim in summer. Head back in mid-spring if necessary	Very neat habit.
Trim in summer. Head back in mid-spring if necessary	There are numerous varieties.
Trim in summer. Head back in late winter if necessary	Scarlet berries.
Trim in summer. Head back in mid-spring if necessary	Very fast growing.
Trim after flowering	Rather tender.
Trim in summer. Head back in mid-spring if necessary	Some have variegated leaves.
Trim in summer. Head back in mid-spring if necessary	Slow growing.
Trim in summer. Head back in late winter if necessary	Like beech.
Trim in summer. Head back in mid-spring if necessary	Prune with secateurs.
Trim in summer. Head back in mid-spring if necessary	Makes thick hedge.
Trim in summer. Head back in mid-spring if necessary	Can be trimmed very thin.
Trim in summer. Head back in late winter if necessary	Makes thick hedge.
Trim in summer. Head back in mid-spring if necessary	Very bright colour.
Trim in summer. Head back in mid-spring if necessary	Grows anywhere.
Trim in summer. Head back in late winter if necessary	Grows anywhere.
Trim in summer. Head back in mid-spring if necessary	Like chamaecyparis.
Trim in summer. Head back in mid-spring if necessary	Slow growing.

GREENHOUSE, FRAME, AND CLOCHE

483. Types and Position There are four main types of greenhouse. A SPAN-ROOFED HOUSE has a ridge-shaped roof, both sides of which are of equal length. The roof stands on walls which may be all masonry or wood, partly or entirely glass. The height of these walls varies from about 30-170cm (1-5½ ft).

A LEAN-TO HOUSE has a roof sloping in one direction only, the back being formed by a wall. In other respects it is similar to the span-roofed type.

A THREE-QUARTER SPAN HOUSE is midway between these two types. The roof is in the form of a ridge, but one side is only about one-quarter the length of the other, and rests against a wall like the lean-to.

The fourth type is THE FORCING HOUSE OR PIT, which has a span roof coming right down to soil level. The floor is excavated about 1m (3ft) below soil level and borders may be built up on this to within a foot of the base of the glass. These houses retain warmth especially well and are useful for forcing crops under high temperatures but are not frequently used by amateur gardeners. Sometimes ordinary span-roofed houses on solid masonry walls are used as forcing houses.

Where possible, span-roofed and forcing houses should have the ridge running north and south; lean-to and three-quarter span houses should face south, the ridge running east and west. Only houses intended for ferns and certain tropical foliage plants should be in an entirely shaded place. All houses should be glazed with horticultural glass or heavy-guage polythene.

484. Temperatures These may be varied within wide limits, but roughly there are four main groupings.

Cold houses are unheated, and in winter the temperature may fall below freezing point, though the average will be in the neighbourhood of 7°C (45°F). This will rise in summer to 16°C (60°F) or considerably more with direct sun heat.

The cool house is artificially heated in winter to a minimum of 7°C (45°F), average 10°-13°C (50°-55°F). In summer it is not heated.

The temperate house has a winter minimum of 13°C (55°F) and summer minimum of 16°C (60°F) and the hothouse has a minimum of 18°C (65°F) winter and 21°C (70°F) summer. Both may need some artifical heat even in summer.

Cold houses can be used in winter only for hardy plants, but many tender plants can be grown in them during the summer. Cool and intermediate houses are the most generally serviceable for the majority of popular greenhouse plants. Hothouses are for really tender plants from tropical regions and for forcing plants into early growth or flower.

485. Heating Hot-water or central-heating boilers connected to water pipes are convenient only when the greenhouse is close to the house. It is important that the greenhouse heating system can still be operated when the heating is not on indoors. Pipes are usually accommodated at the side of the house, low down beneath the stages, if any. Sometimes in carnation houses, where heat is required more to circulate than to warm the atmosphere, the pipes are slung on brackets below the glass, midway between ridge and eaves.

Houses can also be heated directly with paraffin burners. Natural or bottled gas are popular for heating, but all produce potentially harmful gases and increase humidity. For this reason some top ventilation must be provided.

Electrical heating is very reliable and satisfactory, but comparatively costly. Ordinary domestic heaters are not satisfactory, as the source of heat is too concentrated. Low-temperature radiators, low-voltage strip heaters or fan-assisted heaters should be used. Special greenhouse installations such as soil-warming cables are made by many manufacturers of electrical equipment, and expert advice should always be obtained regarding their installation.

Thermostatic control can be applied very easily both to electrical heaters and to gas-heated boilers. The instrument is set to keep the heat of the greenhouse constant within certain limits, usually three or four degrees. Thermostatic control cannot prevent rises of temperature caused by sun heat.

486. Capacity of Electrical Heaters This is expressed in terms of the watts or kilowatts (1000 watts or units) of electricity the heater consumes. To raise the inside temperature of a 2·4 x 1·8m (8x6ft) greenhouse 14°C (25°F) above the outside temperature a 1·5kW heater is required. For a 3·6 x 2·4m (12x8ft) greenhouse a 2kW heater will ensure the same increase in temperature. All electrical installations should be fitted by a qualified contractor.

487. Staging This is essential in houses with solid side walls more than 60cm (2ft) in height and is useful in all houses in which pot plants or seedlings are to be grown. Its object is to keep plants near the glass where the light intensity is greatest and also to bring them close to hand so that they can be easily inspected, watered and tended.

Staging may be permanent or removable. If the latter, it is usually made of wood; if the former, it may be of wood, brick, or concrete. Open-slat staging is best for plants that like a dry atmosphere and free circulation of air, eg pelargoniums and perpetual-flowering carnations. Solid staging covered with clean gravel or small, sifted cinders is to be preferred for moisture-loving plants, eg tuberous-rooted begonias and gloxinias.

488. Ventilation Ventilators should be fitted in the ridge of every house - on both sides in the case of span-roofed houses – about 60cm (2ft) in depth and in total length equivalent to at least half the total length of the house. Houses with part glass and part brick or wood sides should have ventilators of large size in the glass and it is an advantage if they can have small box ventilators with hinged or sliding wooden doors in the brick walls also. Greenhouses standing on brick or wood sides only should have such box ventilators every 1m (3ft) along these walls.

The purpose of ventilation is to allow as free a current of air as possible, without severe draughts, to assist in the control of temperature and humidity. As a rule, top ventilators alone are used in winter, and then only by day when the weather is reasonably fine. They may be opened 2–3cm (1in) for three or four hours around midday, according to outside conditions. In summer, when the weather is really hot, top and side ventilators may be opened widely to let currents of air pass through the house from bottom to top. Automatic ventilator openers are available which can be adjusted to operate at required temperatures. An alternative is to use extractor fans, which can be thermostatically controlled, usually fitted high up in the end walls of small greenhouses.

In unheated or moderately heated houses it is often possible to trap enough sun heat to keep the air warm throughout the night if all ventilators are closed an hour or so before sun-down. Note that in the spring a clearing sky and falling wind towards evening is usually a warning sign of a sharp frost.

489. Atmospheric Moisture This is required in very varying degree by different plants. Cacti like a comparatively dry atmosphere, whereas most tropical plants need one that is saturated with moisture. The majority of popular greenhouse plants stand midway between these extremes. Excessive humidity will encourage mildew (667), damping off (667), and other fungal diseases. Excessive dryness will result in scorching of the leaves and stems, often mistaken for disease. Scorched leaves develop brown patches which are dry and parchment-like without any sign of mould. Ventilation usually increases the dryness of the air especially if combined with some artificial heat.

The necessary moisture is maintained in three ways: by spraying the plants themselves, by damping down the paths, walls, and stages, and by placing water in shallow evaporating trays over hot-water pipes or soil-warming cables.

Spraying must be practised only with plants known to like moisture and should be discontinued while plants are in flower or are ripening fruits. As a rule it is done in the morning when the temperature has begun to rise, but before the sun is shining fiercely. In some cases several sprayings may be required each day. Avoid spraying late in the evening, as this lowers the temperature and encourages condensed moisture on the foliage early in the morning which, in turn, causes scorching. Tepid water is to be preferred to cold.

Damping down can be done with any plants if moisture is required. Again it is advisable not to work late in the evening nor to use very cold water.

Evaporating trays are used mainly in hothouses and vineries, and have much the same effect as damping down, except that the moisture is given off night and day.

490. Watering Plants require varying quantities of water according to their nature and period of growth. In a general way plants with very small leaves, eg heaths, require less water than those with large leaves, eg caladiums, while cacti and succulents require less water than those of ordinary character. The maximum quantity of water is required while plants are in full growth and producing flowers and fruit. Most plants have a resting season when little or no water is required. It is most marked in plants with bulbous or tuberous roots, many of which can be kept completely dry for several months each year after their foliage has died down.

No hard-and-fast rules can be given regarding the quantity of water required. This will depend upon many changing factors, such as the weather, time of year, state of growth, and type of soil. It is never wise to wet the surface soil and leave lower layers dry. When water is given it must be in sufficient quantity to moisten the soil right through. If top watering is being practised with watering-can or hose, application usually should not be repeated until there are definite signs of dryness. To tell this the pot may be lifted and its weight judged, since damp soil weighs more than dry, but usually a little experience will enable the gardener to judge requirements by sight alone.

Automatic watering systems are also available of which one of the easiest to install is the capillary bench. This is a 2-3cm (1in) deep layer of sand and pea gravel on a perfectly level, water-retentive surface such as polythene film, kept constantly wet so that pot plants placed on it draw water upwards by capillary attraction as they require it. Capillary matting is also available. Various devices are available for feeding water to such beds.

Water may be applied from a watering can either with or without a rose. The rose should be used only when watering seed pans, seedlings, or freshly potted plants. The drawback is that water flows slowly, the surface becomes deceptively wet and foliage is unnecessarily splashed. Established greenhouse plants are almost invariably watered direct from the spout, which should be held close to the soil to prevent splashing.

Watering by complete immersion of the pot in a tub of water is useful for established plants which require abundant moisture, eg hydrangeas. Watering by partial immersion, ie by holding the pot or pan almost to its rim in a tub of water so that water rises from below through the drainage hole, but does not flow over the surface, is useful for seed receptacles, especially if they contain very small seedlings liable to be disturbed by top watering. Partial immersion should be continued until the surface of the soil is darkened by the rising moisture.

491. Shading Only ferns and a few foliage plants require permanent shading, but many greenhouse plants, even normally sun-loving varieties, may require temporary shading from strong sunlight in the summer. This is particularly so in small houses which are heated rapidly by the sun and may become excessively hot in summer even with maximum ventilation.

Shading is of two types, semi-permanent and temporary.

SEMI-PERMANENT SHADING is obtained by painting or spraying the glass with a proprietary shading compound. A home-made alternative is made from one part of flour to six of water mixed to a paste.

TEMPORARY SHADING is obtained with blinds of hessian or plastic netting. These are attached to rollers fixed to the outside ridge of the house so that they can be pulled down over the glass as required. As a rule such shading is needed on the sunny side only.

492. Propagating Frames Some seedlings and cuttings need a hotter or moister atmosphere than that of the greenhouse. To obtain this a propagating box or frame is used. In its simplest form this is a box of any convenient size and about 30cm (1ft) in depth placed over the hot-water pipes or heating apparatus at the warmest end of the house and covered with panes of glass. The box is half filled with sand or granulated peat in which pots containing the seeds or cuttings are plunged. The purpose of the fibre is to retain heat and moisture. More elaborate propagators and propagating frames contain their own heating or soil-warming devices.

493. Seed Raising under Glass It is not necessary to employ numerous composts for raising seeds of different plants. One good mixture will serve for all. That known as the John Innes Seed Compost (JIS for short) can be bought easily, or made as follows:

2 parts by loose bulk of medium loam.

1 part by loose bulk of good peat.

1 part by loose bulk of coarse silver sand.

To each 35 litres (bushel) of this mixture add:

50g (1$\frac{1}{2}$ oz) of superphosphate (16% phosphoric acid) (79).

25g ($\frac{3}{4}$ oz) of ground limestone or chalk.

Pass all ingredients through a 0·5cm

($^1/_4$ in) mesh sieve. It is an advantage if loam is first sterilized by steam or electricity (631). An alterntive to loam-based compost is peat-based, all-peat, or peat-substitute compost of which various brands are available.

Seeds may be sown in earthenware or plastic pans 5-8cm (2-3in) deep and of any diameter, pots, usually 10 or 12cm (4 or 5in) diameter, and in wooden boxes or plastic trays 3-5cm ($1^1/_2$ -2in) deep. All must be well supplied with drainage holes or slits, and these must be covered with crocks (broken pots), and small rubble or sphagnum moss. Make soil firm (except for pure peat compost) but do not fill within 1cm ($^1/_2$ in) of the rim. Smooth surface with a planed block of wood and scatter seeds evenly. Cover with a sprinkling of finely sifted compost. A good guide is to cover seeds with twice their own depth of soil; very fine seeds, such as those of begonia and gloxinia, are not covered at all, simply pressed into the surface. Cover seed pans with panes of glass and sheets of paper. Directly seedlings appear, remove paper. A day later tilt the glass panes on pebbles or wooden tallies, and a day or so after that remove altogether. Most seeds will germinate more rapidly if placed in a propagating frame (492), but excessive temperatures are detrimental for some seedlings and may cause damping off (667). Seeds of most popular greenhouse plants germinate well in a temperature of from 16°-21°C (60°-70°F).

Soil in which seeds are to be sown should be moist but not wet. It must not be allowed to become dry while seeds are germinating. Further water may be required and should be given by semi-immersion (490).

494. Pricking Off Almost all seedlings must be pricked off, ie transplanted to other receptacles, as soon as they can be handled conveniently. Exceptions are mainly for bulbous-rooted plants, which may be sown extra thinly and allowed to grow on undisturbed for the first year.

Prick off into compost and receptacles similar to those used for sowing (493). Seedlings are lifted carefully with a sharpened stick, singled out (except with certain annuals) and dropped into dibber holes about 5cm (2in) apart each way. A dibber the thickness of a stout pencil is used. Make soil firm round roots (but not for pure peat composts) and, finally, water freely through a fine rose. Seedlings should be shaded and given reduced ventilation for a few days until established. Subsequently, most kinds may be stood on staging or a shelf near the glass.

495. Cuttings Under Glass Greenhouse stem cuttings, like those taken outdoors (446), (478), are of three main classes, soft, half-ripe, and hard wooded. The first are prepared from young shoots of herbaceous plants or shrubs, the second and third from half-grown and fully grown shoots respectively of shrubs and half-shrubby plants only. Young cuttings must be rooted quickly. For this reason they are usually best in a propagating frame (492), and shaded until rooted. Cuttings are prepared in the same way as those of outdoor plants (446), (478). Bottom heat, ie heat coming from below through the soil (as in a propagating box), is of particular service in helping soft cuttings to root quickly. Root-forming hormones (102) may be used with the same object. Various automatic misting devices are also available and, if used, cuttings need not be shut up in a frame or propagator.

Composts for cuttings are usually very sandy and no fertilizers should be included.

496. Leaf Cuttings The leaves of certain plants, eg gloxinias, *Begonia rex*, streptocarpus, and achimenes, will root. Well-developed leaves are pegged or weighted to the surface of sandy soil in a propagating frame (492), and are kept moist and shaded. Sometimes incisions are made across the main veins. Plantlets are formed at these incisions and at the leaf base. Plantlets also form along the fronds of some ferns, eg *Polystichum angulare* and *Asplenium bulbiferum,* if these are pegged firmly to the soil round the parent plant without being detached.

497. Potting It is not necessary to make a different compost (mixture of soils) for each kind of plant since one general compost will serve for the majority of greenhouse plants. That known as the John Innes Potting Compost (or JIP.1 for short) is prepared as follows:

7 parts by loose bulk of medium loam.
3 parts by loose bulk of good peat.
2 parts by loose bulk of coarse silver sand.

To each 35 litres (bushel) of this mixture add 25g ($^3/_4$ oz) of ground limestone or chalk and 130g (4oz) of base fertilizer prepared from 2 parts by weight of superphosphate (16% phosphoric acid) (79); 2 parts by weight of hoof and horn meal (12·75% nitrogren) (57); and also 1 part by weight of sulphate of potash (78).

For many strong-growing greenhouse plants these quantities of fertilizers and chalk may be doubled when they are moved into pots larger than 11·5cm ($4^1/_2$ in) in diameter, and trebled for 20cm (8in) pots or larger. These stronger composts are often called JIP.2 and JIP.3 respectively.

The limestone or chalk may be omitted for plants known to dislike lime, eg azaleas, rhododendrons, and ericas.

Ingredients should be passed through a sieve only for the smaller plants. For final potting of chrysanthemums, etc, use it

pulled and chopped to pieces so that the largest fragments are about as big as a pullet's egg. Soil should be moist but not wet, and must be at the same temperature as the greenhouse. It is an advantage if loam is first sterilized by steam or electricity (631). Alternatively, propietary peat-based or pure peat composts are available.

Pots must be clean. New earthenware pots should be soaked to take the kiln dryness out of them. Drainage holes may be covered with crocks (pieces of broken pot) or special wire 'stoppers', but no such extra drainage should be used if pots are to stand on a capillary bench (490).

Most plants are potted just as they start to grow. Firm potting is necessary as a rule, but not for ferns, which grow best in soil only moderately consolidated, nor for plants grown in all-peat potting composts. A potting stick made from an old broom handle is used to press down the soil.

When repotting plants, do not disturb the roots unneccesarily. Tap them out of the old pot, remove drainage crocks from the bottom, and then repot.

It is seldom wise to pot direct from small into large pots. As a rule, one size increase is sufficient at first, two sizes later, eg plants in 7·5cm (3in) pots will be moved to 10 or 11.5cm (4 or $4^1/_2$ in) pots, then to 13 or 15cm (5 or 6in), then to 18 or 10cm (7 or 8in). Water rather sparingly for a few days, and shade from strong sunlight.

498. Blueing Hydrangeas Blue flowers on hydrangeas are obtained by growing pink varieties in a rather acid compost (pH 4·0-6·0) treated with alum. Good results have been obtained with the following mixture:

3 parts by bulk of acid loam.
1 part by bulk of oak leaf-mould.

To each 50kg (1cwt) add 1kg ($2^1/_2$ lb) of aluminium sulphate.

Pot plants in this mixture as soon as they come from the propagating frame.

Outdoor plants can be 'blued' by top dressing the soil in late winter with aluminium sulphate at approximately 125g (4oz) per stem, but it is practically impossible to get any result on highly alkaline soils. Markedly acid soils produce blue flowers without treatment.

499. Bulbs in Fibre A special compost made with 6 parts by bulk of peat, 2 parts of oyster shell, and 1 part of crushed charcoal is used when bulbs are grown in bowls without drainage holes. This compost will not become sour, but it contains little or no nutrient and the bulbs lose quality in consequence. It is essential to moisten this fibre before bulbs are planted in it as, when dry, water tends to run off it and not soak in. Subsequently, water must be given occasionally to keep the fibre moist. Bulbs in fibre must be kept in a cool, dark place for at least eight weeks to form roots.

500. Bulbs in Soil All bulbs may also be grown in ordinary compost in boxes or pots if these are drained in the ordinary way (497). In particular, early narcissi, early tulips, hyacinths, and *Iris tingitana* are frequently so grown and forced into flower between early winter and early spring. Bulbs should be potted in late summer or early autumn. They may be almost shoulder to shoulder and just covered with soil. They are then placed outdoors in a cool, sheltered place and covered with 10cm (4in) of sand or ashes. They must remain in this plunge bed for at least eight weeks before they are introduced to a greenhouse. Even the temperature should not exceed 16°C (60°F) at first. Later, when flower stems appear, it may be raised to as much as 24°C (75°F) to rush bulbs into flower.

501. Plunging Plants During the summer months many greenhouse plants, eg azaleas, deutzias, genistas, etc, are better in the open in a sunny, sheltered position. To prevent rapid drying out of the soil, the pots are plunged to their rims in a bed of ashes, sand, peat, or peat substitute.

502. Resting Plants All plants have a season of rest when they make little or no growth, but this is much more marked with some kinds, notably those with bulbous or tuberous roots. Water supply must be adjusted accordingly (490) and as a rule temperature can be reduced considerably. This can often be effected by moving plants to a different part of the house.

503. Starting Plants When growth is about to recommence (or earlier if it is desired to hurry the plant), temperature is raised (see above) and water supply gradually increased. With begonias and gloxinias it is best to arrange the tubers almost shoulder to shoulder in shallow boxes filled with ordinary potting soil (497) when they have made two or three leaves each.

504. Pruning Greenhouse Plants Shrubby, half-shrubby, and climbing plants often need to be pruned to prevent them from becoming straggly or occupying too much space. This is usually done in late winter or early spring unless plants are then in full growth or flower, when it is deferred until after this. An exception is made for regal and show pelargoniums, which are pruned in mid- to late summer. Method of pruning will depend upon requirements and type of growth. Climbers can, as a rule, have some of the oldest growths removed if over-crowded, and others shortened a little. Most shrubby plants can be cut back severely if it is desired to restrict size. Hard cutting must be avoided with hydrangeas, as it limits flowering, although again, method used depends upon type.

FRAMES

505. Types Frames may be permanent or portable and they may have span or lean-to roofs as in greenhouses. The pitch of the frame light (covering glass) is usually much less than that of the greenhouse, but must never be quite flat. Depth of frames varies greatly according to requirements but is not as a rule less than 22cm (9in) at the lowest point or more than 1m (3ft) at the highest.

506. Maintaining Temperature An unheated frame, known as a cold frame, will not be proof against frost in winter. In consequence, tender plants cannot be kept in it with complete safety. Matters can be improved by covering it heavily with sacks or mats during frosty weather, but these are mainly of use at night, for if kept on for long by day, plants will become drawn through lack of light.

Heating can be effected by running hot-water pipes through the frames, placing small electrical or oil heaters in them, or by heating the air or soil with electrical warming cables. The cable is attached to the inside walls of the frame or buried a few inches deep in the soil. Alternatively the frame may be placed on a hotbed, ie a heap of decaying manure. Fresh manure is required and should be turned once or twice as for mushroom beds (148). As it starts to ferment it will heat. When the temperature in the centre of the heap has subsided to 24°-27°C (75°-80°F), it is trodden into a pit at least 45cm (18in) deep and a little larger than the frame, or alternatively it is built up into a rectangular mound of this size and 45-60cm (18-24in) high. About 15cm (6in) of soil is placed on top and then the frame is set in position. Seeds can be sown or cuttings inserted either in the soil or in boxes and pots plunged in it.

507. Ventilation This can be given in three ways, by sliding the lights, by tilting them, or by removing them altogether. All are useful according to weather and condition of growth. When tilting lights, always do so on the side away from the wind. Frames are especially useful for hardening off half-hardy plants. This is done during mid- and late spring, and ventilation is gradually increased until the lights are removed altogether by day and finally by night as well.

508. Watering General rules are the same as for watering in greenhouses (490). During rainy weather it is often wise to remove the lights for a time and let the plants get their moisture naturally, but do not do this if the rain is very cold or the plants of a kind that do not like moisture on their foliage.

509. Seed Raising in Frames General rules are the same as for greenhouses, but seeds may be sown direct in a bed of soil prepared in the frame instead of in boxes or pots, if preferred. As a rule this is desirable only with strong-growing plants, such as vegetables and herbaceous perennials. Late winter and early spring are the periods when the frame is most in use for seed sowing, but it may also be required in early summer and again in late summer to early autumn.

510. Cuttings in Frames General remarks regarding cuttings in greenhouses (495) apply. Frames are particularly serviceable for cuttings of hardy plants which need a close atmosphere, eg spring and summer cuttings, or those that appreciate shelter, eg evergreen shrubs. No attempt should be made to strike tender cuttings in frames unless they can be moved before cold weather arrives or the frames can be heated.

511. Frames in Summer From early summer to early autumn inclusive, frames can be used for many greenhouse plants that do not like high temperatures. A shaded frame will be serviceable for cyclamen, greenhouse primulas, calceolarias and cinerarias, and a sunny one for perpetual-flowering carnations, pelargoniums, etc. For some of these plants it may be necessary to increase the height of the sides.

CLOCHES AND HANDLIGHTS

512. Types There are bell glasses, which are made entirely of glass and are shaped like a bell; handlights of varying pattern, but usually rectangular with span or pyramidal top glazed with glass or glass substitute, and continuous cloches which are open ended, and so may be placed end to end to cover a row of any length. These continuous cloches are the most useful for rearing seedlings and growing crops. Bell glasses and handlights are superior for striking summer cuttings, as the atmosphere within them is closer.

Continuous cloches can be made of sheets of horticultural glass or clear plastic held together by special wire frames or clamps. They can be dismantled easily and stored flat when not required. Breakages are easily made good. These cloches can be had in several forms, the two most important being the tent, made of two panes of glass set together like an inverted V, and the barn, made of four pieces set together like the end view of a barn. Plastic cloches of many different patterns are also available and yet another method is to stretch lengths of polythene film over wire supports to make long, tunnel-like protectors held in place by wooden pegs.

513. Ventilation Bell glasses and handlights are ventilated by tilting them on a block of wood. Continuous cloches may be ventilated in two ways according to the weather and needs of plants: by leaving the ends of the row of cloches open, or by spacing the cloches out a lit-

tle. In this way a great range of ventilation can be obtained. There are also special designs of cloches in which provision is made to open the sides or tops for ventilation.

514. Watering Seeds and plants in cloches or handlights must not be allowed to get dry, but as a rule they do not require watering as freely as those in frames because water runs down the glass and then soaks in from the surrounding soil. Cloches may be placed fairly close together over ground in late winter and early spring, to enable the surface to dry off and so make seed sowing possible.

515. Plants to Grow in Cloches In spring they are serviceable for early seedlings of flowering plants and vegetables and for early crops of salad vegetables, tomatoes, and strawberries. In summer they are used for cuttings of all kinds; in autumn for more cuttings, seedlings of hardy annuals, broad beans, Brussels sprouts, and cauliflower, for ripening tomatoes and also crops of lettuce, endive, parsley, and radish. In winter cloches are useful as protection for small plants of doubtful hardiness such as some alpines and bulbs, also on the seedling crops already raised under them in the autumn.

CARNATIONS (PERPETUAL-FLOWERING)

516. Propagation Cuttings may be taken at any time from early winter to early spring. They are rooted in pure silver sand or very sandy soil in a propagating frame, temperature 16°C (60°F). Cuttings are prepared from side growths on the flowering stems. Those mid-way up these stems are the best ones to take. They are simply pulled off with a heel attached and this is then trimmed up.

517. Potting Cuttings are potted singly in 7·5cm (3in) pots as soon as they are rooted. Subsequently, they are potted on as necessary until by late spring or early summer they reach the 15 or 18cm (6 or 7in) pots, in which they will flower. At first use an ordinary potting compost such as JIP.1 (497). For the later potting use JIP.2. Alternatively carnations may be grown in rings of soil on an aggregate base. Pot firmly.

518. Stopping This is first done when the cutting has made seven joints. The top joint is broken off to encourage side growths to form.

The plants are stopped a second time when side growths resulting from the first stopping have made about eight joints. Two joints are broken out. Complete this second stopping by midsummer if flowers are required by early – mid-winter.

519. Routine Cultivation From mid-autumn to late spring plants must have the protection of a greenhouse, but during the summer they may be placed in a frame and ventilated freely. Stand the frame on bricks to give height and allow air to enter from below as well as above. Cool, airy treatment is necessary throughout. Even in winter, heat is used more to dry than to warm the atmosphere, but frost must be excluded. By taking cuttings over a long period (516) plants may be had in flower most of the year. Water moderately in summer, sparingly in winter. Excessive heat encourages thrips and red spider (667).

CHRYSANTHEMUMS

520. Types and Classification There are annual and hardy perennial chrysanthemums which are dealt with elsewhere (407) and (450). Here we are only concerned with the florist chrysanthemums developed over many centuries from plants of Chinese and Japanese origin. For garden purposes these are broadly divided into three main groups. Early

Flowering or Border which normally flower in the open before mid-autumn, Mid-season and Late Flowering or Indoor which normally flower under glass between late autumn and mid-winter.

Within each division the varieties are classified according to flower characteristics. Singles have up to five rows of petals and a button-like disk. Anemone-centred varieties are similar except that a low, soft cushion of very short petals replaces the button-like centre. Doubles have so many petals that no central disk is visible until the flower fades.

Doubles are split into three groups according to the form of the petals. In Incurved varieties these all curl inwards making a ball-like flower. Reflexed varieties have outward or downward-curling petals. Intermediate varieties have the inner petals curling inwards and the outer petals curling outwards. For exhibition purposes there are further sub-divisions of each group according to the normal size of the flower.

There are also some other special classes. Pompons have very small, fully double flowers produced freely in clusters. Thread-petalled or Rayonante are doubles with petals rolled lengthwise like thin quills. In Spoon-petalled varieties petals are partly rolled but open out at the end like little spoons. Cascade varieties have lax growth and can be trained as hanging plants. Charm varieties are very branching, compact and have numerous small single flowers. Korean and Rubellum varieties have very numerous single or semi-double flowers but are relatively hardy and may be grown outdoors all the year in mild places and on light soils. All other chrysanthemums, even the Early Flowering or Border varieties, are likely to need winter protection in temperate climates.

521. Propagation Though chrysanthemums can be raised quite easily from seed, seedlings are very variable in quality and this method is therefore hardly ever adopted, except with Cascade and Charm (small single-flowered) varieties. Seed is sown in late winter in a warm greenhouse and subsequent treatment of seedlings is similar to that of half-hardy annuals (397-400).

Cuttings are almost invariably employed for other chrysanthemums and selected Cascades. These are taken from mid-autumn until late spring; the earliest cuttings are taken for exhibition varieties and especially those to be flowered on second crown buds (523), and the latest cuttings for dwarf plants. With the exception of late cuttings, which are often prepared from the tops of plants rooted earlier in the year, all cuttings are made from sucker growths, ie shoots coming direct from the roots through the soil. Shoots growing from the old woody flower stems will not make good cuttings. Cuttings are 5-8cm (2-3in) in length, trimmed below a joint and the lower leaves are removed. They are inserted 1-3cm (½-1in) deep in sandy soil, usually in pots or boxes, and are rooted on the cool greenhouse staging or in a propagating frame (492). Great heat is undesirable as it encourages disease.

522. Potting As soon as cuttings are rooted and growing, they are potted singly in 7·5cm (3in) pots and ordinary potting compost (497). Pot rather firmly and shade for a day or so until established. Subsequently, grow on in full sun and average temperature of 13°-15°C (55°-60°F). Pot on as smaller pots become moderately full of roots, using similar compost throughout but coarser in texture as plants get bigger. For final potting in late spring or early summer into 20-25cm (8-9in) pots, the loam used may be

in lumps as large as a small hen's egg. To this final compost, basic chrysanthemum fertilizer (92) should be added instead of the general potting fertilizer. Pot firmly throughout. Early-flowering and Korean chrysanthemums are not usually potted beyond 7·5cm (3in) pots, in which they are hardened off (507) in a frame and planted outdoors 30cm (1ft) apart in rows 60cm (2ft) apart in late spring.

523. Stopping This means pinching out the growing tips of the plants. It is practised for two distinct reasons: (i) to make the plants more bushy, and (ii) to obtain buds and flowers at the right time. The first purpose is necessary only for decorative varieties, singles grown for decoration, late-flowering varieties grown as large specimen plants, early-flowering types grown for garden decoration or small flowers in sprays, and Koreans. As a rule two stoppings are then given, the first when the young plants are 15 or 18cm (6 or 7in) in height and the second when the side growths produced as a result of the first stopping are 20cm (8in) long. For exhibition purposes, early-flowering chrysanthemums are usually grown with one stopping only during mid – late spring.

When stopping to time blooms for exhibition, each variety must be treated according to its peculiarities. Catalogues issued by trade specialists usually give instructions which may need to be modified to suit the locality. Left to itself the cutting will, after a few weeks, produce a flower bud at the tip of the stem. This bud prevents further extension of the main stem and forces the plant to produce side growths. It is, in consequence, known as a BREAK BUD. Some time later the side growths will produce flower buds, known as FIRST CROWN BUDS. Further shoots appear below them, themselves terminating in flower buds some weeks later. These are SECOND CROWN BUDS. Again, the process is repeated, but the third batch of side growths will end in clusters of flower buds, not in one flower bud surrounded by further shoots. The plant has reached the end of its development and these buds are in consequence known as TERMINAL BUDS. By pinching out the tips of shoots a little before each stage in this sequence would occur naturally, the next stage can also be advanced by a few days. Since the sequence of growth and bud formation is controlled by the interaction of warmth and day length it is subject to modification according to the time at which cuttings are taken. It can also be modified by artificial control of temperature and by the use of blackouts or lighting to shorten or lengthen the days, and it is by these means that commercial growers are able to produce chrysanthemum cut flowers throughout the year. However, not all varieties respond equally well or in a similar manner and for good results it is essential to be able to control the lighting and heating very accurately.

A special system of stopping and training is necessary for Cascade chrysanthemums. After the first stopping of the rooted cutting, the uppermost new shoot is tied to a bamboo cane sloping north to south at an angle of 45°, pointing downward towards the direction of cool shade, and is not stopped again. The plant must be stood on a shelf or raised bench both in the greenhouse and when outdoors from early summer to early autumn (525). All other growths are stopped after the fourth leaf. If they form secondary growths, these are stopped in turn at the fourth leaf. No growths are stopped after early autumn. When the plants are brought into the greenhouse the main stems are lowered so that they hang perpendicularly.

524. Bud Taking This signifies the gardener's decision that the particular flower bud just formed will develop into a bloom at the right time and so must be

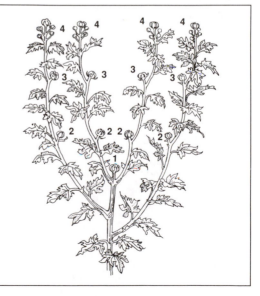

Stopping chrysanthemums.
This illustration shows the desired results of correct stopping (523).
1: break bud
2: first crown bud
3: second crown bud
4: terminal bud

526. Table of Greenhouse Flowering Plants

NOTE – Letters indicating habit:

An	Annual, or treated as such (402)	Cl	Climbing
Bn	Biennial (421)	·Tr	Trailing
Hb	Herbaceous (443)	Bl	Bulbous or tuberous
Sh	Shrubby (473)	Su	Succulents
HSh	Half-shrubby		

Other methods of propagation: *(d)* – division, *(g)* – grafting or budding, *(l)* – layering
(lc) – leaf cutting

Name	Colour	Season of interest	Habit
Abutilon	various	all year	Sh, Cl
Acacia	yellow	late win – mid spr	Sh
Achimenes	various	early sum – early aut	Bl, Tr
Aechmea	red and blue	late sum – early aut	Hb
Agapanthus	blue or white	early sum – early aut	Hb
Agathaea	blue	late spr – mid aut	HSh
Allamanda	yellow	mid spr – early aut	Cl
Allium neapolitanum	white	late spr – early sum	Bl
Anthurium	red or pink	late spr – early aut	Hb
Aristolochia	various	mid sum	Cl
Arum (Zantedeschia)	white or yellow	early win – mid spr	Bl
Astilbe	white to crimson	late spr – early sum	Hb
Auricula	various	early spr – mid spr	Hb
Azalea indica (*Rhododendron simsii*)	white to crimson	early win – early spr	Sh
Balsam	various	early sum – mid aut	An or Hb
Begonia (fibrous)	white to crimson	early sum – mid aut, late aut – late win	Hb
Begonia (tuberous)	various	early sum – early aut	Bl, some Tr
Beloperone	pink and white	early sum – late sum	Hb
Billbergia	pink and green	early sum – late sum	Hb
Bougainvillea	rose, crimson, orange	early sum – mid aut	Cl
Bouvardia	white to scarlet	early aut – mid win	Sh
Browallia	white and blue	mid sum – early win	An
Brunfelsia	blue	all year	Sh
Calceolaria (herbaceous)	various	mid spr – early sum	An
Calceolaria (shrubby)	various	early sum – early aut	Sh
Calystemon	red	early spr – mid sum	Sh
Camellia	white to crimson	mid win – mid spr	Sh
Campanula isophylla	blue, white	early sum – early aut	Tr
Campanula pyramidalis	blue, white	early sum – mid sum	Bn
Canna	yellow to red	mid sum – mid aut	Bl
Carnation (perpetual)	various	all year	Hb
Cassia	yellow	early sum – mid aut	Cl

Letters indicating treatment:

U	Cold (unheated) house (484)	I	Intermediate atmosphere (489)
C	Cool house (484)	W	Wet atmosphere (489)
T	Temperate House (484)	R	No water during resting period
H	Hothouse (484)	G	Water moderately during resting
D	Dry atmosphere (489)		period (490, 502)

Treatment	Season of propagation		
	Seed	Cuttings	Other
CIG	early spr	early spr – mid sum	
CIG	early spr	early sum – mid sum	
TIR	mid win – late win	mid spr, mid sum	d late win
TWG			d early spr
CIG			d early spr
TIG	early spr – early sum	early aut – mid aut	
HIG		early spr	
CIR			d mid aut – late aut
HWG			d early spr
H or TIG	early spr	early sum – mid sum	
C or TWR			d late sum
U or CIG			d mid aut
CIG	early spr – early sum		d early sum
CIG		early sum – mid sum	g early spr
CWG	early spr – late spr	mid spr – late spr	
TIG	late win – early spr	late win – mid spr	
C or TIR	mid win – early spr		d early spr – mid spr
C or TIG		mid spr	
C or TIG			d early spr – mid spr
C or TIG		early sum – mid sum	
T or HIG		early spr – mid spr	
TI	late win – early spr		
T or HIG		early sum – mid sum	
TI	late spr – early sum		
CIG	early spr	early aut – mid aut	
CDG		mid sum – late sum	
U or CIG	early spr	early sum – mid sum	l early spr, early aut g early spr
U or CIG		early spr – mid spr	
U or CIG	late win – early spr		
TIR	late win – early spr		d late win – early spr
CDG	late win – early spr	late aut – early spr	
C or TIG		early spr – early sum	

▶

Name	Colour	Season of interest	Habit
Celosia	yellow, red	mid sum – early aut	An
Celsia	yellow	mid spr – mid aut	Hb
Chrysanthemum	various	mid aut – mid win	HSh
Cineraria	various	late aut – late spr	An
Clerodendrum fallax	scarlet	late spr – late sum	Hb
Clerodendrum (others)	white, red	mid sum – early aut	Cl
Clianthus puniceus	red or white	late spr – early sum	Sh
Clivia	yellow, orange	early spr – late spr	Bl
Cobaea	purple	mid sum – mid aut	Cl
Coronilla	yellow	late spr	Sh
Crinum	white, pink	mid sum – late sum	Bl
Cuphea	scarlet	early sum – late sum	Hb
Cyclamen	white to crimson	late aut – late win	Bl
Daphne odora	pink	late win – early spr	Sh
Datura	white, orange	early sum – mid sum	Sh
Deutzia gracilis	white	late win – late spr	Sh
Dicentra	rose	mid spr – late spr	Hb
Diplacus	orange to red	late spr – early aut	Sh
Dipladenia	white to pink	late spr – early aut	Cl
Eccremocarpus	orange	mid sum – mid aut	Cl
Epacris	white to red	late aut – mid win	Sh
Erica	white to red	mid aut – early sum	Sh
Eucharis	white	mid win – mid spr	Bl
Euphorbia fulgens	scarlet	late aut – late win	Hb
Exacum	lavender	late sum – early win	An
Francoa	white and red	mid sum – early aut	Hb
Freesia	various	early win – early spr	Bl
Fuschsia	white, red, purple	late spr – mid aut	Sh
Gardenia	white	all year	Sh
Genista	yellow	early spr – mid spr	Sh
Gerbera	yellow to red	late spr – early aut	Hb
Gloxinia	various	late spr – early aut	Bl
Haemanthus	red or white	early win – mid spr	Bl
Hedychium	white, yellow, red	mid sum – late sum	Bl
Heliotrope	mauve	early sum – early aut	Hb
Hibiscus rosa-sinensis	yellow to crimson	late spr – early aut	Sh
Hippeastrum	red to white	late aut – early sum	Bl
Hoya	pink	mid sum – late sum	Cl
Humea elegans	brown	mid sum – mid aut	Bn
Hydrangea	white, pink, blue	late spr – mid sum	Sh
Ipomoea	various	mid sum – mid aut	Cl, An
Jacobinia (Justicia)	various	mid aut – mid win	Hb
Jasminum	white, yellow	late aut – early spr	Cl
Kalanchoë	red to white	all year	Su
Lachenalia	yellow, orange	late win – mid spr	Bl
Lantana	various	early sum – mid aut	HSh

Treatment	Season of propagation		
	Seed	Cuttings	Other
C or TI	late win – early spr		
CIG	early spr – mid sum	early spr – mid spr	
CDG	late win – early spr	late aut – late spr	
CI	mid spr – early sum		
T or HIG	early spr		
T or HIG		mid win – early spr	
CDG	early spr	early sum – mid sum	
TIR	late win – early spr		d late win, early sum
CIG	late win – early spr	mid sum – late sum	
CIG		mid spr, late sum	
CDR	early spr		d early spr
TIG		mid spr – mid sum	
CIR	late sum		
U or CIG		early aut – mid aut	
TWG	early spr	early spr – mid spr	
U or CIG		early sum – mid sum	
U or CIG			d early spr
CIG		mid spr – mid sum	
T or HWG		early spr	
U or CIG	late win – mid spr		
CDG		late spr – early sum	
CDG		mid spr – mid sum	
T or HIG			d late spr
T or HIG		mid spr – late spr	
U or CI	early spr – early aut		
U or CIG	early spr – mid spr		d early spr
CIR	early spr – early sum		d late sum
U or CIG	early spr	early spr, early aut	
T or HWG		mid win – mid spr	
U or CIG	early spr – mid spr	early sum – mid sum	
CDR	early spr – mid spr		
TWR	mid win – late win		
TIR			d mid spr
T or HIR			d early spr
C or TIG	late win – early spr	mid spr, early aut	
T or HWG		early spr – mid spr	
C or TIR	late sum		d mid win – early spr
TIG		early spr – late spr	l early sum – mid sum
CIG	mid spr – mid sum		
U or CIG		mid spr – mid sum	
CI	late win – early sum		
H or TIG		mid spr	
T or HIG		mid spr	
CDR	early spr	late spr – early aut	
CDR	early spr		d late sum – early aut
CIG	late win – early spr	early spr, late sum	

▶

Name	Colour	Season of interest	Habit
Lapageria	white to crimson	early sum – mid aut	Cl
Lilium	various	early spr – mid aut	Bl
Luculia	pink	early win – mid win	Sh
Nerine	white to scarlet	early aut – late aut	Bl
Nerium (Oleander)	pink or white	early sum – late sum	Sh
Orchids, cattleya	white to purple	early spr – early sum	
– O. cymbidium	white, pink, buff, etc.	early spr – late spr	
– O. cypripedium	blush, green, chocolate	mid win – mid spr	Hb
– O. dendrobium	yellow, pink, mauve	late win – late spr	
– O. miltonia	white, crimson	mid spr – mid sum	
– O. odontoglossum	white, yellow to maroon	late win – late spr	
– O. oncidium	yellow to brown	late win – mid sum	
Pancratium	white	early sum – late sum	Bl
Passiflora	various	mid sum – early aut	Cl
Pelargonium (geranium)	white to crimson	mid spr – mid aut	HSh
Plumbago	blue	mid sum – mid aut	Cl
Poinsettia	scarlet, pink	late aut – mid win	HSh
Primula malacoides	pink, red, mauve	late win – mid spr	An
Primula obconica	various	mid aut – mid spr	An
Primula sinensis	various	early win – early spr	An
Rehmannia	rose	late spr – late sum	Hb
Rose	various	all year	Sh, Cl
Saintpaulia	violet, pink, white	all year	Hb
Salvia	scarlet, blue	late sum – late aut	Hb or HSh
Schizanthus	various	mid spr – mid aut	An
Smithiantha	yellow to red	mid sum – early aut	Bl
Solanum capsicastrum	red berries	late aut – mid win	Sh
Solanum jasminoides	white	mid sum – late sum	Cl
Sparmannia	white	all year	Sh
Statice	white, pink, blue	late sum – mid aut	Hb and An
Stephanotis	white	all year	Cl
Strelitzia	blue and orange	late spr – early sum	Hb
Streptocarpus	various	early aut – early sum	Hb
Streptosolen	orange	mid spr – mid sum	Cl
Thunbergia alata	orange	early sum – early aut	An
Thunbergia (others)	various	late spr – mid aut	Cl
Tibouchina	violet	late spr – mid aut	Sh
Trachelium	blue	early sum – early aut	An
Tropaeolum	yellow to scarlet	early sum – mid aut	Cl
Tuberose	white	mid sum – mid aut	Bl
Vallota	scarlet	late sum – early aut	Bl
Veltheimia	yellow and red	late aut – mid spr	Bl
Vinca rosea	pink, white	all year	Sh

Treatment	Season of propagation		
	Seed	**Cuttings**	**Other**
CIR			l early spr, early aut
U or CIR	late win – early spr		d early aut – mid aut
ClG	late spr – early sum	mid spr – late spr	
CDR			d late sum
ClG		mid sum – late sum	
H or TIR	early spr – mid spr		d early spr – mid spr
C or TIR	early spr – mid spr		d late spr
C or TIG	early spr – mid spr		d mid spr
H or TIR	early spr – mid spr		d mid spr – late spr
T or HIR	early spr – mid spr		d early sprly spr
TIR	early spr – mid spr		d mid spr – late spr
TIR	early spr – mid spr		d mid spr
CIR			d early spr
C or TIG	late win – early spr	early spr – mid spr	
CDG	late win – early spr	mid sum – early aut	
CIG	mid spr – late spr	late spr – early sum	
HWR		mid spr – late spr	
Cl	mid spr – mid sum		
Cl	early spr – early sum		
Cl	early spr – early sum		
CIG	late win – early spr		d early spr
U or CIG			g early sum – late sum
H or TIG	late win – early spr		lc early sum – late sum
CIG	late win – early spr	early spr – mid spr	
U or CI	mid win – early aut		
C or TIR	late win – early spr		d late win – early spr
C or TIG	late win – early spr		
CIG		early sum – late sum	
CIG		mid spr – mid sum	
U or CIG	late win – early spr	early spr – mid spr	
HWG		early spr – mid spr	
T or HIG			d early spr – mid spr
C or TIG	late win – early sum		d early spr
CIG		mid spr – mid sum	
U or Cl	early spr – mid spr		
HWG	early spr – mid spr	early spr – early sum	
C or TIG		mid spr – mid sum	
Cl	early spr, mid sum		
CIG	early spr	early spr –mid spr	
T or HIR			d late win
CDR			d early spr
CIR			d late sum – early aut
T or HIG	late win – mid spr		

527. A Table of Greenhouse Foliage Plants

NOTE – Letters indicating habit:

Hb   Herbaceous (443)
Sh   Shrubby (473)
Cl   Climbing

Other methods of propagation: *(d)* – division.

Name	Colour	Habit	Treatment
Aralia	green, bronze	Sh	T or HIG
Araucaria excelsa	green	Sh	CIG
Asparagus plumosus	ferny, green	Hb	CIG
Asparagus sprengeri	trailing, green	Hb	CIG
Aspidistra	green and white	Hb	CIG
Begonia rex	marbled	Hb	C or TWG
Caladium	marbled	Hb	HWR
Chlorophytum	green and white	Hb	CIG
Cissus	purple, green, variegated	Cl	C or TIG
Coleus	green, crimson, yellow, etc.	Hb	C or TIG
Croton (codiaeum)	green, yellow, orange, etc.	Sh	HWG
Dracaena	red, orange, green, etc.	Sh	TIG
Fatsia	green	Sh	UIG
Ferns	green	Hb	U to HWG
Ficus	green and yellow	Sh	TIG
Grevillea	green	Sh	CIG
Palms	green	Sh	C or TWG
Pandanus	green and white	Hb	TWG
Sansevieria	marbled	Hb	T or HIG
Selaginella	green, bronze, etc.	Hb	CWG
Smilax	green	Cl	CIG
Tradescantia	variegated, trailing	Hb	TIG

NOTE All the above with the exception of caladiums are evergreen

kept. All other buds or side growths surrounding or immediately beneath it are rubbed out. Usually buds of intermediate or reflexed varieties required for exhibition in late autumn should be taken towards the end of summer while incurves may be a week or fortnight later. Buds that appear a little too soon can be retarded by leaving side growths round them for a week or fortnight.

Bud selection is also sometimes determined by the type of flower required since first crown buds tend to produce flowers with more petals than second crown buds which, in time, have more petals than do flowers from terminal buds (522).

525. Cultural Routine Chrysanthemums are almost hardy but the flowers

Letters indicating treatment:

U	Cold (unheated) house (484)	W	Wet atmosphere (489)
C	Cool house (484)	R	No water during resting period
T	Temperate House (484)	G	Water moderately during resting
I	Intermediate atmosphere (489)		period (490, 502)
H	Hothouse (484)		

Season of propagation			
Seed	Cuttings	Other	Potting
	early sum – late sum		early spr
early spr			early spr
early spr		d early spr	early spr
early spr		d early spr	early spr
		d early spr	early spr
early spr – mid spr		d early spr	early spr
		d early spr	early spr
		d early spr	early spr
	mid spr – mid sum		early spr – mid spr
late win – early spr	mid sum – late sum		early spr
	late spr – early sum		early spr
early spr	early spr – mid spr		early spr
	early sum – mid sum		early spr
early sum		d early spr	early spr
	mid spr – early sum		early spr
late win – early spr			early spr
early spr			early spr
		d early spr	early spr
		d early spr	early spr
		d early spr	early spr
early spr			early spr
	early spr – early sum		early spr

and flower buds of all kinds except the very hardy Korean varieties may be damaged severely by frost. They require cool greenhouse (484) protection from mid-autumn until late spring in temperate climates. During the remaining months they are best outdoors in a sunny position. Old roots are discarded and only the rooted cuttings retained. These are watered moderately at first, but more freely as weather becomes warmer. In summer, water is supplied freely. Feed with chrysanthemum summer fertilizer (92) from midsummer till flower buds show colour.

When plants are stood outdoors, pots should be placed on boards, slates, or a gravel or ash base to assist drainage and to keep out worms. Stake and tie each plant securely.

Alternatively, decorative varieties may be planted out in late spring in ordinary well-dug soil 45cm (18in) apart in rows 75cm (2½ ft) apart. They are then lifted with good balls of soil in the autumn and replanted in the greenhouse either in beds or boxes. Planting of border and Korean varieties has already been described (522). These may be left in the open all through the winter in well-drained soil, but a few plants should be lifted in mid-autumn into a frame with old potting soil to give cuttings. After flowering, cut down all plants to within about 10cm (4in) of soil level. Chrysanthemums can be grown quite successfully using the ring culture method.

Chrysanthemums are frequently attacked in summer by aphids and capsid bugs and flowers may be damaged by earwigs. All can be kept under control with suitable insecticides (see Section 8). Diseases include rust and mildew, also grey mould (botrytis) which is highly likely to damage expanding flowers causing them to decay. This disease thrives in a cold, damp atmosphere and is best controlled by good ventilation coupled with some artificial heat to dry the air and keep it on the move. Other diseases can be controlled by occasional spraying or dusting with fungicide (see Section 8).

CALENDAR OF GARDEN OPERATIONS

GARDEN OPERATIONS

Work for mid-winter

528. Seeds to Sow in Warmth *Vegetables*: French beans, cress, shorthorn carrots, leeks, lettuces, mustard, onions, radishes, tomatoes. *Flowers*: antirrhinums, begonias, cannas, gloxinias, scarlet salvias, streptocarpus, sweet peas, verbenas.

529. Plants to Start in Warmth *Flowers*: achimenes, tuberous begonias, clivias, gloxinias, hippeastrums, hyacinths, bulbous irises, lilies, narcissi, pot-grown roses and shrubs, tulips. *Fruits*: early vines, peaches, and nectarines. *Vegetables*: chicory, early potatoes, rhubarb, seakale.

530. Vegetables to Force Outdoors Rhubarb, seakale.

531. Cuttings to Take in Warmth Perpetual-flowering carnations, greenhouse chrysanthemums.

532. Root Cuttings to Take in Frame Anchusas, gaillardias, perowskia, oriental poppies, *Phlox decussata*, romneyas, perennial statices, perennial verbascums.

533. Pruning Outdoors Apples, apricots, cherries, currants, gooseberries, nectarines, peaches, pears, plums.

534. Pruning under Glass *Flowers*: *Plumbago capensis*, passion flowers (passiflora), climbing roses. *Fruits*: late vines.

535. Miscellaneous *Vegetables*: dig, trench, work in bulky and slow-acting manures and fertilizers, mulch asparagus beds with dung, protect broccoli curds. *Fruit*: spray fruit trees with tar-oil wash, protect fruit buds from birds.

Work for late winter

536. Seeds to Sow in Sheltered Places Outdoors Onions, parsley, parsnips, early peas, turnips.

537. Seeds to Sow in Warmth *Vegetables*: French beans, broad beans, Brussels sprouts, shorthorn carrots, cress, cucumbers, celery, cauliflowers, leeks, lettuces, mustard, onions, radishes, tomatoes. *Fruit*: melons. *Flowers*: Antirrhinum, ageratum, anagallis, begonias, brachycome, balsams, cobaea, cosmeas, cannas, celsia, celosia (including cockscomb), *Clerodendrum fallax*, carnations, dahlias, *Dianthus heddewigii*, eccremocarpus, fuchsias, gloxinias, *Impatiens holstii, I. sultanii*, kochia, lobelia, marigolds (tagetes), marguerites, mimulus, nicotianas, nemesias, *Phlox drummondii*, petunias, pelargoniums, *Rehmannia angulata*, streptocarpus, scarlet salvia, sweet peas, salpiglossis, schizanthus, annual statices, ten-week stocks, trachelium, verbenas.

538. Planting Outdoors *Vegetables*: Jerusalem artichokes, chives, spring cabbage, garlic, onion sets, autumn-sown onions, early potatoes (in very sheltered place), shallots. *Fruits*: apples, apricots, blackberries, cherries, currants, figs, grape vines, gooseberries, loganberries, medlars, mulberries, nectarines, nuts, pears, plums, peaches, raspberries. *Flowers*: tuberous-rooted anemones, lilies (except *Lilium candidum* and *testaceum*), roses, ranunculuses, deciduous trees and shrubs (except magnolias).

539. Plants to Start in Warmth *Flowers*: achimenes, tuberous begonias, clivias, cannas, dahlias, gloxinias, hyacinths, hippeastrums, bulbous irises, lilies, narcissi, pot-grown roses and shrubs, tulips. *Fruit*: apricots, nectarines and peaches, mid-season vines. *Vegetable*: seakale.

540. Planting and Potting Under Glass *Flowers*: autumn-sown annuals for the greenhousle, started begonias and gloxinias, rooted chrysanthemums, border chrysanthemums, perpetual-flowering carnations.

541. Cuttings to Take in Warmth Winter-flowering begonias, greenhouse chrysanthemums, border chrysanthemums, perpetual-flowering carnations.

542. Pruning Outdoors Late-planted fruit trees, cobnuts and filberts, autumn-fruiting raspberries. *Flowers*: *Cornus alba*, clematises of the jackmanii, lanuginosa and viticella types, *Hydrangea paniculata, Hypericum moserianum, Spiraea aitchisonii, arborea, ariaefolia, bullata, japonica, lindleyana, menziesii* and *salicifolia, Tamarix pentandra.*

543. Pruning Under Glass Bougainvilleas, *Diplacus glutinosus*, fuchsias, gardenias, zonal and ivy-leaved pelargoniums.

544. Miscellaneous *Vegetables*: dig, trench, work in bulky slow-acting manures and fertilizers, break down surface of rough dug ground, protect broccoli curds, lift and store parsnips, protect fruit buds from birds, harden off vegetable seedlings in frames, prick off early seedlings under glass. *Fruit*: pollinate early flowers in vinery and orchard house, and spray outdoor peaches and nectarines with fungicide.

Work for early spring

545. Seeds to Sow Outdoors *Vegetables*: broccoli, Brussels sprouts, broad beans, early carrots, cabbages, cauliflowers, lettuces, leeks, onions, peas, parsnips, parsley, radishes, summer spinach, spinach beet, turnips. *Flowers*: annual alyssum, bartonia, calendulas, annual candytuft, annual chrysanthemums, clarkias, collinsia, *Convolvulus tricolor*, annual coreopsis, cornflowers, eschscholzias, godetias, annual gypsophila, larkspurs, *Lavatera rosea*, limnanthes, linums, annual lupins, malopes, nemophilas, nigellas, phacelias, cardinal and Shirly poppies, annual rudbeckias, roses, annual saponaria, annual sunflowers, Virginia stock, ornamental trees and shrubs, viscarias.

546. Seeds to Sow under Glass *Vegetables*: Brussels sprouts, broccoli, cress, celery, celeriac, cucumbers, cauliflowers, herbs, mustard, radishes, tomatoes. *Fruits*: melons. *Flowers:* as late winter. Also asters, hardy annuals (for pot culture in greenhouse), coleus, exacum, herbaceous perennials, *Solanum capsicastrum*, zinnias.

547. Planting Outdoors *Vegetables*: Brussels sprouts, spring cabbages, pickling cabbages, cauliflowers, chives, garlic, mint, onion sets, autumn-sown onions, potatoes, horse-radish, rhubarb, shallots, seakale. *Fruits*: as late winter. Also strawberries. *Flowers*: Alpines, hardy climbers, border carnations, Canterbury bells, double daisies, forget-me-nots, gladioli, montbretias, herbaceous perennials, polyanthuses, sweet peas, roses, ornamental trees and shrubs (deciduous and evergreen), tigridias, wallflowers.

548. Planting and Potting under Glass *Vegetables*: early cucumbers and tomatoes. *Flowers*: *Asparagus plumosus, A. sprengeri*, aspidistras, begonias, coleus, crotons, cacti and succulents, chrysanthemums, perpetual-flowering carnations, ferns, fuchsias, gloxinias, heliotropes, marguerites, palms, pelargoniums (geraniums), smilax. Bedding plants.

549. Plants to Start in Warmth *Flowers*: as late winter. *Fruits*: apricots, nectarines, peaches, vines.

550. Cuttings to Take in Warmth *Flowers*: as late winter. Also ageratum, dahlias, fuchsias, heliotropes, lobelias, marguerites, pelargoniums, scarlet salvias.

551. Cuttings to Take in Frame Delphiniums, perennial coreopsis, lupins, perennial scabious.

552. Pruning Outdoors *Flowers*: *Buddleia davidii*, hardy fuchsias, hybrid tea, floribunda and climbing roses. Clip ivy on walls.

553. Spraying Outdoors *Fruit*: apples, pears and plums with a winter wash against capsid bugs and with insecticide against red spider, capsid bug, aphids, etc; loganberries, raspberries, and blackberries with fungicide against cane spot.

554. Miscellaneous *Vegetables*: prick off seedlings raised under glass as soon as they can be handled. *Fruit*: train and pinch young growths of grape vines. Pollinate grapes, peaches, and nectarines in bloom. Protect blossom outdoors. Graft apples and pears. *Flowers*: increase herbaceous perennials by division, stop Japanese and incurved chrysanthemums and perpetual-flowering carnations, turf lawns.

Work for mid spring

555. Seeds to Sow Outdoors *Vegetables*: asparagus, globe artichokes, globe beetroot, broad beans, broccoli, sprouting broccoli, Brussels sprouts, cabbage, carrots, cauliflowers, cress, endive, kale, kohl rabi, lettuce, mustard, parsley, peas, radishes, salsify, savoy, spinach beet, turnips. *Flowers*: hardy annuals as early spring. Also, late in the month, nicotianas, aster, calandrinia, canary creeper, dahlias, dimorphotheca, jacobaea, layia, leptosiphon, *Mesembryanthemum criniflorum*, nasturtiums, salpiglossis, sweet sultan, *Tagetes signata pumila*, ursinia, venidium, zinnias, lawn grass seed.

556. Seeds to Sow under Glass *Vegetables*: French beans, runner beans, celery, cucumbers, vegetable marrows, tomatoes. *Fruits*: melons. *Flowers*: cinerarias, coleus, exacum, *Primula kewensis, P. obconica, P. sinensis*. Annuals (hardy and half-hardy for flowering in pots).

557. Planting Outdoors *Vegetables*: asparagus, artichokes, broad beans, cauliflower, leeks, lettuces, onions, peas, potatoes. *Flowers*: alpines, antirrhinums, evergreen shrubs, gladioli, herbaceous perennials, montbretias, pansies, penstemons, sweet peas, violas, violets.

558. Planting and Potting under Glass *Vegetables*: celery, cucumber, tomato. *Flowers*: achimenes, azaleas, annuals or plants treated as such sown in late winter and early spring, begonias, bedding plants generally, carnations, chrysanthemums, camellias, cyclamen, dahlias, eupatorium, gloxinias, haemanthus, jasminum, luculia, perlargoniums.

559. Plants to Start in Warmth *Flowers*: as late winter. *Fruit*: late vines.

560. Cuttings to Take in Warmth As early spring. Winter-flowering begonias of the Lorraine type, poinsettias.

561. Cuttings to Take in Frames As early spring.

562. Pruning Outdoors As early spring. Also evergreen foliage shrubs, forsythias, *Leycesteria formosa, Perowskia atriplicifolia*, romneyas, willows grown for bark.

563. Pruning under Glass Azaleas, deutzias, genistas.

564. Spraying Outdoors Blackcurrants and gooseberries with fungicide against mildew and insecticide against big bud; apples and pears with fungicide against scab.

565. Miscellaneous *Vegetables*: train and top dress cucumbers, lift celery and leeks, feed spring cabbages, protect early potatoes, harden off celery. *Fruits*: train and pollinate melons, train and stop vines, thin and disbud peaches and nectarines,

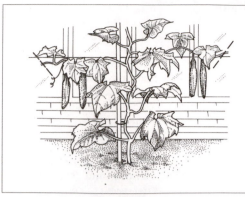

Training cucumbers.
The fruit-bearing laterals
have been stopped some time
previously by pinching out
their tips. Further laterals are
allowed to form all up the
stem which is stopped when
it reaches the ridge.

graft fruit trees, remove grease bands from fruit trees. *Flowers*: sow grass seed, apply fertilizer to roses, harden off bedding plants and half-hardy annuals, stake sweet peas, feed lawns and apply selective lawn weed-killer if necessary.

Work for late spring

566. Seeds to Sow Outdoors *Vegetables*: French beans, haricot beans, runner beans, beetroots, chicory, cress, ridge cucumbers, endive, kohl rabi, lettuces, vegetable marrows, mustard, peas, radishes, spinach, turnips. *Flowers*: asters, hardy annuals (as mid-spring), zinnias and other half-hardy annuals for autumn flowering.

567. Seeds to Sow under Glass *Flowers*: Calceolarias, cinerarias, humea, greenhouse primulas.

568. Planting Outdoors *Vegetables*: French beans, early broccoli, Brussels sprouts, cauliflowers, celeriac, leeks, onions, peas, potatoes. *Flowers*: alpines, antirrhinums, aquatics, bedding plants (towards end of season), border chrysanthemums, dormant dahlia tubers, magnolias, pansies, penstemons, seedling hardy perennials, violas, violets.

569. Planting and Potting under Glass *Vegetables*: cucumbers, tomatoes. *Fruits*: melons. *Flowers*: begonias, perpet-

ual-flowering carnations, chrysanthemums, gloxinias, streptocarpus, spring-rooted cuttings of pelargoniums, fuchsias, etc.

570. Pest Control Outdoors *Vegetables*: spray onions and peas with fungicide if mildew appears; spray with insecticide if any vegetables are attacked by aphids (greenfly, black-fly, etc) or caterpillars; dust soil around onion and cabbage seedlings with insecticidal dust to kill eggs of onion and cabbage flies. *Fruit*: apples with insecticide against codling moth, and apple sawfly, and fungicide against scab; pears with fungicide against scab, raspberries, loganberries and blackberries with fungicide against cane spot; strawberries with fungicide against mildew. *Flowers*: spray with insecticide any that are attacked by caterpillars or aphids, spray roses with fungicide against black spot.

571. Miscellaneous *Vegetables*: thin seedlings, earth up potatoes, stake peas, train and feed tomatoes and cucumbers coming into bearing, start to blanch early leeks, cut asparagus, prick off celery. *Fruit*: mulch fruit trees with manure, disbud and thin peaches, nectarines, and vines under glass, train and feed melons, ring unfruitful apples and pears, straw strawberries, start to pick gooseberries at end of month, thin out new raspberry canes. *Flowers*:

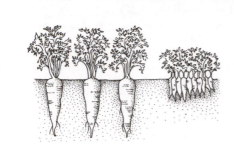

A lesson in thinning. The evils of overcrowding are evident on the right.

stop chrysanthemums according to growth, clear beds of spring bedding, heel in tulips, daffodils, hyacinths, etc, train sweet peas, thin and stake herbaceous plants, thin roses, apply lawn sand, feed plants in growth.

Work for early summer

572. Seeds to Sow Outdoors *Vegetables*: French beans, shorthorn carrots, coleworts, cress, endive, lettuces, mustard, parsley, early peas, radishes, summer spinach, turnips. *Flowers*: tuberous anemones, *Alyssum saxatile*, aquilegias, aubrietas, Canterbury bells, campanulas and other miscellaneous hardy biennials, perennials, and rock plants, perennial coreopsis, double daisies, delphiniums, forget-me-nots, foxgloves, hollyhocks, lupins, Oriental poppies, Iceland poppies, Brompton stocks, sweet williams.

573. Seeds to Sow under Glass Calceolaries, cinerarias, greenhouse primulas.

574. Planting Outdoors *Vegetables*: French beans, runner beans, broccoli, Brussels sprouts, cabbage, cauliflowers, celeriac, celery, ridge cucumbers, kale, leeks, vegetable marrow, savoys, tomatoes. *Flowers*: abutilons, auriculas, tuberous begonias, cannas, dahlias, heliotropes, flag irises (immediately flowers fade), maize, polyanthuses, primroses, ricinus, scarlet salvias, mossy saxifrages, bedding plants.

575. Potting under Glass Auriculas, perpetual-flowering carnations, chrysanthemums, early-sown greenhouse primulas and cinerarias.

576. Pruning Outdoors *Fruit*: red and white currants, gooseberries. *Flowers*: brooms, *Clematis montana*, *Chaenomeles speciosa*, evergreen ceanothus (all as soon as possible after flowering). Remove faded flower trusses from rhododendrons and azaleas. Cut back aubrietas, arabis, and perennial candytufts. Trim hedges.

577. Pest Control Outdoors *Vegetables*: spray onions and peas with fungicide against mildew, spray peas with insecticide against thrips, spray with insecticide any vegetables attacked by caterpillars or aphids. *Fruit*: spray or dust raspberries with insecticide when first fruits of Lloyd George start to colour, spray apples and plums with fungicide against scab and mildew, spray pears with fungicide against scab, spray with insecticide any trees attacked by caterpillars or aphids. *Flowers*: spray roses with fungicide against black spot, spray with insecticide any plants attacked by aphids.

578. Miscellaneous *Vegetables*: blanch leeks, earth up potatoes, train and feed cucumbers and tomatoes, thin seedlings, start to dig early potatoes, draw soil from shallot bulbs, pinch broad beans, stop cutting asparagus about middle of month. *Fruit*: start to thin apples and pears, train and feed melons, complete thinning of peaches, nectarines, and vines, remove runners from strawberries. *Flowers*: remove runners from violets, disbud roses and border carnations, rest arums, cyclamens, and pot-grown roses and shrubs outdoors, bud roses, take cuttings of hardy pinks.

Work for mid summer

579. Seeds to Sow Outdoors *Vegetables*: spring cabbage, shorthorn carrots, coleworts, cress, endive, lettuces, mustard, parsley, early peas, radishes, turnips. *Flowers*: forget-me-nots. Brompton stocks.

580. Seeds to Sow under Glass Calceolarias, cinerarias, greenhouse primulas.

581. Planting Outdoors *Vegetables*: broccoli, Brussels sprouts, cabbage, cauliflowers, celery, kale, leeks, savoys. *Flowers*: seedlings of biennials and perennials raised from seed sown in early summer, colchicums, autumn-flowering crocuses, *Lilium candidum*, sternbergias.

582. Potting under Glass Seedling greenhouse primulas, cinerarias, and calceolarias as soon as the smaller pots become filled with roots. Also pot the late spring-struck cuttings of pelargoniums.

583. Pruning Outdoors *Fruit*: apples, apricots, trained cherries, red and white currants, gooseberries, nectarines, peaches, pears, plums. *Flowers*: brooms, evergreen ceanothuses, deutzias, helianthemums, philadelphuses, hybrid tea roses, weigelas, wisterias - all after flowering.

584. Cuttings to Root in a Frame or Cool Greenhouse Hardy Shrubs and shrubby alpine plants generally.

585. Propagation Outdoors Bud roses and fruit trees, layer border carnations, shrubs, and clematises; peg down strawberry runners.

586. Pest Control Outdoors *Vegetables*: spray potatoes with fungicide against blight and peas against mildew, spray peas with insecticide against thrips, spray with insecticide vegetables attacked by caterpillars or aphids, spray tomatoes under glass with insecticide against white fly or try biological control. *Fruit*: spray apples with fungicide against scab, and vines against mildew, saw off plum branches attacked by silver leaf, burn straw used on strawberry beds. *Flowers*: spray roses with fungicide against black spot, any plants attaked by mildew, or other fungal disorders and with insecticide any plants attacked by caterpillars or aphids.

587. Miscellaneous *Vegetables*: blanch leeks, lift and store shallots and autumn-sown onions, lift early potatoes as required, gather and dry herbs, commence to earth up celery, make outdoor mushroom beds, cut globe artichokes. *Fruit*: allow atmosphere to dry in vineries carrying fruit starting to colour, begin to pick early apples and pears, pick cherries, plums, currants and gooseberries in season, remove unwanted runners from strawberries. *Flowers*: lift and store daffodils and bulbous irises, tulips and hyacinths, remove faded flowers from annuals and bedding plants, remove runners from violets, disbud dahlias and roses.

Work for late summer

588. Seeds to Sow Outdoors *Vegetables*: spring cabbage, pickling cabbage, cress, endive, lettuces (for transplanting later to a frame), mustard, onions, radishes, winter spinach, spinach beet, lawn grass seed.

589. Seeds to Sow under Glass *Flowers*: cyclamen, mignonette (for pot

Layering a strawberry runner.
Peg it down into a pot of soil sunk in the ground near the parent plant.

culture), winter-flowering stocks, schizanthus.

590. Planting Outdoors *Vegetables:* late broccoli, winter cabbage, coleworts, kale, savoys. *Fruit:* strawberries. *Flowers: Lilium candidum, L. testaceum,* colchicums, autumn crocus, sternbergia.

591. Potting under Glass Winter flowering begonias, calceolarias, cinerarias, cyclamen (old corns), freesias, Roman and 'prepared' hyacinths, lachenalias, arum lilies, greenhouse primulas.

592. Pruning Outdoors. *Fruit:* same as midsummer. Also summer-fruiting raspberries. *Flowers:* show and regal pelargoniums, evergreen shrubs and hedges, hydrangeas.

593. Cuttings to Root in Frame or Cool Greenhouse. Hardy shrubs and shrubby alpines generally, fuchsias, hydrangeas, bedding pelargoniums (geraniums), show and regal pelargoniums, calceolarias, penstemons.

594. Propagation Outdoors. As midsummer. Also tip layer blackberries and loganberries.

595. Pest Control Outdoors *Vegetables:* as midsummer. *Fruit:* spray gooseberries and currants with insecticide as soon as crop has been gathered, brush methylated spirits into white woolly patches on apples attacked by American blight. *Flowers:* as midsummer. Also set traps for earwigs.

596. Miscellaneous *Vegetables:* lift second early potatoes as required. Earth up leeks and early celery, bend over leaves of spring-sown onions, blanch early endive when well grown, lift and store early beetroot when large enough. *Fruit:* as midsummer. *Flowers:* remove faded flowers from annuals and bedding plants,

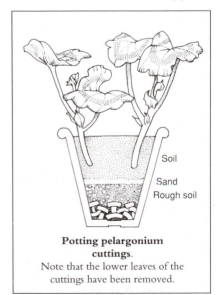

Soil

Sand
Rough soil

Potting pelargonium cuttings.
Note that the lower leaves of the cuttings have been removed.

remove runners from violets, disbud dahlias and roses, 'take' chrysanthemum buds, start nerines, cyclamen, and arum lilies.

Work for early autumn

597. Seeds to Sow Outdoors *Vegetables:* Brussels sprouts, cauliflower (to a frame later). *Flowers:* annual alyssum, calendula, candytuft, clarkia, annual coreopsis, cornflower, godetia, larkspur, nigella, Shirley and cardinal poppies, annual scabious, viscaria, lawn grass seed.

598. Seeds to Sow under Glass *Vegetables:* cress, endive, lettuces, mustard, radishes. *Flowers:* annuals for flowering in pots in the greenhouse.

599. Planting Outdoors *Vegetables:* late winter and spring cabbage, late kales, savoys. *Fruit:* strawberries. *Flowers:* anemones, rooted border carnation layers, crocuses, daffodils (narcissi), bulbous irises, lilies, muscaris, scillas, snowdrops, other spring-flowering bulbs, all herbaceous plants not actually in flower, evergreen shrubs.

600. Potting or Planting under Glass *Vegetables:* parsley (seedlings raised outdoors). *Flowers:* as late summer. Also cyclamen seedlings, daffodils (narcissi), hyacinths, bulbous irises, lilies, tulips, violets (in frames).

601. Pruning Outdoors *Fruit:* blackberries, blackcurrants, loganberries, summer-fruiting raspberries (as soon as crop is gathered). *Flowers:* rambler roses (as soon as flowers are faded).

602. Cuttings to Root in a Frame or Cool Greenhouse Bedding calceolaries, fuchsias, gazanias, mesembryanthemums, pansies, zonal pelargoniums (geraniums), penstemons, verbenas, violas, violets, and hardy evergreen shrubs generally (many hardy evergreen shrubs will root in a sheltered place in the open).

603. Pest Prevention Outdoors Spray with insecticide any vegetables, fruits, or flowers attacked by mildew, fix grease-bands around fruit trees.

604. Plants to be Removed to Shelter at First Sign of Frost Agapanthus, Indian azaleas, camellias, perpetual-flowering carnations, greenhouse chrysanthemums, fuchsias, gazanias, genistas, heliotropes, hydrangeas, arum lilies, marguerites, mesembryanthemums, pelargoniums, double-flowered tropaeolums.

605. Miscellaneous *Vegetables:* lift beetroots, carrots and potatoes for storing, continue to blanch leeks, celery and endive. *Fruit:* allow grapes, peaches, melons, etc, to ripen as rapidly as possible. Continue to pick apples and pears as they part readily from the trees. *Ornamental garden:* turf lawns, apply worm-killer if necessary.

Work for mid-autumn

606. Seeds to Sow Outdoors Sweet peas.

607. Planting Outdoors *Vegetables:* spring cabbage, coleworts. *Flowers:* hardy perennials, biennials, and evergreen shrubs generally. Also spring bedding plants such as double daisies, forget-me-nots, polyanthuses, and wallflowers. Hardy bulbs as early autumn. Also hyacinths, lily of the valley, and tulips.

608. Planting or Potting under Glass *Vegetables:* box mint roots for forcing. *Flowers:* hardy plants, bulbs, hardy annuals and evergreen shrubs for the greenhouse. Calceolarias, cinerarias, greenhouse primulas.

609. Pruning Outdoors Blackberries, currants, gooseberries, loganberries.

610. Cuttings to Root Outdoors *Fruit:* currants, gooseberries. *Flowers:* roses and deciduous shrubs generally.

611. Cuttings to Root in a Frame or Cool Greenhouse As early autumn.

612. Plants to be Lifted and Stored in a Frost-proof Place Tuberous-rooted begonias, dahlias, gladioli, *Lobelia cardinalis*, choice montbretias and *Salvia patens*.

613. Miscellaneous *Vegetables:* dig vacant ground, working in lime or manure where necessary. Lift and store potatoes, carrots, beetroots, turnips, and swedes. Cut back asparagus and globe artichokes, complete blanching of leeks and celery, blanch endive as required, protect cauliflowers. *Fruit:* gather and store all remaining apples and pears, prepare sites for fruit trees. *Flowers:* prepare ground for trees and shrubs, including roses, turf and repair lawns, disbud perpetual-flowering carnations, stop feeding chrysanthemums.

Work for late autumn

614. Seeds to Sow Outdoors Long-pod broad beans, hardy culinary peas.

615. Planting Outdoors *Fruit:* all the hardy kinds with the exception of strawberries. *Flowers:* hardy bulbs as mid-autumn. Also hardy deciduous trees, shrubs, and climbers, including roses.

616. Potting under Glass Azaleas, brooms, deutzias, hydrangeas, lilacs, roses, and other flowering shrubs required for the greenhouse. Also astilbes and other herbaceous perennials.

617. Pruning Outdoors *Fruit:* all hardy varieties, including canes if not already dealt with. *Flowers:* all deciduous hedges.

618. Cuttings to Root Outdoors As mid-autumn.

619. Pruning under Glass Apricots, nectarines, peaches and vines as soon as they have lost their leaves.

620. Miscellaneous *Vegetables:* dig and manure or lime all vacant ground, protect cauliflower and broccoli curds from frost, blanch endive as required, lift and store Jerusalem artichokes, horseradish, parsnips and salsify, lift chicory, rhubarb, and seakale for forcing. *Fruit:* cut and store late grapes, ventilate vineries and peach houses freely, root prune excessively vigorous fruit trees. *Flowers:* tidy up herbaceous borders, cut back outdoor chrysanthemums and remove a few plants of each kind to a frame, bring early potted bulbs into the greenhouse, protect tender or woolly-leaved alpines with panes of glass.

Work for early winter

621. Cuttings to Take under Glass Perpetual-flowering carnations, greenhouse chrysanthemums.

622. Planting Outdoors As late autumn, when weather and soil conditions are favourable.

623. Pruning Outdoors As late autumn. Also prune *Clematis jackmanii*.

624. Pruning under Glass Vines, peaches, nectarines, and apricots. Lower vine rods to check flow of sap. Ventilate vineries freely.

625. Miscellaneous *Vegetables:* continue to protect curds of broccoli and cauliflowers, continue to blanch endives, continue to force seakale, rhubarb, and chicory. *Flowers:* cut back chrysanthemums as they pass out of flower, pinch tips out of sweet pea seedlings, examine all plants and tubers in store.

PESTS, DISEASES AND WEEDS

MISCELLANEOUS INFORMATION

626. Controlling Pests and Diseases It is not always necessary to know precisely what pest or disease is attacking plants in order to apply effective remedies. Frequently it is sufficient to be able to fit it into one or other of a few main groups. First decide whether it is a pest, eg insect, or other creature, or a disease, eg fungus, or other low type of vegetable organism. Pests are treated with insecticides or acaricides (mite killers), diseases mainly with fungicides.

Sometimes a simple change in the way a plant is being grown can help. For example, over-feeding with nitrogen can result in lush and sappy growth that is irresistible to aphids and other pests. Equally, hot and dry conditions can favour the spread of certain fungus diseases. For serious infestations, however, chemical control may be the best solution.

If it is an insect which is attacking the plant above soil level, eg leaves, stems, flowers, or fruits, it is probable that an insecticide such as derris (644) will give reasonable control because it is poisonous to a wide range of insects including beneficial ones, though not always as effective against particular insects as other chemicals which are more specific in their action.

Soil pests, such as cutworms, leatherjackets, wireworms, and millepedes, cannot be destroyed by spraying but must be attacked with a soil insecticide such as gamma-HCH (649) or chlorpyriphos (637). Slugs can be controlled by metaldehyde (653) or aluminium sulphate (633).

Red spider mites, which are not insects, can be killed by using pirimiphos-methyl (659) in various forms or with malathion (651), derris (644), or horticultural soap (662).

For plants grown under glass, biological control of pests can be very successful. Certain plant pests have specific predators that will kill the pests without damaging the plants. The predators can be bought from specialist suppliers and released in the greenhouse. In the garden, beneficial insects and other animals can be encouraged by planting, providing a suitable environment and by using garden chemicals with discretion. Bats, hedgehogs, frogs, toads, slow-worms, some birds, hoverflies, and ladybirds are all of benefit in the garden. There are many others, too, so take care not assume that everything that moves is a pest.

If the trouble is due to disease, decide whether this is caused by a fungus, eg black spot, rust, mildew, etc, or bacterium or virus, eg streak, mosaic, etc. Fungi usually cause dark dampish spots, or patches of decay or outgrowths of mould, rusty coloured spots, etc. Bacterial and virus diseases usually cause drier spotting or streaking without obvious outgrowth (624), but are in general more difficult to identify. Fungal diseases may be treated by spraying with reliable fungicides such as Bordeaux mixture (636), or with carbendazim (640), mancozeb (652), or by dusting with sulphur (663). Bacterial and virus diseases cannot as a rule be treated (628).

627. Trapping Rats and mice can be caught in spring or cage traps baited with cheese or fat. Moles may be caught with steel traps set across the burrows. Gloves must be worn while setting the traps to avoid leaving human scent on them. Soil removed to set the traps must be replaced so that burrows are dark. Traps should be set across main burrows and those leading to water. Cockroaches can be caught in proprietary traps baited with bran. Earwigs may be trapped in inverted flower pots stuffed with hay, hollow broad bean stalks, slightly opened matchboxes, or any other similar dark hiding place. Leatherjackets and slugs can be trapped under wet sacks or heaps of damp vegetable refuse laid on the soil. Millepedes and wireworms can be collected from sliced carrots and potatoes buried just beneath the surface of the soil. For tree bands, see (178).

628. Incurable Diseases and Infestations Not all diseases and pests can be controlled as yet. In some cases the only way of preventing further damage is to remove and burn affected plants as soon as detected. Even with diseases that can be treated, it is generally advisable to remove and burn specially bad plants or portions of plants. On no account should these be placed on the compost heap or left lying about. This applies, among other diseases, to plum silver leaf, all collar and root rots, club roots, aster wilts, coral spot and brown rot of fruits.

629. Virus Diseases A large class of diseases caused by ultra-microscopic organisms which infect the sap. Symptoms vary from a slight mottling or rolling of the leaves to intense dry brown spotting or complete collapse. Such names as aucuba mosaic, bronze leaf, streak, leaf roll, yellow edge, etc, describe outstanding symptoms of different viruses. External applications have not proved very satisfactory in controlling these diseases. Infection is carried largely by sucking insects, especially aphids, eg greenfly, blackfly, etc, and these must be kept

down by spraying with suitable insecticides such as derris (644), dimethoate (646), fenitrothion (648) or malathion (651). Virus may also be carried on knives, secateurs, etc, used in pruning, and these should be disinfected by dipping in a good household disinfectant. Badly infected plants should always be burned.

Some varieties of plants subject to virus disease are resistant to infection and some are tolerant, ie they show no adverse symptoms. Tolerant plants can become unnoticed sources of infection for sensitive plants.

630. Eelworms Microscopic, transparent, eel-like creatures which often infest roots or stems of certain plants in great numbers, causing knots, goutiness, and distortion. Much larger, transparent nematode worms are frequently mistaken for them and are allied but are harmless, as they feed on decaying matter in the soil and are frequently found in manure, compost, or leafmould.

Eelworms are principally found in phloxes, chrysanthemums, narcissi, tomatoes, cucumbers, potatoes, and onions. Usually there is no satisfactory remedy and plants should be destroyed. Eelworms on potatoes form very small white or brown cysts on the roots. There is no remedy, infected plants and tubers should be destroyed. Plant only resistant varieties.

Infected narcissus bulbs can be cleared of eelworms and fly larvae by keeping the bulbs for three hours in water maintained at 43°C (110°F) followed by immediate cooling in cold water but special apparatus is required for this. Infected chrysanthemum stools from which all stems have been cut can be heated in a similar manner but for 20-30 minutes only. For strawberry runners, the time is five to six minutes and the water temperature 46°C

(115°F). Clean stock of phlox can usually be obtained from root cuttings (446). It is always advisable to sterilize the soil if practicable with steam (631) or chemicals, or to replace soil in the area to be replanted.

631. Sterilization by Heat In addition to treatment with chemicals such as phenolic emulsions, which should be used with great care, following the manufacturer's instructions, soil can be sterilized by raising the temperature. Four methods may be employed, namely electrical heating, baking, steaming, and scalding.

ELECTRICAL STERILIZATION requires special apparatus, and manufacturer's instructions must be followed in the use of this.

BAKING of small amounts of soil can be done by spreading soil thinly in an oven or in trays in a special apparatus. The danger is that soil may be charred. This risk can be lessened if the soil is thoroughly moistened first. The temperature of the soil should be raised slowly until it is between 96° and 99°C (205° and 210°F) and maintained at this for 15 minutes. This is rarely tackled by amateur gardeners.

STEAM sterilization must be done with special apparatus. Steam under pressure is forced through the soil until the temperature is raised to between 93° and 96°C (200° and 205°F). It is maintained at this for $1/2$ hour.

SCALDING is a simple method for home use. Soil is placed dry in a sack and this is suspended in a copper containing a little water. The water is then boiled rapidly for $1/2$ hour.

Soil that has been sterilized by heat shows a falling off in fertility for a few months. This can be counteracted by using the John Innes formulae for seed and potting composts (493), (497).

632. Systemic Chemicals Some chemicals when applied to plants remain on the outside, on leaves, stems etc. They are known as non-systemic chemicals in contrast to systemic chemicals, which are absorbed by the plant and enter into its sap in which they may be carried from one part of the plant to another. Systemic insecticides, fungicides and weed-killers are known. Advantages are that it is not necessary to cover the whole plant with the chemical to get a good result; that the chemical is not removed by rain; and with insecticides that it is less likely to harm useful insects since these do not feed on the plant. Drawbacks are that systemic chemicals cannot be wiped or washed off, that some persist for a considerable time and may render a crop unusable until they have been dispersed or decomposed.

INSECTICIDES AND FUNGICIDES

633. Alum As a pesticide it is aluminium sulphate that is used primarily for killing slugs and snails. Aluminium ammonium sulphate can be used to deter animals and birds from lawns, beds, trees and shrubs.

634. Benomyl A fungicide that can be used to control a wide range of diseases both in the garden and the greenhouse.

635. Borax Sometimes used to kill ants. It is available mixed with a sugary gel for use inside and outdoors or as a powder mixed with carbaryl (639).

636. Bordeaux Mixture This is a useful fungicide against potato and tomato blight, peach leaf curl, rust and canker.

637. Chlorpyriphos An effective insecticide for controlling soil pests, including cabbage- and other vegetable root flies.

638. Captan A synthetic chemical used with gamma-HCH formulated as a powder in seed dressings to protect seedlings from damping off and other soil-borne diseases. Captan is also used with 1-naphythylacetic acid in power form in hormone rooting preparations – often with added fungicide to protect against fungal rots.

Captan is harmful to fish.

639. Carbaryl A synthetic insecticide effective against a fairly wide range of pests including leather-jackets, wireworms, caterpillars, chafers, earthworms and ants. Carbaryl is harmful to bees and fish, so should not be used when plants are in flower and should be kept out of streams and ponds. It is moderately persistent and should not be used with alkaline mixtures such as Bordeaux.

640. Carbendazim A fungicide used for a wide range of diseases of fruit, vegetables, shrubs, flowering plants, bulbs and lawns. It is particularly useful for cases of powdery mildew, botrytis and leaf spot.

641. Cheshunt Compound A fungicide used chiefly for the prevention or check of damping-off disease in seedlings. It is based on copper sulphate.

642. Copper Various formulations of copper compounds, including copper sulphate and copper oxychloride, are sold as 'copper fungicide' or under trade names. They may be employed for much the same purposes as other copper sprays, such as Bordeaux mixture (636) might be used.

643. Cresylic Acid A powerful sterilizer for use as a liquid pruning compound or to cure canker on trees.

644. Derris An insecticide that is effective against many pests including aphids, leaf hoppers, thrips, caterpillars of many kinds, apple-blossom weevil, pea and bean weevil, raspberry beetle, gooseberry sawfly, flea beetles and red spider mites. Though relatively harmless to

human beings, warm-blooded creatures and bees, it is recommended that at least one day elapse between use on edible crops and harvesting. It is very poisonous to fish and harmful to adult ladybirds.

Derris is available as a dust, ready for immediate use, and as a liquid, ready made up or to be diluted with water and used as a spray according to manufacturer's instructions. The effectiveness of derris depends on the percentage of rotenone it contains and this may diminish with age.

645. Diazinon An insecticide used primarily to kill aphids, capsid bugs, leaf miners, thrips, red spider mites, mealy bugs, scale insects, springtails and mushroom flies. It is poisonous to warm-blooded animals, including man, and the manufacturer's instructions must be followed carefully. It should not be used on crops. Special care should be taken if other chemicals of the organo-phosphorus group, to which diazinon belongs, have been used, as accumulation of these chemicals within the body can be harmful.

646. Dimethoate A systemic insecticide, ie one that is absorbed into the sap of plants. It is used primarily to control aphids, apple and pear sucker, plum sawfly, woolly aphid and red spider mites. It should be used according to manufacturer's instructions. Edible crops treated with dimethoate should not be harvested for at least one week. Special care should be taken if other chemicals of the organophosphorus group, to which dimethoate belongs, are being used, as accumulations of these in the body can be harmful. Dimethoate should not be used on chrysanthemums.

647. Dinocap A fungicide used primarily to control powdery mildews on many plants, particularly roses. It is available mixed with foliar feed and fungicide as a complete treatment. Dinocap is not very poisonous to warm-blooded animals, including man, but care should be taken not to inhale it nor to get the concentrated chemical on the skin.

648. Fenitrothion This insecticide can be used to control a variety of insect pests on ornamentals, fruit and vegetables, including greenfly, blackfly, capsid bug, caterpillars, codling moth and sawfly, and raspberry beetle. A gap of 14 days should elapse between application and cropping, but just seven days for raspberries.

649. Gamma-HCH An insecticide used as a dust to control rootfly, wireworms, beetles and leatherjackets in the soil, or as a smoke to control pests in the greenhouse. It is also available combined with a fungicide for general treatments.

650. Lime This is mainly of value to correct soil acidity for which purpose it can be of great use in the control of club root of cabbages and other brassicas, since this disease thrives in acid soils. It is also used as a slug and snail deterrent.

Hydrated lime is easy to handle and is most effective when fresh. It can also be applied at 250–500g per square metre ($\frac{1}{2}$–1lb per yd^2) either as a top dressing or worked into the soil.

651. Malathion An insecticide effective against many pests including aphids, leaf hoppers, thrips, suckers, scale insects, mealy bugs, leaf miners, white flies, mushroom flies, gooseberry sawfly, raspberry beetle, pollen beetles and red spider mites. It is poisonous to warm-blooded animals, including man, also to bees and fish but protective clothing is not necessary when it is used. As it belongs to the organo-phosphorus group special care should be exercised if other chemicals of this group are being used because of the danger of cumulative effect. Four days should elapse between use of malathion and harvesting of edible crops.

Malathion is available as an aerosol and a dust, both for immediate use and as a liquid for dilution with water and application as a spray according to manufacturer's instructions. It should not be used on antirrhinums, crassulas, ferns, fuchsias, gerberas, petunias, pileas, sweet peas or zinnias.

652. Mancozeb A synthetic fungicide which is particularly good for the control of downy mildews, rose black spot, potato blight, tomato leaf mould, rust, apple and pear scab and peach leaf curl. At least one week should elapse between its use on outdoor edible crops and harvesting, but three weeks for lettuce. It is available as a wettable powder to be stirred into water at the rates directed by the manufacturers.

653. Metaldehyde (Meta) Used as a poison bait for slugs and snails in the form of pellets, tape or liquid.

654. Methiocarb A chemical used to kill slugs and snails, leatherjackets, millipedes and woodlice, and said to be more efficient than metaldehyde under damp conditions. It is available, ready for use, as small pellets or tablets to be sprinkled around plants liable to be attacked, or wherever slugs or snails are likely to be. It is harmful to fish, and poultry should be kept off treated ground for at least seven days.

655. Naphthalene Pellets of naphthalene mixed with volatile, scented oils can be scattered on the ground to deter cats and dogs from fouling in the garden. Pepper dust can be used for the same purpose (656).

656. Pepper Dust This may be sprinkled freely on the leaves and flowers of plants. It is chiefly useful to keep cats and dogs at bay, but is also of some service against slugs and earwigs.

657. Permethrin A widely used insecticide used either alone or in combination with other insecticides, or foliar feeds and fungicides, in liquid, aerosol, powder or smoke form (for use under glass). It is used to control many insect pests, including caterpillars (including the egg stage), whitefly, ants and other crawling insects, wasps, greenfly, blackfly, thrips, red spider mite, mealy bugs, scale insect, and pea maggot. When formulated for use on fruit and vegetable crops, one day must elapse between application and harvesting.

658. Pirimicarb An insecticide available in aerosol or liquid form, sometimes combined with fungicide as a complete pesticide treatment for roses and other ornamentals. Alone, it can be used to control greenfly and blackfly on crops either in the garden or under glass. Three days must elapse between application and cropping, or 14 days for lettuce grown under glass.

659. Pirimiphos–methyl An insecticide available as a dust, aerosol or liquid, either alone or with additional insecticide for the control of whitefly, red spider mite and other garden and greenhouse pests. When used on crops, seven days must elapse between application and cropping. It is also sometimes used on house plants.

660. Pyrethrum An insecticide prepared from the flower heads of certain tropical plants. It is not very poisonous to warm-blooded animals, including man, but acts very rapidly on many insects, including aphids, capsid bugs, leaf hoppers and thrips, giving a knock-down effect but not always a complete kill, for which reason it is often combined with slower but more certain insecticides. It is poisonous to fish and may harm ladybirds. Pyrethrum is available as a dust ready for use or as a ready-to-use liquid, or to be diluted with water and applied as a spray according to manufacturer's instructions.

661. Quassia A natural non-poiso-

nous insecticide chiefly used against aphids and sometimes available mixed with derris, in which form it is also effective against caterpillars and thrips.

662. Soft Soap Mainly used as a spreader but has some insecticidal properties and is occasionally used to control aphids and red spider mites. Insecticidal soaps have a stronger action against a wider range of insects, but can also harm beneficial insects.

663. Sulphur A fungicide particularly useful against mildews and storage rots. It is available as a fine powder for use direct or in various colloidal or wettable formulations to be mixed with water and applied as a spray according to manufacturer's instructions. It is also available as a smoke to control moles, rats and mice outdoors.

664. Tar–oil Wash Proprietary sprays made from tar distillate and used to clear fruit trees of caterpillar and aphid eggs, scale insects, lichen, moss, etc. Can only be applied with safety while trees are dormant in early or mid-winter. Manufacturer's instructions should be followed carefully. Other tar preparations are used to clear moss or slime from hard surfaces or lawns, or as glasshouse sterilants. As tar-oil scorches foliage, care must be taken when applying it to trees underplanted with green crops.

665. Thiophanate–methyl A useful fungicide available in liquid form for control of disease on garden and greenhouse ornamentals, fruit and vegetables, houseplants and lawns. There is no interval required between spraying and cropping. It can also be used as a preventative measure for clubroot on brassicas.

666. Thiram A fungicide effective in controlling a wide range of diseases including rose black spot, grey mould (botrytis), tulip fire, some rusts, apple and pear scab, downy mildew, raspberry cane

667. Table of Pests and Diseases

Method: Figures in (brackets) refer to numbered paragraphs throughout the book

Name	Notes	Treatment	
		Period	Method
American blight	See Aphid, woolly		
Antirrhinum rust	See rust		
Ants	Soil disturbed, aphid encouraged	all year	(635, 639, 649, 659)
Aphids (blackfly, greenfly, greyfly, rosy apple aphid, etc)	Lice suck juices, carry virus, and cripple young growth	early win – mid win	(664)
		late spr – mid aut	(644, 645, 646, 651)
Aphid, root	Lice suck juices from roots of lettuces and auriculas	late spr – mid aut	(637, 649)
Aphid, woolly	Lice, protected by white, woolly covering, on stems and roots. Paint with methylated spirits in summer	early win – mid win	(664)
Apple blossom weevil	Grubs 'cap' and destroy blossom	mid spr – late spr	(639)
		mid win	(664)
Apple blossom wilt	Fungus kills blossom and spurs	mid spr	(634)
Apple canker	Festering wounds encircle branches	mid win	(664)
		early spr – late aut	(642)
Apple codling moth	Caterpillars eat into fruits	late spr – early sum	(639, 178)
Apple sawfly	Maggots eat into fruits	late spr – early sum	(648)
Apple and pear scab	Black spots on leaves and fruits later cracked	mid spr – mid sum	(636, 634)
Apple sucker	Lice deforms leaves and kill blossom	mid spr – late spr	(648, 651)
Aster wilt	Annual asters rot at soil level	late spr – mid sum	(631)
Bacterial soft rot	Celery, etc, rots at the heart	early sum – mid aut	(642)
Bacterial canker (cherry and plum)	Round holes in leaves, gum oozes from bark, branches die	late sum – mid aut	(636)
Bean anthracnose	Sunken black spots on pods	early sum – mid sum	(636, 634)
Bean beetle	See Pea beetle		
Bean chocolate spot	Leaves and stems of broad beans blotched	late win – late spr	(636, 642)
Bean halo spot	Angular spots on leaves	mid spr – late sum	(628)
Bean rust	See Rust		
Bean weevil	See Pea weevil		
Blackfly	See Aphid		
Botrytis (grey mould)	Black decay followed by white mould	late spr – early aut	(634, 640, 663, 665)
Brown rot	Fruits of apples, plums, etc, mummified with rings of white mould	mid win	(664)
Brown scale	See scale		
Cabbage caterpillars	Leaves skeletonized	early sum – mid aut	(648, 639, 644, 649)

Name	Notes	Treatment Period	Method
Cabbage gall weevil	White maggots in galls at soil level	late spr – mid aut	(649)
Cabbage root fly	White maggots eating roots	late spr – mid sum	(637, 645)
Cabbage white blister	White blisters on stems and leaves	early spr – early aut	(636)
Cabbage white fly	Tiny white flies fouling leaves	early aut	(659, 651)
Cane spot	See Raspberry cane spot		
Canker	See Apple, Bacterial or Rose canker		
Capsid bug	Active lice on fruit trees. Leaves distorted, fruits marked	late win – early spr mid spr – early aut	(648, 646)
Carnation spot	Leaves yellow and curled	all year	(652)
Carrot fly	Maggots eat roots	late spr – mid sum	(637, 645)
Caterpillars	Leaves and stems of many plants eaten	early win – mid win mid spr – early sum	(649, 664) (649, 639, 644)
Celery fly	See Leaf miners		
Celery heart rot	See Bacterial soft rot		
Celery spot	Numerous spots on leaves	early sum – early aut	(642, 634)
Chafers	White larvae attack roots of many plants	all year	(639, 649)
Clematis wilt	Stems wither and die	mid spr – late spr	(636, 642)
Club root	Roots of cabbage tribe swell and decay	early spr – mid aut	(665, 634)
Cockroaches	Seedlings eaten	all year	
Codling moth	See Apple codling moth		
Collar rot	See Aster wilt, Damping off, Tomato collar rot		
Cranefly larvae	See Leather-jackets		
Cuckoo spit (froghopper)	Lice covered with froth on leaves and stems of many plants	late spr – late sum	(649, 651)
Currant big-bud	Buds swollen by mites within	early spr – mid spr	(634)
Currant clear wing moth	Shoots tunnelled by caterpillars	early sum – mid aut	(628)
Currant reversion	Leaf veins reduced in number, little fruit produced	all year	(628)
Cutworms	Caterpillars in soil eat stems and roots of many plants	all year	(649, 639)
Damping off	Seedlings rot at soil level	all year	(641)
Didymella	See Tomato stem rot		
Die back	Stems of roses and gooseberries die, especially in winter	early win – late win early spr – mid sum	(78) (636)
Earwigs	Flowers and young leaves of dahlias, etc, eaten	mid sum – mid aut	(649, 639)
Eelworms	Roots and stems infested by microscopic 'worms'	all year	(630, 631)
Flea beetles	Leaves of cabbages, turnips, etc, riddled with small round holes	early spr – mid aut	(649, 639, 644)

Name	Notes	Treatment	
		Period	Method
Foot rot	Stem decays at base	all year	(636, 666)
Frog flies (leaf hoppers)	Pale larvae suck juices from leaves	late spr – early aut	(644, 651)
Gladiolus scab	Leaves decay at soil level, corms spotted and split	mid aut – early spr	(634, 638)
Gladiolus dry rot	Leaves wither from tips, corms spotted	late spr – mid aut	(634)
Gooseberry mildew, American	Felt-like mildew on leaves, stems and fruits	early spr – early sum	(634, 640)
Gooseberry mildew, European	See Mildew		
Gooseberry rust or cluster-cup	Reddish blister-like swellings on leaves and fruits	early spr – mid sum	(636, 652)
Greenfly	See Aphid		
Grey mould	See Botrytis		
Gumming	See Bacterial canker		
Gummosis	Cucumber fruits ooze gum and crack	early sum – early aut	(652)
Hollyhock rust	See Rust		
Honey fungus (armillaria)	Roots die, white fungus under bark	all year	(628, 631)
Iris rhizome rot	Plants rot at base	early spr – early sum	(642)
Lawn diseases (dollar spot, red thread and fusarium)	Grass develops pale or pinkish patches	early spr – mid aut	(634)
Leaf hoppers	See Frog flies		
Leaf miners	Small maggots burrowing leaves	all year	(649, 651)
Lettuce grey mould	Stems rot and become mouldy	all year	(640)
Leather-jackets	Blackish larvae in the soil eat roots and stems of many plants including grass	all year	(649, 659)
Lily disease	See Botrytis rot		
Lily mosaic	See Mosaic		
Mealy bug	Juice sucked from vines and other greenhouse plants	all year late aut – early wint	(644, 651) (664)
Mice	Bulbs, corms and seeds eaten	all year	(627, 663)
Mildew, Powdery	Powdery white outgrowth on stems and leaves of many plants	late spr – mid aut	(665, 663)
– Downy	Leaves yellow, shrivelling, faintly powdered	late spr – early aut	(642, 640)
Millepedes	Whitish to black, many-legged soil pests which feed on the roots of the plants	all year	(634, 649)
Mint rust	Rusty spots on leaves and stems	early sum – early aut	(628)
Moles	Tunnels in soil and mounds of soil	all year	(627, 663)

Name	Notes	Treatment Period	Method
Mosaic	Yellow mottling of leaves caused by virus	late spr – early aut	(629)
Mushroom maggots	Mushrooms holed and maggoty	all year	(649)
Mussel scale	See Scale		
Narcissus basal rot	Base of bulb decays	late sum – mid aut	(634)
Narcissus fly	Maggots eat interior of bulb	mid sum – late sum	(649)
Nut weevil	Maggots feed in kernels	late spr – early sum	(649)
Onion fly	Maggots eat plants just beneath soil	early spr – mid sum	(649, 639, 637)
Onion neck rot	Top of bulb decays	early aut – early win	(628, 634)
Onion smut	Black stripes on leaves	late spr – late sum	(628)
Onion white rot	White mould and decay at base of bulb	early sum – late sum	(628)
Pea beetle	Seeds holed. Reject bad seeds		
Pea moth	Small caterpillars eat peas in pod	early sum – late sum	(648)
Pea and bean weevil	Holes eaten in leaf edge	late spr – mid sum	(644)
Peach leaf curl	Leaves curled and red	late win – early spr	(636)
Pear leaf blister mite	Reddish blister on leaves	late win / mid spr	(628) / (634)
Pear midge	Maggots eat interior of fruitlets	mid spr	(648, 649)
Pear sawfly	See Caterpillars		
Pear scab	See Apple and pear scab		
Potato blackleg	Black decay of stems from soil	early sum – early aut	(628)
Potato blight	Damp, black blotches on leaves, brown decay in tubers	mid sum – early aut	(636, 628, 652)
Potato eelworm	White cysts on tubers	late sum – early win	(628, 630)
Potato scab (common)	Scabs on skin of tubers. Avoid liming soil. Diseased tubers keep and are fit for use. Dig in leaf-mould or peat		
Potato storage rot	Dry brown rot after lifting	early aut – mid aut	(628)
Potato wart disease	Wart-like outgrowths which destroy tubers. Plant resistant varieties	mid sum – mid aut	(628)
Raspberry beetle	White maggots eat fruits, beetles eat flower buds	late spr – early sum	(644, 648)
Raspberry cane blight	Canes wither and snap off near ground level	late spr	(636)
Raspberry cane spot	Purplish decay encircling canes. Also attacks blackberries and loganberries	early spr – late spr	(634, 665)
Raspberry mosaic	See Mosaic		
Raspberry midge	Pink grubs in rind of young canes	late spr	(644, 648)
Red spider mites	Minute reddish mites, suck juices from leaves of many plants	early sum – early aut	(657, 644, 662, 651)
Rhododendron bud blast	Flower buds die, control leaf-hoppers	early sum – late sum	(648, 649)

Name	Notes	Treatment	
		Period	Method
Ring spot	Circular spots on leaves of cabbages and other brassicas	early sum – early aut	(666, 652)
Root maggot	Small maggots in roots of chrysanthemums and lettuces	late spr – early aut	(644, 649)
Root rot	Roots and lower stems of many plants killed	all year	(666, 641)
Rose black spot	Circular black spots on leaves. See also (39)	late spr – early aut	(638, 652)
Rose canker	Festering wounds encircling branches	all year	(628)
Rose sawfly	Leaves curled	late spr – mid sum	(648)
Rust	Rusty spots on under surface of leaves	early sum – early aut	(666, 652)
Scale	Scale-covered insects on branches of fruit trees, etc	all year	(645, 651)
Silver leaf	Leaves of plum, apples, cherries, peaches, etc, silvered. Branches killed	early sum – mid sum	(348, 628)
Slugs	Leaves, stems, and fruits of many plants eaten	all year	(633, 653)
Slugworms	Black maggots eating leaf surface of fruit trees, roses, etc	early sum – early aut	(648, 644, 651, 659)
Snails	Damage and treatment. See Slugs		
Sooty mould	Black coating on leaves	all year	(644, 651)
Spotted wilt	Plants stunted. Brown spots on leaves	all year	(634, 665)
Springtails	Minute white insects in soil	early aut – early spr	(649)
Strawberry leaf spot	Reddish spots on leaves	late spr – mid sum	(647, 652)
Strawberry yellow edge	Virus, dwarfs and curls leaves and turns edges yellow	late spr – early aut	(629)
Streak (sweet pea, tomato)	Leaves and stems deformed and streaked	early sum – early aut	(629)
Tarsonemid mite	Mites suck juices from young leaves of strawberries, cyclamen, etc	early sum – late sum	(628)
Thrips	Small active insects, deform leaves, flowers, etc, and cause silvery streaking of many plants	all year	(648, 651, 646, 648)
Tomato blossom end rot	Black decay of fruit at end opposite to stalk. Encouraged by underwatering	late spr – mid aut	
Tomato leaf-mould	Khaki mould on underside of leaves	early sum – early aut	(640)
Tomato sleepy disease	Plant flags but recovers when temperature is raised above 75° F	all year	(628)

Name	Notes	Treatment	
		Period	Method
Tomato stem rot	Stems shrink and rot	early spr – late sum	(652)
Tulip fire	Leaves and flowers scorched	early spr – late spr	(652, 666)
Turnip flea beetle	See Flea beetle		
Vine mildew	See Mildew		
Virus	See (629)		
Wasps	Ripening fruits eaten	mid sum – early aut	(659, 644)
Weevils	Notches in leaves, grubs in roots	all year	(648, 649, 659)
White fly	Small white 'flies' on many plants	all year	(644, 657, 659)
White rust	White 'felt' on stems and leaves of brassicas, wallflowers and stocks	all year	(628)
Winter moth	Caterpillars eat young leaves of apples, etc	mid win	(644)
		mid spr – late sp	(644)
		early aut	(178)
Wirestem	Stem of young brassicas wither	early spr – early sum	(641)
Wireworm	Yellow hard-skinned larvae eating roots of many plants	all year	(637)
Woodlice	Seedlings eaten	all year	(649, 654)
Worms	Mainly beneficial but drainage of pot plants blocked and lawns fouled	mid spr – late spr early aut – mid aut	(639)

spot and tomato leaf mould, as well as some soil-borne diseases such as damping off and pea and bean foot rot. It is sometimes included in hormone rooting preparations and is available ready-mixed with insecticides as a general treatment for a wide range of garden plants. Manufacturer's instructions must be followed. Thiram should not be used on fruit intended for deep freezing because of a tendency to taint.

WEEDS AND WEED-KILLERS

668. Mechanical Destruction All weeds can be killed in time by digging and hoeing. Frequently these are the best means, though laborious. Deep-rooted weeds such as bindweed, dock, coltsfoot, and ground elder can only be destroyed by repeated applications of chemical herbicides. If their roots are dug out to a depth of 45-60cm (18-24in) and top growth is prevented for one whole spring and summer by hoeing and removing all regrowth, no further trouble is likely.

Annual and biennial weeds such as groundsel, chickweed, and common purple thistle can be exterminated quickly by hoeing only, if this is done before they ripen seeds.

Most surface-rooting weeds eg creeping buttercup, nettles, and couch grass, can be killed by burying them 45cm (18in) deep.

669. Types of Herbicide Some chemicals kill almost all kinds of plants and are called 'total herbicides'. Some kill particular types of plant but are more or less harmless to other types and are called 'selective herbicides'. Some kill plants by being scattered or sprayed over them, some are applied to the soil and some are effective applied in either of these ways. Herbicides which kill only the parts of the plant they touch are known as 'contact herbicides' in contrast to 'translocated' or 'systemic herbicides', which enter the plant either by leaves or roots and are carried round in the sap. Herbicides which remain active in the soil for a considerable time, preventing the growth of seedlings or small plants, are known as 'residual herbicides'. Scientists prefer the term 'herbicide', meaning plant killer, to 'weed-killer' since no chemical can distinguish between a garden plant and a weed. The user, by selection of an appropriate chemical and choice of the right method and time for application, ensures that weeds, not garden plants, are killed.

670. Application of Herbicides Dry, gel, stick and liquid chemicals are available. Some of the forms are applied direct to weeds, others are dissolved in water and applied as sprays or from sprinklers. Dry herbicides may be spread by hand but care is needed to ensure even distribution and correct dosage. The manufacturer's instructions must always be followed. Some manufacturers prepare lawn fertilizers blended with chemicals to kill lawn weeds, thus doing two jobs in one.

Liquid herbicides, after dilution with water, may be sprayed with any garden spraying equipment but there is often danger of spray drifting where it is not wanted. Herbicides are more safely applied from a watering-can or special applicator fitted with a fine rose or sprinkler bar, from which the liquid can be delivered almost in contact with the weeds or soil. Sprinkle bars of different widths are available to suit particular requirements eg a very narrow 7–8cm (3in) bar for applying herbicides between garden plants or in awkward places and a wide 45cm (18in) bar for covering lawns or large areas of vacant ground.

All equipment should be well washed after use. It is best to keep equipment solely for application of herbicides, thus reducing the risk of the chemicals getting on to garden plants.

671. Alloxydim-sodium A herbicide specifically used for controlling couch grass and other weed grasses among ornamental plants. It is available in the form of soluble granules.

672. 2,4-D A translocated selective weed-killer which will kill a good many weeds in lawns without injury to the grass. It is often mixed with other herbicides, such as mecoprop (681) to widen its band of efficacy. It is most effective if applied when grass and weeds are growing actively. Lawns should not be cut for a few days after application to give the chemical time to act. It is harmful to most garden plants other than grass and also to fish, so care should be taken to prevent drift. It is not persistent in the soil. It is available in various forms to be used according to manufacturer's instructions.

673. Dalapon A translocated selective herbicide which will kill grass, including couch grass, also reeds, sedges and other monocotyledons but is much less toxic to dicotyledons. It is particularly useful for killing grass in orchards and around bush fruits. It should not be used near Apple Cox's Orange Pippin in winter. Sensitive plants should not be planted on treated ground under six weeks. Dalapon is sold as a powder to be dissolved in water according to manufacturer's instructions and applied as a spray or sprinkle to the weeds.

674. Dicamba A translocated selective herbicide used either alone or in combination with other herbicides such as MCPA (680) for the control of weeds in lawns. It is supplied as a liquid to be diluted with water or aerosol. It is harmful to most plants, other than grass, and also to fish.

675. Dichlobenil A total residual herbicide which can be used to keep paths, drives etc clean for many months or in carefully limited doses can also be used to prevent growth of seedlings and small weeds around established shrubs, trees, roses, etc. It is purchased in granular form for application direct according to manufacturer's instructions.

676. Dichlorophen Used for the control of moss, lichen and algae on turf, paths, walls, roofs and fences. It is also useful in the control of lawn diseases and liverwort.

677. Dichlorprop A common ingredient of weed-control mixes for lawns, it is a selective herbicide, killing broad-leaved weeds but not grasses, although scorching may occur. It should not be used in windy conditions, because of the risk of damage to other plants through spray drift. It is sometimes included in herbicide and fertilizer (weed-and-feed) combinations.

678. Diquat A total weed-killer, available as a mixture with paraquat and some other herbicides, which is inactivated by contact with the soil. It is not itself poisonous to plants but is changed into a poisonous substance in the plant leaf by photosynthesis. Light is therefore essential for its action which is most rapid in warm, bright weather. It is available as a liquid for dilution and can be used to clear ground for sowing or planting or to kill weeds around growing plants, provided care is taken to apply it to the leaves of the weeds and to keep it off the leaves or green stems of garden plants. It does not matter if it falls on the soil.

679. Glyphosate A useful systemic herbicide for the control of annual and perennial weeds. It is available in liquid or gel form, and is inactivated on contact with soil. It is most effective when used during periods of active growth, preferably in sunny conditions.

680. MCPA A translocated selective herbicide used mainly in gardens for the control of weeds on lawns. For this purpose it may be used alone or in combination with other selective herbicides such as 2,4-D (672) or dicamba (674). Both it and these mixtures are used in the same way as 2,4-D.

681. Mecoprop A translocated selective herbicide chiefly used in gardens for the control of weeds in lawns. It is more effective than either 2,4-D (672) or MCPA (680) in killing clover and is often offered in mixture with 2,4-D to provide a weed-killer with a wide band of effectiveness. Method of use, either alone or in mixture, is the same as for 2,4-D.

682. Paraquat A total herbicide allied to diquat (678) and with similar properties. It is a better grass killer than diquat and mixtures of the two are offered to provide a herbicide with the widest possible band of effectiveness.

683. Simazine A residual herbicide which in heavy doses will inhibit the growth of all plants and can be used to keep paths, drives, etc clear of weeds for long periods. In smaller, carefully controlled doses it can be used selectively to prevent growth of weeds in rose beds, round ornamental trees and shrubs, in orchards, around bush and cane fruits, etc. It is available as a powder for dissolving in water and application as a spray or sprinkle direct to the soil according to manufacturer's instructions. It moves about very little in the soil, but on light, sandy soil it may affect adjacent plants.

684. Sodium Chlorate A total herbicide which is both translocated in the plant and also effective in the soil. It is useful for clearing waste land and for keeping paths, drives, etc clear of weeds. Drawbacks are its readiness to move about in the soil where it may easily be carried to places where it was not intended to be; the difficulty of knowing just how long it will remain effective, since it is easily washed out by rain yet may be retained for a long time in heavy soils or in dry weather; and its inflammability. To counter this last danger sodium chlorate is often mixed with a fire depressant. It is applied both as a powder (or granules) for use dry or for solution in water and application as a spray or sprinkle either to the weeds or to the soil. It can be corrosive to metal. Clothing wetted with sodium chlorate may become inflammable.

685. Sulphate of Iron This is sometimes used as a moss killer and fertilizer on lawns, either by itself or in combination with other chemicals such as sulphate of ammonia, to make lawn sand (99).

SPECIAL TECHNIQUES

686. Ring Culture Some plants, notably tomatoes, chrysanthemums and carnations, grow well in bottomless 'pots' standing on a bed of gravel or ashes. Real pots with the bottoms knocked out can be used but most ring culture is carried out in special rings made of bitumenised cardboard or 'whalehide'. Rings 22cm (9in) in diameter and 22cm (9in) deep are suitable for strong-growing plants. They are filled with ordinary potting soil and are stood on a bed of clean washed gravel or well-weathered boiler ashes at least 15cm (6in) deep. The plants are raised in the normal way from seed or cuttings and are planted in the rings while still quite small. After planting they are well watered in so that the soil in the 'rings' is moist throughout. Subsequently all water is applied to the gravel or ash base from which it is drawn up into the soil by capillary attraction. Any solid or liquid food required is applied to the soil in the rings.

The plants make two quite distinct root systems, one of fine feeding roots in the soil, the other much coarser, moisture-gathering roots, in the aggregate base. At the end of the season the plants and roots are removed, the soil is discarded, to be replaced by fresh soil the following year, and the aggregate is flushed with water, perhaps with the addition of a little disinfectant.

687. Mist Propagation Various appliances are now available for keeping cuttings constantly moist and cool by automatically spraying them with water at fairly frequent intervals. Broadly these devices may be divided into two types, those that are controlled by the actual rate of water evaporation and those that work on a simple time basis. Rate of evaporation may be determined by electrical contacts placed in the cutting bed. As long as these contacts remain moist current flows between them. As soon as they become dry the flow of current ceases and a sensitive electronic control unit switches on more powerful current which operates a solenoid valve which itself turns on the water supply to the misting jets. These wet cuttings and electric contacts alike so that after a few seconds current flows between the contacts, the electronic control unit switches off the current to the solenoid valve and the water stops.

Time switches can as a rule be set to give any sequence of stop and flow desired but are not sensitive to changing conditions of evaporation. A third alternative is a device which measures the amount of light reaching the cuttings and controls the frequency of mist bursts accordingly. Other devices work purely mechanically, as by water dripping into a little 'bucket' which, when full, tips a valve to start the water flow and at the same time empty itself; or a tiny sponge on the arm of a balance which, when dry, allows it to rise and turn on the water.

Mist propagation is most satisfactory in spring and summer. The cuttings are not kept close but are usually rooted on the floor or staging of a greenhouse. Coarse sand and peat is the most satisfactory rooting medium and the best results are obtained when this is warmed to about 18°-21°C (65°-70°F) from below as, for example, with an electrical soil-warming cable. Cuttings should be removed to ordinary compost or soil, sand and peat as soon as they are rooted.

INDEX